ADVANCE PRAISE FOR

Walt Whitman's Multitudes

Walt Whitman's Multitudes

PETER LANG
New York • Washington, D.C./Baltimore • Bern
Frankfurt am Main • Berlin • Brussels • Vienna • Oxford

Jason Stacy

Walt Whitman's Multitudes

Labor Reform and Persona in Whitman's Journalism and the First *Leaves of Grass*, 1840–1855

PETER LANG
New York • Washington, D.C./Baltimore • Bern
Frankfurt am Main • Berlin • Brussels • Vienna • Oxford

Library of Congress Cataloging-in-Publication Data

Stacy, Jason
Walt Whitman's multitudes:
labor reform and persona in Whitman's journalism
and the first Leaves of Grass, 1840–1855 / Jason Stacy.
p. cm.
Includes bibliographical references and index.
1. Whitman, Walt, 1819–1892—Political and social views.
2. Whitman, Walt, 1819–1892—Knowledge—Economics.
3. Whitman, Walt, 1819–1892—Knowledge—United States.
4. United States—In literature. 5. Labor in literature. I. Title.
PS3242.P64S73   811'.3—dc22   2007030623
ISBN 978-1-4331-0153-3 (hardcover)
ISBN 978-1-4331-0383-4 (paperback)

Bibliographic information published by **Die Deutsche Bibliothek**.
Die Deutsche Bibliothek lists this publication in the "Deutsche
Nationalbibliografie"; detailed bibliographic data is available
on the Internet at http://dnb.ddb.de/.

Cover photo courtesy of the Ed Fulsom Collection

The paper in this book meets the guidelines for permanence and durability
of the Committee on Production Guidelines for Book Longevity
of the Council of Library Resources.

CONTENTS

ACKNOWLEDGMENTS

No book would exist without the generous support and assistance of many people. Dan Larsen expressed confidence in this project at its inception. Ed Folsom and David Reynolds supplied encouragement at critical moments. Felicia Campbell and *Popular Culture Review* provided a forum for the article that eventually became this book. James Sabathne helped hone the core arguments through his friendly and compelling challenges. Lewis Erenberg, Timothy Gilfoyle and Susan Hirsch gave their expertise and support while the manuscript went through many revisions. The referees for the 2006 American Journalism Historians Association annual conference offered helpful suggestions for secondary sources in journalism history. Bruce Bardarik and the Paterson Free Library in Paterson, New Jersey contributed their time and holdings of the *New York Aurora*. Southern Illinois University Edwardsville funded this project with a summer research fellowship and grants through the College of Arts and Sciences, the Graduate School, and the Department of Historical Studies. Douglas Noverr gave critical suggestions for the final revision. Throughout, Michelle Stacy proved to be the best of friends and the most relentless of readers. I am especially thankful to my parents, who made Walt Whitman a member of the family.

Cover: Daguerreotype of Walt Whitman (circa 1848-1854) provided by Ed Folsom.

INTRODUCTION

Do I contradict myself?
Very well then....I contradict myself;
I am large....I contain multitudes.
                            -Walt Whitman, *Leaves of Grass*, 1855

For most readers, there are two Walt Whitmans. One is our bard who declares the United States a "nation of nations." Poems like "O Captain, My Captain!" are ringing calls to communal memory and patriotic reflection. The other Walt Whitman is our earliest modern poet who exhibits all the trappings of this loose title: rebelliousness, individualism in the face of the crowd, a daring use of form and ideals antagonistic to mainstream America. Whitman molds to his situation and metamorphoses into what we want of him. On the Fourth of July, he is our drum-beating patriot. In our moments of quiet doubt, he whispers to our desires.

Both lie at the heart of Whitman's works. If, as the poet claimed, the United States is "essentially the greatest poem," everything within is, in effect, poetic. Nothing is to be dismissed or reduced. All conflicts and resolutions are a product of the same poetic dynamic. Righteousness and sin, freedom and oppression, the soul and the body are all parts of the same churning verse. As a native of Brooklyn and son of a skilled artisan, Whitman felt keenly the upheaval of the new market economy and watched as the economic and moral debates around slavery engulfed the nation. He tried to resolve these conflicts through words.

Between 1840 and 1855, Walt Whitman formulated a cohesive labor reform program that he intended to authentically unify the United States through a celebration of the nation as it was, rather than as it should be. The editorialist, and later poet, tried to introduce his readers to their essential equality without overthrowing the established economic order and social hierarchy; to do so would force him to admit that the promises of the nation's founding had gone awry. Many of Whitman's writings, then, were an attempt to uncover a still living republic of equality and liberty in the face of dramatic economic and social change. Rather than elevating liberty and equality to a spiritual plane above economics, Whitman envisioned labor and capital as equal in their place. In this seeming contradiction, he united the ideologies of radical labor reformers (those that supported an economic leveling) and conservative reformers (who accepted hierarchy and an "organic" economy) in order to maintain a cohesive version of the republicanism of his father's generation. To this end, he sought to convince his readers that their republic was the best the cosmos had to offer and that affectation and hubris, rather than social and economic forces, were the origins of injustice and immorality. Economic conflicts disappeared when citizens recognized this truth.

Whitman made this argument in print by taking on three distinct personas: the Schoolmaster, the Editor, and the Bard. In these roles he constructed public voices that were distinct from Walter Whitman, Jr. and sought to "teach" Americans about their inherent equality and freedom. As the Schoolmaster, he cited the prevalence of "fashion" in the new market economy as the cause of his readers' confusion. As the Editor, he attacked public sectarianism, pretensions toward European "high" culture and, later, slavery. Finally, as the Bard, Whitman redefined the labor theory of value as a means to equality without leveling. In this final persona, he presented a novel melding of free-soil and abolitionist arguments prevalent in the decade preceding the Civil War. Though Whitman's personas and arguments changed over time, his central thesis remained the same: America was perfect; one needed only recognize its perfection. Thereafter, confusion (fashion, sectarianism, or slavery) fell away. In this way, Walt Whitman sought to enlighten his readers of their equality within the status quo and educate the Republic as to its own true nature.

Many literary critics who explore Whitman's ideas about labor find his proposals mystical and utopian. For example, Newton Arvin, in *Whitman* (1938) notes the influence of Whitman's father's ideological heroes (Thomas Paine, Frances Wright, Robert Owen), and argues, from a Marxist perspective, that his "transcendental or mystical tendencies...drag on his materialist leanings."[1] Though Arvin calls the poet "highly affirmative...of American middle-class culture in the era of Emerson, of Vanderbilt, of Lincoln" he also senses "something more" in Whitman's "appeal...to the future."[2] In commenting on Whitman and the slavery question, for example, Arvin remarks that:

> Whitman was less close to the humanitarian idealists than he was to thousands of ordinary Americans with whom his fellow-feeling was more instinctive: less close to Parker and Thoreau than to many a Northern farmer, shopkeeper, or workman of those decades. His opposition to slavery was essentially...the opposition felt to it in

the North...by the men who raised corn and hogs, by the workers in the mill and mine, by the skilled artisans and the trade unionists.[3]

This is a common and significant beginning to literary historicist work on Whitman and labor. Arvin takes Whitman's proletarian background, rhetoric, and political status and implies that *Leaves of Grass* is, in effect, a working-class, radical polemic that falls short of its own "leanings." Whitman had an interest in working-class issues, but from a subtler and, at times, paternalistic position. There was more class ambivalence in Whitman that class-consciousness. As Schoolmaster, Editor, and Bard, Whitman sought to unify his conservative tendencies with his egalitarian ideals in a way that connected all facets of nineteenth-century America with the revolutionary idealism of a generation past. Arvin faults Whitman, on the one hand, for bourgeois mysticism and, on the other, for not being the universalist his "mysticism" demanded of him. The accusation that Whitman did not live up to his own standards is a common charge leveled against him by modern literary critics.

M. Wynn Thomas' seminal The *Lunar Light of Whitman's Poetry* (1987) considers many of the subtleties in Whitman's ideas about labor that are often missed by heavy-handed studies such as Arvin's. For Thomas, a celebration of the soul is Whitman's way to poetically reclaim an ideal artisan republic. By spiritualizing democracy, "an individual's worth is constant, since it relates to his existence as a soul, and not to the vagaries of his life as a social and economic being."[4] Accordingly, Whitman overcame working-class alienation through his universalism.

Whitman's universalism is ultimately unsatisfying for Thomas, "somehow or other a system of untrammeled economic competition is supposed to produce a harmoniously cooperative and egalitarian social order." This is "a contradiction which lies at the very heart of Whitman's convictions and which manifests itself in everything he writes."[5] Whitman only overcame this contradiction by including the "financier and connoisseur" in "Song of Myself" for "inclusiveness's sake."[6] Thomas finds in Whitman's attempts to unite individual and mass, high and low, the wishful thinking of a disoriented artisan.

Taking Whitman's working class sympathies further, Betsy Erkkila in *Whitman the Political Poet* (1989) sees in the poet's work a radical agenda. According to Erkkila, Whitman's verse represented a political program opposed to contemporaries like Matthew Arnold who used high conceptions of art to "counteract the tendency to anarchy." Whitman created an art of "perfect equality" and, in this way, acted as both poet and activist.[7] According to Erkkila, the split between [poet and activist] has been at least partly the construction of critics who, under the influence of the Modernist and New Critical insistence on the separation of politics and art, have been eager to rescue Whitman's poems from the charge of political contingency....[8]

For Erkkila, Whitman's political message and egalitarian ontology express an ideology similar to working-class radicals like Mike Walsh or abolitionist firebrands like William Lloyd Garrison. According to Erkkila, one of Whitman's poems was "the poetic burning of the Constitution."[9] This argument, however, ignores Whitman's own reactionary admiration for the institutions established by the revolutionary generation.

More recently, Andrew Lawson, in *Walt Whitman and the Class Struggle* (2006), traces Whitman's "mixture of self-assertion and anxiety" to "the uncertain position of the lower middle-class as it moved from agrarian folkways to the urban marketplace." For Lawson, Whitman attempted to overcome the class hierarchy of the mid-19th century by "spiritualiz[ing]" it.[10] Amy Schrager Lang finds a similar anxiety in nineteenth-century social theorists and middle class novelists who hoped that American social fluidity and transcendent, supernatural identity might surmount class conflict.[11] For Lawson and Lang, Whitman represented contemporary Americans' attempt to spiritualize away the problem of growing class divisions rather than face the unsettling proposition that harsh economic facts undermined the ideals of the American Revolution.

Whitman's universalism has attracted critics of radical political inclinations, Marxists, labor advocates, and liberation theorists. However, the conflicts within Whitman's own message force many to argue that his claims are half-baked or one-sided. In this regard, they look for the radical who could write in such a radical style. This makes some sense. If an author's context is also his point-of-departure, then his words, their placement, and their meaning-in-context must all say something similar. Whitman does not fit this formula. He slips out of scholars' hands because his conventional politics did not fit his radical poetic form. Some find in Whitman an unwillingness to take his radicalism to its logical end; Whitman was too middle class. For others, Whitman was the fantasist who talked away the nation's problems. Some take Whitman at his word and see only contradictions. Others find ideological uniformity only at the cost of making him into something he was not.

Walt Whitman's politics are an essential facet of his poems. Walt Whitman's poems are an essential purveyor of his politics. Whitman's radical poetic form, however, did not make for radical politics. Ultimately, his political ideas were as conventional as the medium through which he first purveyed them: the newspaper. Looking at Whitman's *Leaves of Grass* and his journalism as primary sources of equal value exposes a cohesive arc to his political and social ideas between 1840 and 1855. Whitman himself welcomed an exploration like this. For him, all undertakings uncovered the origin of poems.[12]

This work reflects recent developments in American cultural and intellectual studies. With the advent of postmodern discursive analyses and the influence of twentieth-century critics like Gramsci, Foucault, and Geertz, works on American culture have taken for granted the struggle for self-definition and power within a cultural discourse. This approach adds to the work of labor historians who have sought to understand the working class as the working class understood itself. Philip Foner's *Organized Labor and the Black Worker* (1974), Herbert Gutman's *Work, Culture and Society in Industrializing America* (1977), Mary Blewett's *Men, Women, and Work* (1988), and David Roediger's *Wages of Whiteness* (1991) are good examples of the new labor history which applies the tools of sociology and anthropology to labor studies. By applying these tools to Whitman, the historian gains further insight into the ways in which the working class defined itself and maintained an abiding devotion to the Republic's founding and the free-market ideology that upheld it.[13] However, instead of uncovering layers of multiple discourses, *Walt Whitman's Multitudes* traces the trajectory of a single voice in the public sphere and reconstructs the personas by which this voice spoke to the times. For this reason, this book reads much like a biography; this is the story of personas meant for public consumption.

Jo Burr Margadant's *The New Biography: Performing Femininity in Nineteenth-Century France* (2000) provides some insight for this work. According to Margandant, "the subject of biography is no longer the coherent self, but rather a self that is performed." With an emphasis on human agency, the biography serves a new role in cultural historiography through the study of a single agent-in-context. For Margadant, the biography provides a means by which the historian analyzes and traces the ways individuals constructed personas in public. Whitman provides a rich and complicated subject for this type of analysis as he wrote the "Sun-Down Papers," his editorials, reviews, and poetry with an explicit "I" as the voice of the people.[14]

David Reynolds' *Walt Whitman's America: A Cultural Biography* (1995) and Rüdiger Safranski's *Nietzsche: A Philosophical Biography* (2001) utilize biography within cultural and intellectual history. Both Reynolds and Safranski construct a "life" of their subjects without the traditional attempt to raise the dead. For example, Reynolds uses Whitman as a lens through which to survey the

American cultural landscape. Whitman's words and actions echo the conflicting voices of his times. This allows Reynolds to avoid the affected timelessness and objectivity of traditional biographies.[15] Safranski also reworks the traditional biography in his attempt to trace Nietzsche's intellectual trajectory rather than his physical and psychological life. In doing so, he finds the philosopher's actions less interesting than the changes and subtleties in Nietzsche's written ideas. This saves Safranski from psycho-historical over-speculation because he does not seek to discover what lies behind Nietzsche's theories as much as he reveals change-over-time in the philosopher's ideas.[16]

John Emerson Todd's *Emily Dickinson's Use of the Persona* (1968) and Don Florence's *Persona and Humor in Mark Twain's Early Writings* (1995) provide a framework for an analysis of Whitman's earliest personas. Todd reconstructs Dickinson's "Little Girl" and "Lover-Wife-Queen" personas in context while Florence argues for an end to the psychoanalytical search for the "real" Mark Twain in Samuel Clemens. Likewise, William Pannapacker, in *Revised Lives: Walt Whitman and Nineteenth-Century Authorship* (2004), takes Whitman's construction of the bard persona in *Leaves of Grass* seriously and compares it to the "revised" lives of Abraham Lincoln, James Russell Lowell, and Edgar Allan Poe. Instead of masks to be torn away, these scholars assume an author's personas are themselves personalities worth knowing.[17] This book places Whitman's earliest personas in a narrative where *Leaves of Grass* is only part of the story.

Cultural historians Lawrence Levine and Richard Lyman Bushman also contribute here. Though traditionally understood as standing at opposite ends of the debate regarding the origin of high and low culture in the early Republic, Whitman's attitude toward culture reflected the theories of both of these cultural historians. Levine argues that competing ethnicities, classes, and regions produced tensions in nineteenth-century urban culture that slowly split between the "highbrow" and the "lowbrow" varieties in the mid-to-late 19th century.[18] Bushman, on the other hand, sees culture as a marker of status from the inception of the Republic.[19] Whitman exhibits the truth in both theories. In the 1840s, he transformed the *Brooklyn Daily Eagle* from a political broadsheet to a conduit of culture to the masses. In this way, he managed to be both egalitarian and elitist.

Historians, however, have thus far largely ignored Walt Whitman. Typically, he serves to provide the convenient quote for labor historians and not much else.[20] However, the public Whitman wrestled intimately with the debates of his day: conspicuous consumption, nativism, slavery, and, through it all, labor and the status of the new working class. Whitman scholars typically read the historical record backward from *Leaves of Grass* and use the journalism to fill out a life story or to function as a poetic primer. This book reads the historical record forward and traces ways in which Whitman searched for a proper voice and forum through which to purvey his ideas about a nation in ideological and social crisis. It maps the trajectory of Whitman's thinking, follows trends, interprets turns, and analyzes revisions in its quest for other "Walt Whitmans." This rejects Emerson's statement that the editorials represent a "long foreground" which culminated in 1855.[21] Instead, it considers the Bard to be only one of Whitman's many public personas and finds significance in each. A forward-looking analysis, from editorials to first edition, asks what were the means and processes by which Whitman constructed these identities on paper. In doing so, it looks to the social, economic, and political upheavals of Whitman's time as the canvas upon which he painted himself many times over.

PART ONE

ARTISAN AND SCHOOLMASTER

1819–1841

CHAPTER ONE

ARTISAN UNDEFINED

When Walter Whitman Jr. was born on May 31, 1819, he could trace his family's origins in the New World back nearly two hundred years. His ancestors' fortunes waxed and waned with those of New York. Brothers John and Zachariah Whitman arrived on the *True Love* to Weymouth, Massachusetts sometime between 1635 and 1637 and lived as semi-subsistence farmers for a generation. In 1657, the family migrated to Huntington, New York and, with the help of slave labor, became moderately prosperous farmers. By the birth of Walt Whitman, Sr. on Bastille Day, 1789, however, the family fortunes shifted downward, and the Whitmans became one of many subsistence farmers along Long Island just as New York City became a major metropolis and temporary seat of the new national government

Walter Whitman, Sr.'s adulthood reflected the economic uncertainty and upheaval common to artisans on the cusp of the new market economy. Walter courted his wife in 1816 after living in New York City as an apprentice and journeyman carpenter, but relocated the family numerous times throughout Walter Jr.'s childhood, first to West Hills, New York, later to burgeoning Brooklyn, and then back into the Long Island countryside because of Walter, Sr.'s ongoing inability to find profit in real estate speculation.[1]

The bustling economy of the early-19th century bred this economic uncertainty. Unlike New England, the industrial revolution in New York began in small shops that shifted from craft to industrial production.[2] After 1815, Brooklyn industry established itself in small frame and brick houses near the waterfront and produced light consumer goods: playing cards, pocketbooks, combs, tinware, etc. In these small shops, the artisan economy broke down as masters became employers and, in an attempt to keep up with steam-powered competition from New England factory towns, employers packed workrooms with apprentices and low-wage female workers, none of whom they expected to become journeymen in their own right. By the early 1830s, this type of production took over the clothing trades and "ready wear" clothing, formerly the reserve only of the poorest as "slops," dominated the clothing market.[3]

Walter Whitman, Sr. worked on the edge of this rift between the artisan and the wage-labor economy. Between 1823 and 1831, the elder Whitman tried to make it as a master carpenter and nascent capitalist: buying property, building a house, selling and buying more property. However, by 1831, Walter worked for wages and Walter, Jr. later recalled that two of the four houses his father built were mortgaged and later lost to creditors.[4]

Thirty years after his father's death, Whitman remembered Walter, Sr. as hot-tempered, stern, and, perhaps, alcoholic.[5] Though Whitman implied an emotional distance between himself and his father, Walter Sr.'s artisan republicanism (and his admiration of Thomas Paine) inculcated in his son a visceral sympathy for the "farmer, laborer, and tradesman."[6] The names Walter, Sr. chose for his children reflected this artisan ideology. After naming his oldest son after his father (Jesse, born 1818), and his second oldest after himself (1819), Walter Whitman, Sr. chose patriotic names for the rest of his sons: Andrew Jackson (born 1827), George Washington (1829), and Thomas Jefferson (1833). Whitman's democratic and largely secular political ideology had its foundations partly in the artisan republican ideology of his father.

On his maternal side, Whitman's ancestors prospered in New York colony. His mother, Louisa, grew up on the well-to-do farm of Captain Cornelius Van Velsor who, among other business pursuits, successfully bred horses for sale throughout the colonies and new republic.[7] Louisa was the emotional touchstone and spiritual center for the young Whitman.[8] Raised in a Quaker household, she grew up in the spiritually fertile atmosphere that eventually produced Elias Hicks and the "Hicksite Reformation" that split many monthly meetings after 1827.[9] This brand of "Hicksite" Quakerism maintained the individual spirituality and silent worship of seventeenth-century Quakers in reaction to the rising evangelicalism and textual fundamentalism of urban Friends, predominately in the Philadelphia Yearly Meeting.[10] Louisa's father, Captain Van Velsor, was a personal friend of Hicks.[11]

Elias Hicks shaped the theology of the "Liberal" branch of the Society of Friends and opposed to the "Orthodox" branch of the Arch Street Meeting in Philadelphia. However, these titles are problematic. Hicks and his adherents did not see themselves as reformers against Quaker orthodoxy. Instead, Hicks revolted against the evangelicalization of the Philadelphia Yearly Meeting during the early days of the Second Great Awakening. The Awakening's religious fervor convinced many Friends that the Society needed rejuvenation through a more fundamentalist reading of scripture, a "programmed" (or led) as opposed to "unprogrammed" (or silent) religious service, the belief in an immediate, rather than arduous rebirth in Christ, and a rejection of the

Quaker conception of the "inner Light" or "inner Christ" as the means to personal revelation. According to Hicks and his followers in rural New York and New England, the Quakers swept up in the Methodist-style revivalism of the Second Great Awakening went astray from the tenets of traditional Friends. Though the evangelized Philadelphia Yearly Meeting on Arch Street took the moniker "Orthodox," the followers of Hicks believed themselves the ones who maintained the traditional, unaffected ways of the original Quakers.[12]

No record exists of Louisa Whitman ever formally becoming a Quaker. Walter, Jr., therefore, had only a tenuous relationship with the Friends of Long Island and the schismatic Elias Hicks. However, he remembered fondly hearing Hicks speak in the ballroom at Morrison's Hotel in Brooklyn Heights in November 1829 and recalled that both his mother and father attended the sermon. It was still one of his seminal memories in 1888, nearly sixty years after the event.[13]

Whitman's earliest statements about the Quakers show some ambivalence toward the Society. One of his articles in the *New Orleans Crescent* expressed opposition to Quaker tenets, as they "can never become the creed of the race." According to Whitman, most people could not abide by Quaker pacifism; "you might as well expect all men to adopt the...plain phraseology of the followers of [George] Fox, as to hope that their principles of peace will ever become the law of men's opinions and actions."[14] In one case Whitman tried to disguise Quaker influence on him; he changed the title of a lecture he gave in the 1840s from "Elias Hicks" to "On the Religion." Next to the new title, he penciled a note to "make no allusion to him [Hicks] at all."[15] Whitman's audience was the reason for this reticence. Both the *Eagle* and the *Crescent* catered to highly patriotic, Democratic readers, many of whom supported James K. Polk and the Mexican-American War. Any public celebration of Quaker values situated Whitman on the outskirts of the mainstream. As editor and writer for the popular press, he had to remain within certain margins.[16] However, late in life, Whitman claimed that he had considered joining the Society, but decided he "was never made to live inside a fence."[17] In 1888, he began to write an extended piece on Hicks. In an essay entitled "Notes (such as they are) founded on Elias Hicks," Whitman described Hicks as a Quaker version of himself; "He gives the service of pointing to the foundation of all naked theology,...namely in *yourself* and your inherent relations."[18] This suspicion of affectation, and a sense that transcendent truth lies buried in each individual remained a common theme for Whitman throughout his years as an editor and poet.[19]

Regarding Whitman's parents and their beliefs, one could argue that his writings attempted to unite his father's secular democratic politics with his mother's spiritually tolerant and mystical faith. Such speculation supposes that Whitman elevated democratic politics into the realm of the religious and presented a radical social vision founded on the radical artisan politics and Quaker mysticism of his parents.[20]

However, Whitman's parents had another possible effect on him. Walter Sr.'s artisan politics and Louisa's Hicksite Quakerism were *both* radical *and* conservative in their outlook. Whitman's father looked back to the founding of the Republic and saw an intimate connection between his artisan status and the Revolution's promise. The naming of his children after the founders and his admiration of Paine point to this grounding in the Revolution. This echoed the arguments of Democrats like Andrew Jackson who claimed to resurrect what was just and original in the American founding.[21] Likewise, Hicksites like Louisa saw themselves as conservatives; rather than revolutionizing the Society of Friends, Hicks' apostles hoped to maintain original, "unprogrammed," and mystical Quakerism in the face of evangelical fundamentalism.

This presented not two opposing views of reform, one secular, one religious, that Whitman reconciled but, instead, two very similar world-views as to the nature of change: things were worse now than they were in the past. The world (religious, economic, political) had taken a turn from the essential truths upon which the Republic and the faith were founded. Reform was a return, not a revolution. These commonalities between Walter Whitman, Sr.'s artisan republicanism and Louisa Van Velsor Whitman's Quakerism served similar ends in the writings of the editor and poet.

Artisan Undefined

Whitman claimed his true education happened in the print shop.[22] In 1831, after only a few years of formal education, his family's connection to Elias Hicks helped to secure eleven-year old Walter a position as an apprentice at Samuel E. Clements' *Long Island Patriot*. Clements, a devout Hicksite Quaker, was fired in 1830 from his position as postmaster of Brooklyn after seeking to remove Elias Hicks' corpse from its resting place to clandestinely make a bust of the famous preacher.[23] Between 1832 and 1835 Whitman continued his apprenticeship on Alden Spooner's Whig newspaper, the *Long Island Star*.[24] Later in life, Whitman recalled his days in the print shop: "you get your culture direct: not through borrowed sources—no, a century of college training could not confer such results on anyone."[25]

By the year that Whitman began working for Alden Spooner, the terms "artisan" and "mechanic" could still seem eternal and self-evident. Craftsmen like Whitman's father used an artisan-centered version of the American Revolution and the political rhetoric of Jeffersonian republicanism to define themselves. New York Jeffersonian-Republicans appealed to the large artisan population of a generation previous by claiming that the American democracy depended on the well-being of "middling producers" and that Federalists sought to "rob the mechanics and laborers of their independence of mind" and to "wantonly...take away [their] rights."[26] This rhetoric drew its inspiration from the American Revolution and an egalitarian ideal that artisans viewed as elemental. Craftsmen cited examples such as the Sons of Liberty during the Stamp Act crisis and the Boston Tea Party as empirical evidence of artisan investment in the Revolution. In 1819, the year of Whitman's birth, this form of republicanism bound masters, small masters, and journeymen in a politico-economic unity against perceived "aristocrats" who sought to take away workingmen's rights. Like subsistence farmers in the countryside, tradesmen formed the backbone of the American Revolution because, like the small landholder, the craftsman owned the means to his prosperity. This made him a free man. Unlike the leisured aristocrat of Europe or the parasitic speculator and merchant of New York City, the artisan's work intimately connected him to his prosperity. He had a direct hand in the production of goods that were of tangible benefit to the Commonwealth.[27]

In this regard, artisan republicanism exhibited a careful balance between outright egalitarian leveling and hierarchical individualism. The mechanic's middling status bred individual pride and proved "more congenial with the nature of our government and conducive to the general happiness."[28] Likewise, the apprenticeship process required a veneration of private property and a respect for shop hierarchy between master, journeyman, and apprentice. Ideally, artisans based this hierarchy on practical compassion and mutual need. The shop floor had all the attributes of the ideal republic in this regard: property rights, brotherly benevolence, civic responsibility, organic hierarchy, and essential egalitarianism. This republican rhetoric, however, masked an acute and widening rift within the artisan class itself.[29] By the 1830s, this rift became an ideological chasm.

The origins in this rift lay in an argument over Adam Smith's Labor Theory of Value first formulated in *An Inquiry into the Nature and Causes of The Wealth of Nations* (1776). The growth from an artisan to an industrial economy created a disconnection between the formerly mutually dependent distinctions of master, apprentice and journeyman and replaced them with the seemingly unbridgeable gap between capital and labor. Within the context of the British artisan and mercantile system of the late-18th century, Smith's theory had a certain logical consistency; rich and poor were determined by the degree to which they could "enjoy the necessaries, conveniencies, and amusements of human life." Those of wealth could afford a superior standard of living and, therefore, Smith defined the rich by their ability to consume necessities and luxuries.[30] The price consumers paid for an item, however, did not determine its value. Ultimately, labor was the "real measure of the exchangeable value of all commodities." The by-product of one person's ability to control another's labor was wealth, but "labor...is alone the...real standard by which the value of all commodities can at all times and places be estimated and compared. It is their real price; money is their nominal price only."[31]

This theory worked within the context of an artisan and mercantile economy. All value derived from the hands of those who produced necessities. Wealth went to those who had the ability to own these necessities. A merchant profited from the labor of others. A master craftsman, on the other hand, lent value to the item he produced. Though he employed journeymen, he was the master-laborer of a shop which produced "necessaries and conveniences" of life.

The advent of an industrial economy created a new kind of wealth. Whereas in an artisan economy the master craftsman maintained an intimate connection to his labor through his expertise and ability to pass along his skill to journeymen, the capitalist generated his wealth specifically by his separation from labor. The owner of a factory was an *employer*. What defined the value of an employer's labor when he organized the production and the sale of a product that someone else made? He did not make a useful product, but disseminated goods made by his employees. Unlike a merchant (who also disseminated goods made by others' hands), he considered himself the *manufacturer* of the product, and, by Smith's labor theory, determined its value through his labor. However, because he did not labor at the object of value himself, what "real standard" labor did the capitalist do?

The creation of a working class without direct ownership of the fruits of its labor raised a number of questions when viewed through Smith's labor theory. What was the laborer's relationship to the "non-producing" class of capital? Had capital usurped his value? Or, did a laborer's value lie in more "nominal" realms (his ability to negotiate contracts, his mobility, his flexibility)? If a laborer had the skills to produce, but his employer owned the product of his labor, what determined the absolute value of the product (and, implicitly, the producer) in such a system?

Conservative and Radical in New York City

When he left Alden Spooner's shop and came to New York to work as a journeyman printer in 1835, Whitman entered a city where the unified ideology of artisan republicanism broke into two broad, rival ideologies: conservatives, who saw in the new market economy a continuation of the old apprentice system, and radicals, who argued that a parasitic class of capitalists sought to rob workingmen of their natural dignity.

Conservative reformers who embraced the new market economy formulated a modified version of the traditional master-journeyman relationship. Whereas the master and journeyman traditionally shared one shop and common duties, capital and labor now worked in partnership with particular, exclusive means to a common end, namely, profit. This required a harmony of interests between capital and labor. Accordingly, labor would find its new place in the Republic by becoming a class whose values and interests proved conducive to the profitable production of goods for universal economic benefit. The nation could achieve this ideal by "uplifting" the American working class and creating responsible, virtuous citizens. Rather than a blemish on labor and its value, capitalists and master craftsmen played the same role.[32] Like the master craftsman and the journeyman, the employer and employee had obligations to each other that benefited both.

When conservatives rejected the economic egalitarianism of radical reformers, they did so with the argument that in the organic relationship between master and apprentice, there had always been those who led and those who followed. Status was not tyranny, and employers were not parasites. Instead, conservatives assumed that employees properly looked to their employers for moral guidance as apprentices formerly looked to their masters. This rhetoric of moral benevolence borrowed heavily from the language of the Second Great Awakening. For example, the General Society of Mechanics and Tradesmen, working hand-in-hand with the New York Temperance Society, sought, by the 1820s, to establish "that systematic and methodical arrangement of business so indispensable to the good regulation of every establishment."[33] In 1830, Joseph Brewster, a skilled master hatter turned capitalist, declared his conversion to evangelical Christianity, joined the General Society, and formed, with the master bookbinder Charles Starr, the Association for Moral Improvement of Young Mechanics.[34] This organization encouraged the city's laborers to fulfill their obligations "to the City and to God"[35] and promised employers that temperance, Christian habits, and a dedication to home and church would improve their profits by twenty-five percent.[36] For conservatives, moral persuasion protected "the security of republican institutions from a drunk, corruptible electorate."[37] To this end, the General Society founded a mechanics' school and apprentices' library (which young Whitman visited in the 1830s) for moral and educational uplift.[38] Conservatives like Brewster denied through their actions that the fundamentally different relationship between employer and employee undermined the practical benevolence of the traditional craftsman's workshop.

In the aftermath of Jackson's destruction of the Second National Bank in 1833, conservative labor reformers found in the Whig Party a national platform in which to invest these local interests. Henry Clay's "American System," with its program of a National Bank, federally-funded internal improvements and tariffs, saw the economy, as Daniel Webster put it, united in a "great chain of being" where a "national community" rewarded and benefited from individual initiative.[39] Webster compared the circulation of money through the economy to the flow of blood through an organism.[40] Blessed with equality of opportunity, wage laborers, under the protection of the government, acquired "a stake in the welfare of [the] community."[41]

In New York, local Whigs, like Alexander H.H. Stuart, applied these ideals to everyday debates, "...we have no necessity for factory bills....Here a competency is within reach of every man who is disposed to exercise ordinary industry and frugality; and the labouring population is prosperous and happy."[42] According to Stuart, because New World wage earners already earned more than those in the Old World, legislatures did not need to pass laws to promote economic equality. Equal opportunity united capital and labor; both had the same goal and served the same end from different relative positions in the national economic body.[43] The Whig platform fell on sympathetic ears. After 1846, the party gained control of seven wards in New York City, five of them working class.[44] This support came primarily from artisans who successfully adjusted to the new market economy and joined the Republicans after the dissolution of the Whigs in the 1850s.[45]

New York radicals answered the questions raised by the new economy differently. Generally, radical reformers took Adam Smith's definition of value literally: those who worked established an item's intrinsic value. These radical reformers rejected the argument that willful individual appetite produced all social ills; instead, social structures and norms caused poverty.

In the 1830s, labor advocates in the National Trades Union, the Workingmen's Party, and elements of the Democratic Party viewed the transformation of labor's value into the private property of factory owners as the seat of all artisan woe. According to their arguments, the factory system overthrew the traditional value system when it created a class of owners who did not work directly on the products they produced. According to radicals, nascent capitalists were "parasites" on the body of value. The artisan axiom, "He who does not work, neither shall he eat" called for a living wage and subtly critiqued those who lived off the labor of others.[46] Whereas conservative reformers saw industrialization as a natural outgrowth of the artisan system, radical reformers perceived factory owners as subversive to the value of labor itself.

Northeastern intellectuals and labor advocates formed the Workingmen's Party (WMP) in 1829 for reasons similar to the conservative organizations of Joseph Brewster——to tackle the plight of laborers in the face of the new market economy. Where conservatives saw the individual as his own steward, members of the WMP saw laborers pressed by social structures they alone could not modify. Therefore, the WMP advocated institutional reforms like the ten-hour workday, civil service reform, and the abolition of capital punishment.[47] Robert Dale Owen, a founder of the WMP, promoted the reorganization of the American educational system and formed the Association for the Protection and Promotion of Popular Education to lobby for state-funded universal education.[48] According to Owen, universal education facilitated the regeneration and restoration of labor's natural dignity by mixing students of different classes and origins. Likewise, the National Trades Union at its convention in New York (1834) resolved that the American educational system destroyed "that Equality which is predicated in the Declaration of Independence, because of their exclusive character in giving instruction to the wealthy few...."[49] For the National Trades Union, private education created an unrepublican monopoly of knowledge; public education would make true the new market rhetoric of equal opportunity. In the 1840s, Whitman adapted this idea to his own vision of the role of public schools.

Other radical labor reformers saw the unequal distribution of property as the origin of labor's plight. George Henry Evans, in his journal *The Workingman's Advocate*, argued, "all are at birth entitled to equal means to pursue happiness and among these are food, clothing and shelter...which we call property."[50] To this end, he called for a single tax on real property and supported a cooperative system where managers rewarded workers "in direct proportion to what they contributed to society in useful labor."[51] Thomas Skidmore, a former New England schoolteacher and founder of the WMP, pursued a program that challenged the tenets of the market economy itself. In his *The Rights of Man to Property!* he demanded the voiding of all debts, the equal redistribution of property to citizens over twenty-one, and the return of that land to the state upon a citizen's death.[52]

These diverse proposals represented common concerns: the origin of labor's problems lay in a new class of entrepreneurs and the institutions they controlled; the so-called "free" market economy was, in fact, not free at all because laborers could no longer entirely master their own fate. According to radical labor advocates, social conditions necessitated some combination of state intervention and social leveling to reestablish the dignity and prosperity of workers.

Traditionally, the Democratic Party appealed to artisans, but had a very tenuous relationship with radical labor advocates. Though the Party sought gains for the laboring classes, its platform against entrenched wealth worked primarily to fulfill the ideal of an equality of opportunity not so different from the free market rhetoric of the conservatives. Whereas the Whigs envisioned government as the "head" of an organism that fostered national improvement, Democrats, like John O'Sullivan, New York editor of the *Democratic Review*, claimed that "the world is governed too much" and called for a "voluntary principle" where "floating atoms would create a far more perfect and harmonious" order.[53] O'Sullivan, the proponent and originator of the term "manifest destiny," sought progress by calling for a national expansion into "untrodden space."[54] This Democratic policy of untrammeled individual ambition coupled with territorial expansion appealed to an ideal citizen unfettered by oppressive social structures. Though Democrats rhetorically included laborers in this great movement of individuals toward freedom, radicals remained in the outer orbit of the Party.

For example, William Leggett's Loco-foco revolt, which young Whitman followed with great interest as a New York apprentice, sought to unseat established Tammany Hall Democrats in the name of a broader, more inclusive power structure. At the onset, Leggett's reformers sounded radical and egalitarian. In 1837, after a Loco-foco public meeting to protest high flour prices, a crowd of supporters marched to Eli Hart's dry goods store and dumped out all the flour they could find.[55] However, the Loco-foco movement (and the short-lived Equal Rights Party it produced) pursued an end to political cronyism and corruption in Tammany Hall as the means to relieving the plight of the working class. Leggett's diatribes against monopolies, banks, and paper money attracted petty entrepreneurs, Jacksonians-in-exile from Tammany Hall, and workers in search of deflated currency. The General Trades Union (GTU), in fact, avoided throwing in its lot with Loco-focos as Leggett's ideology included a respect for private property, laissez-faire economics and a suspicion of the "monopolistic" tendencies of unions. By the late-1830s, the Equal Rights Party attracted both Loco-focos and reform-minded Whigs like Alden Spooner, Whitman's second employer, to its banner.[56]

By 1836, after a year in New York City, the journeyman printer Walter Whitman, Jr. had set type for three newspapers, visited circulation libraries, read Sir Walter Scott and James Fennimore Cooper, attended the theater, loved Shakespeare (especially *Richard III*),[57] and heard public lecturers like Frances Wright, the Scottish emancipationist and women's rights activist. Two years earlier, his first signed article had appeared in the *New York Mirror*.[58] He still remembered this publication fifty years later, "I used to watch for the big, fat, red-faced, slow-moving, very old English carrier who distributed the 'Mirror' in Brooklyn; and when I got one, opening and cutting the leaves with trembling fingers. How it made my heart double-beat to see *my piece* on the pretty white paper, in nice type."[59] Unfortunately for the journeyman, a fire destroyed much of the publishing district on August 12, 1836 and put master printers out of work. Thereafter, Whitman moved back with his family who had already returned to rural Long Island for financial reasons.

Little is known about Whitman's thoughts on the diverse debates regarding labor, work, and the value of each upon his return to the countryside. By the time he was a teenager, he had lived and worked among artisan republicans, conservative Whigs, Tammany Hall Democrats, Loco-focos, National Trades Unionists, and, at least vicariously, reformers as diverse as Thomas Skidmore, Daniel Webster and Elias Hicks. He had apprenticed with a Quaker and a Whig and identified with the Loco-focos. He admired the famous rebel, Elias Hicks who, himself, claimed to be a conservative against innovation. His father quoted anti-slavery Paine and named one of his sons after slave-holding Jefferson. His parents raised him to believe in a republic that proclaimed equal rights and individual autonomy, but eschewed economic leveling and social hierarchy. He learned that the American Revolution was a radical break with the past; he was taught to venerate this past event.

At seventeen, he also faced an economic shift that threatened to break this diversity into a rift where one either embraced social hierarchy or demanded economic leveling. Artisan sons faced a future that forced them to choose sides. Walt Whitman tried to reconcile them.

CHAPTER TWO

THE SCHOOLMASTER AND ETHICAL AESTHETICS

In the fall of 1836, Whitman took a job as a schoolteacher in rural Long Island. He continued in this capacity until the spring of 1841 and changed locations seasonally throughout these years.[1] A picture taken soon after his years as a teacher shows Whitman, with cane and hat, posing in dandy garb appropriate to a man-about-town without the "rough" persona so important to the later poet of *Leaves of Grass*. With no sense of irony, Whitman played the urbane Loco-foco among rubes in the country.

Whitman taught classes of up to eighty students from ages five to fifteen for nine hours per day. Communities hired teachers for three-month terms and, as was typical, Whitman boarded with the parents of his students.[2] His charges remembered him as both "careless of time and the world, of money and of toil" and as "always musin', and writin', 'stead of 'tending to his proper dooties."[3]

Whitman felt equally ambivalent toward his students. After year in New York City, he probably saw himself as an in-the-know city-dweller stranded in the sticks. He wrote to his friend Abraham Leech in 1840 and described Woodbury, one of the towns in which he taught, as "Devil's den" and "Purgatory Fields."[4] The citizens of this rural village fared not much better,

> I believe when the Lord created the world, he used up all the good stuff, and was forced to form Woodbury and its denizens, out of the fag ends, the scrapts and refuse....[5] [I]gnorance, vulgarity, rudeness, conceit, and dullness are the reigning gods of this deuced sink of despair...[h]ere in this nest of bears, this forsaken of all Go[d]'s creation; among clowns and country bumpkins[,] flad-heads, and coarse brown-faced girls, dirty, ill-favoured young brats, with squalling throats and crude manners, and bog-trotters, with all the disgusting conceit of ignorance and vulgarity.[6]

Whitman clearly had enough by the time he reached his fifth academic year,

O, damnation, damnation! thy other name is school-teaching and thy residence Woodbury.... Time, put spurs to thy leaden wings, and bring on the period when my allotted time of torment here shall be fulfilled.[7]

In Whitestone the next year, he found little more to recommend its citizens, "The principal feather of the place is the money making spirit, a gold-scraping and a wealth-hunting fiend, who is the foul incubus to three-fourths of this beautiful earth."[8]

However, in the same letters to Leech, Whitman expressed an abiding interest in Democratic politics. In one letter regarding the election of 1840, he asked,

is hard cider in the ascendant; or does democracy erect itself on its tiptoes and swing its old straw hat with a hurrah for 'Little Matty?'[9] Down in these parts, people understand about as much of political economy as they do the Choctaw language. I never met with such complete, unqualified, infernal jackasses, in all my life.—Luckily for my self-complacency they are mostly whigs [sic].—If they were on my side of the wall, I should forswear loco-focoism.[10]

Whitman saw no incongruities between his politics and rhetoric. According to the young teacher, his students and their parents needed chiding for their pedestrian tastes; however, as a Democrat, he claimed to be a friend of the common people. Whitman's Loco-focoism had an overtone of ideological snobbery and begs the question: What accounts for this strange melding of democratic politics and overwrought disdain of the farming communities around him?

Loco-foco Democrats themselves were no social radicals. Beyond their claim to hold a "noble impatience" with "palsying conventionalism," William Leggett and Loco-foco Democrats, as stated in the last chapter, acted more as bastions of the Jacksonian ideals of the free market and equality of opportunity than as radical levelers.[11] They were friends of the rising artisan or entrepreneur more than the struggling farmer or the wage-earning mechanic. Loco-focos concentrated on monetary policies against state banks, paper currency, and monopolies. By the late-1830s, when the Van Buren administration adopted many of the policies of the Loco-focos into the mainstream Democratic Party, these breakaway Democrats returned to Tammany and the Party proper. In the fall of 1840, Whitman served as a Democratic campaign worker against banks, money power, and monopoly.[12] As a city artisan and former journeyman for New York newspapers, he brought both an urbane sensibility and contemporary arguments over the labor theory of value and the status of "mechanics" to the countryside. This sensibility justified (at least according to him) his disdain toward the farmers of Queens County.

Though probably unconscious of the contradiction between his politics and his attitude, Whitman understood the possibilities of a schoolmaster persona in print. As both a community member and a resident alien, he invested in the future of the community and brought expertise and skill from the outside world. Whitman utilized the role of schoolteacher in his writing as a means to legitimize his attitude toward the denizens of rural Long Island. A schoolteacher's outsider/insider status made him a useful observer of the people's habits and shortcomings. Starting in the winter of 1840, Whitman began to publish a series of editorials entitled, "Sun-Down Papers—From the Desk of a Schoolmaster." In these ten essays, which he published in three different newspapers until July 1841, the future poet played the role of the Schoolmaster to a population of "students." In this capacity, he portrayed himself as one of the people, yet one who knew them better than they knew themselves. The title of these essays points to Whitman's conscious construction of the Schoolmaster persona. By referring to the setting sun and the desk of a teacher, he created an image before even making an argument. In this case, Whitman imagined himself as a thoughtful educator spending a quiet hour at the end of a day. Still at his desk (probably in the schoolhouse), with the silence of the early evening replacing the din of the children, the Schoolmaster sat down to reflect on the little world around him. This self-referential quality marked Whitman's personas throughout the 1840s and early 1850s. As Schoolmaster, Editor, and Bard, he actively sought to utilize the commonly understood characteristics of these occupations to lend credence to the arguments he made. By calling himself "Schoolmaster" and setting the time and place for his ruminations, Whitman provided his readers with a pre-packaged identity for their consumption.[13]

This leads to another consistent element of Whitman's use of personas during these years; all were professional. Where Emily Dickinson constructed personas out of feminine social roles prominent in the mid-19th century and Mark Twain utilized a certain self-referential humor to bridge different settings and voices, Whitman inhabited professions and, in doing so, expected the reader to accept his arguments based on a shared understanding of the role these professions played.[14] In the case of the Schoolmaster, Editor, and Bard, Whitman rhetorically inhabited these roles because he was, during their creation, a schoolteacher, an editor and a poet. However, Whitman never let these professions speak for themselves. Instead, he took hold of them and tied his profession to his arguments as if the inclinations of the author and the author's profession were necessarily the same. In doing so, Whitman embraced very early the idea that one is what one does.[15] By inhabiting these professions on paper (rather than just doing them in the world), Whitman took the jobs he held and turned them into rhetorical identities. In return, these professional identities gave credence to his arguments.[16] This self-conscious professionalism lent Whitman the power to view, define, and reform America in the midst of economic and social change.[17]

For Whitman, the Schoolmaster was like a secular missionary who saw people's better natures beneath their immaturity and confusion.[18] In this capacity, he portrayed a kind of democratic didacticism that translated into a loose reform ideology. Though unhappy with the reality of teaching, he found the persona of the schoolteacher useful for presenting a reform program that negotiated the social and economic landscape around citizens in the new market economy and defined their place within it.

Ethical Aesthetics

While exploring Whitman's labor ideology and reform theory in the "Sun-Down Papers," it is important to remember that Whitman was only twenty-one when he wrote them. Driven by a youthful understanding of the debates around him, he had no coherent economic or political reform program. Even at this young age, however, Whitman exhibited an interest in social issues, specifically in areas of class and power, through aesthetic theory.

In the "Sun-Down Papers," Whitman presented injustice as ugly. Individuals were beautiful because they were just and just because they were in their natural place. Here, Whitman subtly co-mingled conservative and radical reform ideology. He envisioned no leveling of class, but equalized everyone within an organic social order. Those who refused to embrace this natural order degraded the democracy; one knew them by their ugliness. Though not entirely nostalgic, this order resembled the idealized version of the artisan republic. In this way, Whitman used the "Sun-Down Papers" to celebrate individuals by showing their native beauty in the modern economy.

The "Sun-Down Papers" have been portrayed as "oppressively moral,"[19] "sentimental,"[20] "didactic,"[21] and "prudish."[22] There is some truth in these criticisms. In the context of Whitman's later prose and poetry, they were rather heavy-handed and simple. However, this style proved common in an age when, after 1820, Ralph Waldo Emerson recalled "a certain sharpness of criticism, an eagerness for reform, which showed itself in every quarter."[23] In an era when art could unabashedly serve the goals of reform, these essays proved rather subtle and modest.[24]

Whitman used the "Sun-Down Papers" as an extended exhortation against affectation and consumerism. The first four "Sun-Down" essays critiqued pretense in the working class. According to the Schoolmaster, the softening of class-based etiquette and the advent of conspicuous consumption in the consumers' market caused an identity crisis for the worker. Natural law determined status and, by extension, aesthetics. Any blurring of this aesthetic was bound to be immoral. Essays six through eight established Whitman's vision of the beauty, purity, and wholesomeness of the authentic individual regardless of class.[25] In these three pieces, the Schoolmaster turned from a critic of consumerism to a champion of the citizen unaffected. Essays nine and ten presented a subtle blueprint of a "loafer" republic where this unaffected beauty ruled the day. This allowed the Schoolmaster to put reform in the hands of the citizen rather than in the realm of economic forces beyond his control. By choosing to be himself, the citizen improved his lot.

Pride, Arrogance, Superciliousness, and Effeminacy

Taken individually, the first four "Sun-Down Papers" are as appealing as the wagging finger of a youthful prude. In the first essay, published on February 29, 1840, Whitman described himself sitting in his "elbow chair" and "casting a backward glance...among the mazes of old scenes and times." For the Schoolmaster, there was "something very delightful in using the beautiful power of memory" and that it "passed into axiom, that the old know few occupations of the mind more agreeable than retrospection."

In this vein, Whitman traced "backwards to the originator of...all [ideas]" and marveled at the "wondrous quality...of thought in the human mind!" At the stylistic turn of the essay, the Schoolmaster remembered "actual life around me" and "a saddening influence fell upon my soul." Upon recognizing the "golden hours of youth" passing him by, the author awoke from his reverie rather depressed. However, his mood lightened when he remembered that "it was Sunday evening" a time for "visits from forlorn bachelors to expecting damsels" and left to call on "pretty little Kitty Denton." Thereafter, the author's melancholy dissipated.[26]

Beyond the contrary evidence that Whitman ever courted a woman during his time as a country schoolteacher, this first "Sun-Down" essay presented the beginning of a consistent aesthetic theory.[27] For the author, old age and the memories that delight it endangered youth as it sapped one's vital strength; life was to be engaged in the present. On its own, this first "Sun-Down" essay read like a call for the reader to seize the day; when considered in conjunction with essays two through four, a more coherent aesthetic vision appeared.

The next three "Sun-Down Papers" rose ever increasingly in didactic tone. "Sun-Down Papers no.2" (published March 14, 1840) told the story of the Schoolmaster's two friends: Homer (who Whitman affectionately called "Hom") and Tom Beprim (whose surname told just about all the reader needed to know). Both were bred in the city; both went to "good schools" with "good masters" and kept "good company." Whitman described both as "good looking" with frock coats, straps on their pantaloons, parted hair on the side, and "neither [with] whiskers." Here, Whitman presented two individuals, probably of the middle or upper class, neither of who seemed very different from the other. Also, it is important to note that he wrote this for the rural audience of *The Hempstead Inquirer*; Whitman intentionally presented two individuals "bred in the city" who reflected urbane options for his rural readers.

Hom was natural and unaffected, "open, generous...and frank," whose laugh sounded "like a discharge of small artillery." He was "a total despiser of any thing in the shape of pride, or arrogance, or superciliousness, or effeminacy" and "no foppish pastime ever finds favor in his eyes." In fact, Hom "can swim like a fish; and on horseback...sits as easily as if he were part of the animal itself." Also, Hom enjoyed playing "ball" and "leaping and running." Effortlessly, Hom acted like a gentleman "particularly towards the ladies" and proved "proficient both in music and in dancing."[28]

Pretense, on the other hand, infected Tom Beprim. According to the Schoolmaster, Tom was "all...forms and ceremony." His reading habits ranged from the "Laws of Etiquette" to "The Youth's Guide to Polite Manners" and he knew the mundane rules of appropriate behavior in all social situations common in the works of authors like William Alcott.[29] He danced "like an automaton...yet never misse[d] a step, never [brought] down his foot in the wrong position" and, in his perfect dancing, ruined the idea of dancing itself. Whitman related a "sight" of Tom at an exhibition ball where the other dancers lost their step and stopped dancing while the music continued. Tom, however, "who, with the features as solemn as a mummy...kept moving on, taking the steps in their proper places and doing everything as seriously as if he had been sentencing a criminal to the gallows." Whitman concluded, "there are many who resemble in some degree...Tom [and make themselves] ridiculous in the eyes of all sensible people...." This scourge of pretense was deadly serious; Tom's attitude was "dangerous" and "cumbersome" as authentic action was always more profitable than a "glittering and flimsy bubble."[30]

Whitman's story of Tom and Hom began much like "Sun-Down Papers no. 1," namely, with a recollection and musing. However, by the end of the tale of Tom's silly formality, it turned to a darker lesson: an unnatural devotion to etiquette and pretense sapped away life itself. Whitman presented Tom and Hom as equal on the surface. However, this surface was not superficial; it was, in fact, a mark of their moral nature. Hom did not seek to be anything that he was not. For this reason he was a hearty and forthright friend as well as a good dancer, gentleman, and ladies' man. Any citizen could achieve this easy nonchalance as long as he did not take himself too seriously. Tom, however, was a fraud. He took on the hollow pretense of "etiquette" and, in the end, not only made himself the fool in the dance hall, but also lived a life that was untruthful and "dangerous."

By creating a cursory equality between Tom and Hom, and then presenting an essential difference between them based on their "etiquette," Whitman considered the *pretense* of class immoral rather than the existence of class itself. Hom and Tom came from the same, seemingly "good" background. Hom, however, acted ethically because he acted unaffectedly. Tom, on the other hand, proved ugly and dangerous because he did what no one should: he *acted* superior. Aesthetics equaled essence. Anyone could be Hom regardless of class or upbringing; all stood in danger of falling into the trap of Tom's foppery.

In his essay on Tom and Hom, the Schoolmaster echoed the "sentimental culture" of the period, best exemplified in works like James Fenimore Cooper's *Leatherstocking Tales* or in the Davy Crockett legends.[31] Accordingly, heroes emerged from the wilderness and distinguished themselves by their integrity and character. Middle-class Americans during the 1830s and 1840s idealized this easy grace and sought to cultivate manners that showed an "index of [a man's] soul" rather than the supposedly decadent etiquette of Europeans and con artists.[32] In "Sun-Down Papers no. 2," the Schoolmaster reflected this ethic and, in the form of Hom, transplanted the natural gentleman like Natty Bumppo or Davy Crockett to the streets of an idealized New York and to the readership of rural Long Island. Instead of bringing the unaffected ethics of the wilderness, Hom exemplified the loose grace of a man comfortable in his own skin and honest with those around him.[33]

Whitman began "Sun-Down Papers no. 3" with a damning statement: "Among the things calculated to depreciate mechanics, none is worthy of greater reprehension than the effort to be fashionable...or what is sometimes called 'living genteelly.'" According to the author, the attempt to "keep up" with the "town style" made mechanics "feel the bitter pangs of insult, and, in cases not a few, have brought on bankruptcy and ruin." Though not overtly equating this pretense with Tom, Whitman drew a subtle connection with his last editorial by claiming that living beyond one's station bred mechanics who lost the "keen sense of self-respect" and "noble feeling of independence" that mark the "true gentleman."

What did Whitman mean here by mechanic? By the publication of this editorial, in March 1840, the term had endured a decade of change. In the first quarter of the 19th century, "mechanic" worked interchangeably with "freeman," "artisan," "member of the working classes," "tradesman," and "workingman." In this regard, it blurred the lines between employed and employing artisans.[34] However, by the time Whitman wrote in 1840, the term mechanic no longer encompassed the rift between employer and employee.[35] By the 1830s, the term "boss" applied to a master craftsman who owned a shop that employed artisans permanently assigned to wage earner's status.[36] In using the term "mechanic" here, the Schoolmaster meant someone young, employed and impressionable.

Whitman's mechanic, however, did not lose in a grand economic shift from an artisan to an industrial economy. If he had, the Schoolmaster could logically seek the origins of his degradation in economics or politics. Instead, the danger lay in "living genteelly." Accordingly, the "ambition to be fashionable" tormented the mechanic and set him down a path that led to "disgrace and death." This ambition, born of the "extravagant ideas of children and wives," forced the mechanic to be "ashamed of his calling" and "totally at war with every thing in his proper habits and legitimate sphere of life." Here, Whitman exposed a dilemma that artisans faced with the advent of the Cult of Domesticity. This shift in the nature of the household created an economic paradigm where the ideal family consisted of a producing husband and a consuming wife who devoted her time to rearing children.[37] Whitman, perceptively citing the acute aesthetic dilemma faced by a laborer unable to uphold early-Victorian appearances, argued that in this new context the mechanic became "ashamed of his calling" because he could not "acquire that hundred little refinements which are necessary to acquitting one's-self with credit in that society whose good will he is so anxious after." This aesthetic crisis had social and economic ramifications as it forced "the loss to a workingman of all personal dignity" and threatened his natural identity.[38]

Significantly, nowhere in this article did Whitman uncover any political, social, or economic shift that brought the mechanic to this state. When the young artisan freely chose to move fashionably beyond his station, he fell into debt, disrepute, and danger. Middle-class Hom ("a gentleman in...manners") and the working-class mechanic (a "true gentleman") achieved a natural grace because they eschewed pretense and affectation. Both exhibited noble traits when each maintained the integrity of his status. Here, then, the Schoolmaster presented an egalitarian ideal achieved through a conservative social structure.

For Whitman, the mechanic oppressed himself when he sought, through consumption, to appear to be something more than what he was.

The most didactic and seemingly prudish of the "Sun-Down Papers" is number four. One scholar even dubbed it "a little sermon."[39] Here, Whitman lectured on the ills of tobacco and caffeine. However, when considered within the context of Whitman's first three "Sun-Down Papers," it is clear that these pieces, all published within eight weeks of each other, formed part of a broader argument regarding aesthetics and class. Also worth noting, the *Long-Island Democrat*, a Democratic paper, which opposed the Whig, and later Republican, *Long Island Farmer* throughout the 19th century, published "Sun-Down Papers no. 4." However, Whitman later published the tenth and final of the "Sun-Down Papers" in the Whiggish *Long Island Farmer*. The Schoolmaster, unlike Walter Whitman, Jr., eschewed partisanship.

Whitman began this fourth essay with a dismissal of the "excitement...with regard to the evils created by ardent spirits" and demanded that his audience remember a more "injurious form of intemperance": tobacco. By the fourth paragraph, when he claimed that "the excessive use of tea and coffee, too, is a species of intemperance much to be condemned," Whitman seemed to have become an ardent devotee of Sylvester Graham.[40] However, he justified his critique of tobacco and caffeine in terms akin to his aesthetics of essays two and three. Tobacco use should be condemned because "boys, like monkeys, are generally ambitious of aping their superiors" and that a "segar generally has a *smoky fire* at one end, and a *conceited spark* at the other [Whitman's emphasis]." Likewise, the absurd taking of "hot liquid into their stomachs" showed "what ridiculous lengths can people be led by fashion." Whitman denied damning "any sensual delights, because I think it is a sin to be happy." On the contrary, the author appreciated only what he called "rational gratification[s]...placed here for two beneficent purposes; to fulfill our duty, and to enjoy the almost innumerable comforts and delights which [God] has provided for us."

The Schoolmaster's call for a return to natural luxuries echoed the ethics of his upbringing. For example, the artisan republicanism of his father's generation celebrated the "middling" status of the craftsman as representing the urban version of the Jeffersonian farmer. Accordingly, these two types of "freeman" exemplified the republican ideal of citizens. They were unencumbered by poverty and luxury, both of which proved dangerous to one's freedom; poverty required a freeman to depend on the good will of others; wealth softened the freeman's vigilance that earned him his status in the Revolution. Whitman's "conceited spark" at the end of a cigar gave up this freedom by attempting to be something he was not. A cigar allowed the young smoker to play a role (dandy, aristocrat, or even adult) and to do so with the ease of a few puffs. Contrary to the goals of the act, smoking debased the young man and ultimately led to physical and psychological degradation.

These assumptions also reflected Quaker beliefs. The influence of Quaker theology on Whitman's poetry has been well established.[41] However, few scholars have noted Friends' influence on Whitman's ethics and aesthetics. Hicksites, following the theology of their eighteenth-century brethren, believed in "that [of] God in everyone."[42] This belief shaped Friends' practice of simplicity and pacifism. At the Byberry Meeting House in Philadelphia in December 1824, Elias Hicks presented a sermon that expressed this understanding of the Inner Light and its moral effects:

> We should, therefore unite, with the operation of this divine principle of God in the soul. It is a living principle, it is the light and life, by which all the children of men are enlightened, and shown their condition....[43]

Whitman echoed these sentiments in his "Sun-Down Papers." For Hicks, the truthful and unchanging part of a person was the spirit of God that resided within. This made individuals essentially the same. Though appearances might differ, inside resided an abiding element that was true and unchanging. When people appealed to their inner godliness, they represented the will of God. Likewise, for Whitman, an individual's essential nature was like that of any other. This explains both his assumption that there were "rational gratifications" that appealed to all individuals and his argument that, though of different classes, both Hom and the mechanic could be "natural" gentlemen. For both Whitman and Hicks, one found an inner wisdom and stable identity in quiet reflection rather than in the "exertions and buzzing about" of the world.[44]

There are other connections between Quaker sensibility and the Schoolmaster's critique. In the 1840s, Quakers consciously dressed "plain." Men, for example, dressed in black or grey, with straight coats without collars and buttons and with traditional, broad-brimmed Quaker hats. This plain dress made Quakers appear more and more distinct through the 19th century as fashion trends accelerated with the advent of mass-produced textiles.[45] In 1840, the Quakers provided a *de facto* critique of the rise of consumerism by their dress and testimony to plainness. According to the Society of Friends, plain dress worshipped the Inner Light of God in one's self. Ostentatious display rejected God's truth.

Whitman's diatribes against cigars and coffee and books on etiquette make sense in this context. These consumable, fashionable goods lent a means by which individuals made something of themselves that they were not.

Misguided citizens, through purchasing, owning, and consuming, attempted to find an identity in the world rather than in the self. These goods allowed the mechanic to join an imaginary consensus of consumers rather than embrace his natural place as a producer. Accordingly, the mechanic had no one else to blame but himself for his loss of identity. So, the Schoolmaster scolded him. Whitman ended these three essays by arguing that "nature,...experience, and enlightened reason" all established the danger of tobacco and caffeine. They were bad for the body, but most importantly, they were bad for the soul because they held out the false promise of an easy identity founded on ephemeral goods.[46]

Prettier Customs

In August 1840, the "Sun-Down Papers" turned to an exploration of the ideal aesthetic that Whitman hinted at in essays one through four. Essays six through eight, taken individually, seemingly had little to do with each other. He wrote on subjects as diverse as the use of flowers for burying the dead, the evils of wealth, and the inability of individuals to envision the "Truth." However, as he wrote them all over a relatively short period, published under the same persona of the Schoolmaster, and developed arguments mentioned in the first four essays, a reading of all three reveals an aesthetically just alternative to the dire warnings of February-April 1840.

"Sun-Down Paper no. 6" began with a tone similar to essays one and two;[47] Whitman returned to the pleasant rhetoric of idle rumination. Accordingly, he found "no prettier custom, than that...of strewing the coffins of young people with flowers." The author described the way in which flowers cause "our painful sensations [to] have much about them of gentleness and poetic melancholy." Thereafter, our "grief is not gross, but delicate,...it more resembles the scent of a thick and full blown rose." According to the Schoolmaster, families buried the young with flowers not to comfort the living, but to symbolize the dead. "We are well aware that men who have lived a length of time, must...have had the fine bloom of simplicity and nature nearly rubbed off...." Here, Whitman coupled contemporary theories about the innocence of childhood with his theory of unaffected virtue. The simplicity of the flowers symbolized accurately the innocent nature of the dead themselves. Therefore, burying an aged person with flowers strewn on the coffin made no sense.

The corpse of a person long-lived already had lost its native simplicity because he "respected custom" and "honored the government," "followed fashion" and avoided "glaring transgressions," "stood up or bowed down" at appropriate times and, in the end, lived with a heart that would cause the reader to be "sickened and amazed." These gestures, seemingly of a good man, quietly symbolized his degradation. The Schoolmaster forgave childhood errors because "we know that the worst deeds they ever committed were but child's follies," but the sins of adulthood were the sins of inauthenticity. Though children committed "follies," an adult degraded himself when he acted without consistency between his internal mechanisms and his external actions. Tom's crimes and the crime of the misguided mechanic mirrored each other. The children, like Hom, acted in a natural and unaffected manner that justified all of their "worst deeds."[48]

Scholars often cite the next essay, "Sun-Down Papers no. 7," as Whitman's first implication that he "would compose a wonderful and ponderous book."[49] Though perhaps a prophetic statement of what became *Leaves of Grass*, Whitman more likely imagined a collection of moral essays based on his "Sun-Down Papers." This "ponderous book" aspired to teach its audience one lesson: "[it] is a very dangerous thing to be rich."

The first signs of wealth's danger were aesthetic, "See the sweat pouring down that man's face. See the wrinkles on his narrow forehead. He is a poor, miserable, rich man." Here, the pursuit of material wealth and social status produced ugliness and deviancy contrary to the goals of affluence. Wealth also made people unhappy. Whitman related the story of a "friend" who described life as a long journey by "steamboat, stagecoach, and railroad." This friend noted, "We hardly...adjust...when we are obliged to stop and get into another conveyance.... We are continually on the move." This constant motion forced people to travel lightly. Anyone with "common sense" avoided carrying along "a dozen trunks, and bandboxes, hatboxes, valises, chests, umbrellas, and canes innumerable...." because when "the Grand Engineer" appeared, he admitted "no luggage therein.... Money and property must be left behind."

Here, Whitman implied his ethical aesthetic. At the end of life's journey, "the noiseless and strange attendants gather from every passenger his ticket, and heed not whether he be dark or fair, clad in homespun or fine apparel." Providence rewarded those who lived as they began life's journey both in the end and in transit; "happy is he whose wisdom has purchased beforehand a token of his having settled satisfactorily for the journey!"[50] Instead of expressing an anxiety with the acceleration of life in the 1830s and 1840s, Whitman presented this hurly-burly existence as elemental. Through the modern metaphor of the train, he made a point about eternal reality: life has always been about rush and flux. The wise understand that there is no need to catch up; integrity and unaffectedness guaranteed poise and inner peace. The "Grand Engineer" promised that in the rush of life there was a universal ethic that rewarded neither money nor fashion, but, instead, judged the integrity of a passenger's unaffected inner condition. This inner condition proved portable through life's tribulations and travels, even after death. Whitman's egalitarian ideal put the means to success in the hands of the individual, but turned the rhetoric of the equality of opportunity inside out. All people held the possibility of success and happiness in their hands; they needed only to reject the temptations of the consumer economy to actualize it.

On October 6, 1840, Whitman published a "card" in the *Long-Island Democrat*. Individuals wrote cards as open letters, paid for like advertisements, and published in newspapers often as responses to public challenges. Used commonly in the early 19th century, their origins lay in the masculine culture of dueling and prize fighting. By the 1840s, they became a common public means of answering perceived slights, almost exclusively among men.[51] This card, signed by "Walter Whitman" and published in reaction to an article in the Jamaica Whig organ, *The Long-Island Farmer*, exposes just how consciously Whitman constructed the Schoolmaster for the "Sun-Down Papers." Whitman's "card" answered an article in the *Farmer* that threatened him with "severe...chastisement" for statements he made during a political rally on September 24 where Whitman, serving as the Democratic electioneer for Queens County, debated John Gunn, who represented the Whigs. During the debate, Whitman charged Charles King and other "eminent whigs [sic] with falsehood" for claiming that the Democratic Party and President Van Buren upheld "the doctrine of a 'community of goods, wives and children.'" Unlike the Schoolmaster, who wrote with a bemused distance about his fellow Long Islanders, Walter Whitman Jr., New Yorker, Democrat and Loco-foco, willingly engaged local Whigs in partisan debate.

In defense of the Democrats and his verbal assault on King, Whitman rejected any implication that his politics or party supported leveling of the economic order. Though King exaggerated when he accused the Democratic Party of hoping to share "women and children," the inclusion of "goods" in his critique implied that Democrats had leveling designs on property. In response, Whitman claimed that King "uttered a *lie* and acted as *no gentleman* would act."[52] With his "card," Whitman attempted to defuse a potentially violent situation and still defend his partisan attack on King during the debate. Though Whitman's political virulence in this case reflected the heated political rhetoric and the masculine culture of politics, competition, and debate that shaped campaigns in this period, the Schoolmaster eschewed this kind of partisanship. Between February 1840 and July 1841 he appeared in three newspapers: one not clearly partisan,[53] one Democratic,[54] and one

Whig.[55] In this regard, Whitman affected an apolitical tone to reach the broadest audience possible and to construct an objective position from which to make his arguments. As the Schoolmaster, Whitman began to hone a voice that claimed to speak for all citizens.

The eighth "Sun-Down" paper, published on October 8, 1840, was Whitman's longest and most mystical. It began with the Schoolmaster strolling thoughtfully down a lane and reflecting "on the folly and vanity of those objects with which most men occupy their lives...." Upon sitting down on a grassy bank, the Schoolmaster slipped into a "tranquil sleep" during which his mind went "wandering over the earth in search of TRUTH."

Thereafter, he heard a "voice" which directed him to a vision of paradise, replete with rolling fields, bubbling brooks, flowers, and a Greco-Roman temple. For the Schoolmaster it was "more lovely than the dreams which benignant spirits sometimes weave around the couch of youth and innocence." In fact, the "voice" which led him to this vision demanded that "he seek not...to discover that which is hidden by an all seeing God from the knowledge of mortals" and directed him to "a country different entirely from the one...just described."

In this new country, Whitman saw all the people of the earth straining to see the temple of paradise. Each one held in his hand an "optical glass" and never gazed at the temple except "through this medium." The Schoolmaster noted the different shapes of these optical glasses, the details of which symbolized diverse epistemologies. Some saw the temple with glasses "narrow and contracted." Others had glasses "of one colour, and others a different." Many had optical devices "gross in texture" that hid the temple "completely...from view." It is easy to relate each of these "observers" to certain social, theological, and philosophical types: the philistine who views beauty narrowly, the philosopher whose convoluted theories overshadow the simple contours of truth, the bigot who sees truth in only one color. Some even came "nigh" to seeing the temple unadulterated, but could not because of their useless optics. Only a few of the observers, at the risk of persecution from the others, viewed the temple "without the false assistance of some glass or other." When the voice returned, it explained, "the great light of Truth...can be most truly...contemplated by the plain eye of simplicity." Here, Whitman further expanded his social ideology into universal ethic. [56]

Accordingly, the unpretentious had the stamp of legitimacy from the hand of the Almighty. Simplicity and a lack of affectation generated a natural egalitarianism. The persecuted "few" who observed the temple unadorned by newfangled theories or prejudices appeared different on the surface, but their unaffected observation of the divine exposed their essential equality. No one was better than anyone else. Quakers understood their relationship with God in this light. As in the case of Hom or the honest mechanic or the youthful corpse strewn with flowers or the boy who rejected the fashion of smoking and coffee drinking, equality and difference went hand-in-hand. Fashionable encumbrances of the consumer economy and the limiting ideas of new-fangled theorists divided people. God himself justified those who acted with integrity in their proper social space.

The Loafer Republic

"Sun-Down Papers no. 9," published on November 24, 1840 revealed Whitman's disappointment over the loss of the presidency by Martin Van Buren to the Whig William Henry Harrison.[57] This represented the first example of a trend in Whitman's editorials; at first, Whitman's personas exuded an amused confidence born of an objective stance. Later, however, one-sided, partisan rancor pulled the personas apart. When politics offended Whitman's sensibilities, his anger undermined his affected objectivity.

Whitman's post-election essay of November 1840 began with a statement that was probably meant to shock: "How I do love a loafer!" "Loafer" had only existed in American English since the early 1830s and probably had negative connotations as a derivation of the German word for tramp or vagabond.[58] For the Schoolmaster, the loafer was not "lazy in fits and starts," but a true "philosophick [sic] son of indolence." The Schoolmaster claimed that loafing had an ancient pedigree; both Diogenes and Adam before the fall were loafers,[59] and, because of their essential nature, loafers had "no material difference" between each other. They represented the most static and unchanging element of humanity. A world ruled by loafers would be a paradise; there would be a good deal of sunshine "for sunshine is the loafer's natural element" and there would be "no hurry, or bustle, or banging, or clanging." Best of all, politics did not exist, "your ears ache no more with...the noisy politician...no wrangling, no quarreling, no loco focos, no British whigs." The recent election, completed only two weeks before, and the local political wrangle in which Whitman found himself in the late summer and early autumn, caused the persona of the Schoolmaster to slip a bit.

Nevertheless, he could not resist turning his story to didactic ends. He argued (hopefully ironically) that, "we loafers should organize." Accordingly, "at all events our strength would enable us to hold the balance of power, and we should be courted and coaxed by all the rival factions." Again, Whitman referred cryptically to the recent election, "stranger things than that have come to pass." The Schoolmaster ended this essay with a dark warning; someone threatened loafers, "mysterious intimations have been thrown out...dark sayings uttered, by those high in society, that the grand institution of loaferism was to be abolished." People talked "sneeringly" and "frowningly" of "us." Powerful, "overbearing men" spoke in "derogatory terms" about loafer "rights and dignity." The Schoolmaster warned these individuals to be "careful." If they irritated their mellower brethren, the loafers may "come out at the next election and carry away the palm before both your political parties."[60]

It is easy to imagine that Whitman's interest group of "loafers" was nothing more than the fantasy of a young Democrat in a community controlled by the Whig parents of his students. Even with his sour grapes, the Schoolmaster's "loaferism" ethically echoed previous essays. These loafers did not smoke, drink, or waste the day dancing in perfect form and so fulfilled Whitman's ideals of Hom, the righteous mechanic, and the unaffected youth by living without the constant effort of self-creation. The loafer exhibited the ultimate integrity because his actions reflected his inner nature. He did not seek to get from one place to another; life led, ultimately, only to the place where it began and allowed the individual only the objects with which he started. Loafers lived in a world timeless and unchanging, egalitarian and static. The loafers' republic existed wherever people recognized this truth.

This ideal also exhibited Whitman's ambivalence toward the idea of larger social forces at work in the new market economy. The loafer shared with the noble mechanic and Hom an unaffected grace but not necessarily the same identity or social position. Each embraced the harmonious order of equality and difference. No social engineering was necessary when individuals embraced their unaffected natures. Loafers only became political when threatened; otherwise they just left well enough alone. In this light, partisan politics were themselves an affectation and symptomatic of something amiss in the Republic.

The "Sun-Down Papers" disappeared for seven months after the publication of the ninth essay in November 1840. Some scholars have speculated that this break stemmed from Whitman's disillusionment with rural Long Island in the aftermath of the Election of 1840[61] or with a disagreement with a local family.[62] Nevertheless, by March 1841, Whitman had relocated to Whitestone, Long Island and in a letter to Abraham Leech dated March 25, remarked that he was "quite happy."

"Sun-Down Papers no. 9 *bis*" read like a response to the virulence of essay nine. [63] In his celebration of loaferism, the Schoolmaster warned specific individuals and threatened a loafer revolution that would sweep away both American parties. Number nine *bis*, on the other hand, started where number nine ended, namely, with conflict, and sought to overcome this state. Recalling a walk one evening, the Schoolmaster recounted his meeting with "a man with whom I was bitterly at variance." This bitterness, which broke his pleasant mood, forced him to realize "how evil a thing it is to be at enmity." Thereafter, Whitman meditated on the futility of anger as people were but "the insect of an hour" and that "down in every human heart there are many sweet fountains, which require only to be touched in order to gush forth." Hereafter, the Schoolmaster reconnected with the elemental good nature of all people, "[T]here are hundreds and thousands of men who go on from year to year with their pitiful schemes of business and profit, and wrapped up and narrowed down in those schemes, they never think of the pleasant and beautiful capacities that God has given them." The Schoolmaster, warming up to his former didacticism, "pit[ied] such people" because they "enjoy[ed] no true pleasure;...they [were] all gross, sensual, and low." Forgetting his enemy and the new benevolent feeling he felt toward him, Whitman returned to his former arguments as to the origins of all evil, "I would have men cultivate their dispositions for kindness...." This disposition made everyone "disdain to be hemmed in by the formal mummeries of fashion" and proved "all pleasures of dollars and cents are dross to those of loving and being beloved." Here, he revisited the Schoolmaster's original argument. When we find ourselves through politics, money, fashion, business or the market we lose our way.[64]

In "Sun-Down Papers no. 9 *bis*," Whitman attempted to stabilize the Schoolmaster persona that he had nearly set askew in number nine. When temperate, this persona offered a means by which to prove all conflicting parties were essentially one. Walter Whitman, the country schoolteacher from burgeoning New York, railed against the perceived idiocy of the villagers around him. As Walter Whitman, he competed within a factionalized social order. However, as Schoolmaster, he played above the fracas. From this "neutral" ground he could silence debates by "seeing" the Republic in its singularity. In this respect, the Schoolmaster acted like a very early version of the transcendent Bard in *Leaves of Grass*. It is perhaps too obvious to point out the irony of an author railing against affectation through a constructed persona. Some scholars have pointed out that this dilemma was endemic to sentimental culture itself.[65] Nevertheless, the Schoolmaster allowed Whitman, at least on paper, to play a role that claimed political impartiality and universal good tidings in a social and political environment where faction and partisanship increasingly became accepted as normal.

The Great Clam Excursion

Whitman published the tenth and final of the "Sun-Down Papers" in July 1841 after he returned to Manhattan and gave up a career in schoolteaching altogether.[66] The historical record is silent as to why he published this last piece in the *Long-Island Farmer* (which was the same newspaper that attacked Whitman less than a year before), why he published it after he quit teaching, and why he wrote this last essay still in the persona of the Schoolmaster. Whitman did not publish editorials again until February 1842 and, by then, had left this persona behind. The tone of this last in the series of "Sun-Down Papers" reflected a shift in Whitman's circumstances and formed a bridge to his new public persona, the Editor.

The tenth of the "Sun-Down Papers" centered on the story of a clamming trip to the South Bay of Long Island. This recollection raises some question as to Whitman's location during this experience. A scan of the map of Long Island reveals that the distance between Manhattan and the South Bay coast would force Whitman and his crew of fifteen to traverse a distance that makes a day trip unlikely. Therefore, the timing of Whitman's excursion in this final editorial is in question. The essay could reflect a daytrip taken when Whitman taught in the South Bay town of Babylon in the winter of 1837-1838, making the essay a recollection of events nearly four years before. Whatever the case, Whitman sought to uphold his persona of the Long Island country schoolteacher in this final essay.

For the first time, Whitman introduced characters in short sketches. Bromero had a "narrow-brimed straw hat." "Senor" [sic] Cabinet wore a "sedate face." Captain Sears had his "usual pleasant look." Kirbus brought his gun and breathed "destruction to snipe." Unlike his previous essays, the Schoolmaster's didacticism never appeared. Instead, the narrative unfolded into subtle symbolism. The diverse party of men hoisted the American flag on a "clam-rake handle...very much to our own pleasure, and the edification no doubt of all patriotic beholders." In this way, the gaggle of men represented the masculine American republic writ small.

Mishaps and incidents abounded on the trip: Kirbus came close to shooting a wild duck. Senor Cabinet got the back of his black coat wet in the salt water. The crew sang "Auld Lang Syne" and "Home Sweet Home" to "great taste and effect." Some of the party swam in the water. Others "valorously" searched for clams. One member of the group, Smith, rowed out into the water and "hauling and pulling there nearly an hour" caught only a single clam "and ...was contented to return from whence he came." According to the Schoolmaster, this effort upheld the truth "of the old maxim: 'Let well enough alone.'" The high points of the day included the "astonishing appetite of Cabinet," Bromero's "laughable stories," a hat lost in the water, only to be recovered by Smith at the loss "of a short necked pipe which had for many days before been safely kept…" and the cutting up of the very few clams caught into bits "in the vain hope of nabbing some stray members of the finny tribe." The Schoolmaster passed over these "and other important matters" to relate to the reader that, though empty handed, "we returned home perfectly safe in body, sound in limb, much refreshed in soul, and in perfect good humour and satisfaction with one another."

Through the clam excursion, the Schoolmaster reconstructed his vision of the aesthetically just. The men of this little republic, with their American flag and clam rakes, left the ambitions of their lives and wives behind them. Likewise, they left behind the social hierarchy of the town and allowed their underlying and unaffected qualities to come to the fore. Some sang. Some shot. One member of the "Spouting Club" quoted "specimens of Shakespearian eloquence" and, thereafter, his friends jokingly called him a "whaler." Some things were lost and others found. The hoped-for clams only justified the experience of fraternal good times. To make this point, the Schoolmaster, in a postscript to the essay, informed the reader that the married men of the crew "bought several shillings' worth of eels and clams, probably in order to ward off the danger that would inevitably have followed their return empty-handed." The Schoolmaster implied that wives could not know the joys of an excursion devoid of profit; as natural consumers, they did not understand that work had its own intrinsic fraternal value.[67]

The clam outing proved to be the beginning of a change in Whitman's style, though not a shift in his message. Formerly didactic in the first nine "Sun-Down Papers," the Schoolmaster became subtle in his last essay. Where he previously stated his thesis in no uncertain terms, the truth now unveiled itself. One's identity was in-born and material. Each identity, though different, had equal value. The difference manifested itself in what one did (professionally and socially) and, therefore, one's natural identity determined one's role in the Republic. Some people were "whalers," some dedicated seekers, some storytellers, some swimmers. Sometimes people lost their hat only to find it at the expense of a valued pipe. Sometimes the goal of an excursion proved secondary to the excursion itself. Affectation was both silly and dangerous because it sought to cover what was simple and obviously true and wring value from things that were essentially worthless. In the miniature republic of clam hunters, Whitman did not have to describe his compatriots' true qualities. The facts spoke for themselves.

When Whitman returned to New York City and the printing business in 1841, he had ten "Sun-Down" articles in his portfolio. Instead of re-entering the craftsmen side of printing, he joined the burgeoning and economically precarious profession of journalism. The "Sun-Down Papers" created a niche for Whitman that helped him get a job as an editor. In 1842, the owners of the *New York Aurora*, a Democratic paper, hired him specifically because of his "bold" and "original" writing.[68]

At the *Aurora*, Whitman built a new persona, the Editor, upon the foundations of the Schoolmaster. In this new persona, he avoided the didacticism of his former essays and, ironically for the unhappy schoolteacher, made public education one of his hallmark topics.

PART TWO

EDITOR

1841–1848

CHAPTER THREE

THE OBJECTIVE EDITOR

As the Schoolmaster, Whitman presented an ideology of social improvement that resonated throughout the rest of his persona-driven public career: individuals reformed themselves. Democracy was an elemental and natural state of life itself; it could not be achieved through institutional reform. For the Schoolmaster, personal definition through unaffected living made for a democratic citizenry. In this regard, Whitman reflected many of the reform movements whose origins lay in the conversion methods of Second Great Awakening theologians like Charles Gradison Finney or temperance advocates like the Washingtonians. One month before Whitman took his position as editor at the *Aurora*, Illinois Whig lawyer and state legislator, Abraham Lincoln, applauded the Washingtonians in a speech to their Springfield meeting,

> [W]hen one who has long been known as a victim of intemperance bursts the fetters that have bound him, and appears before his neighbors "clothed and in his right mind," a redeemed specimen of long-lost humanity, there is a logic and an eloquence in it that few with human feelings can resist.[1]

Whitman's rhetoric as the Schoolmaster echoed these sentiments.[2] He used the language of moral persuasion to maintain a balance of individualism and egalitarianism similar to the artisan republicanism of his father's generation. However, he incorporated modern ideology and political discourse to do so.

The newspapers in which Whitman published upon his return to New York were different in scope and interest than those of rural Long Island. Before becoming the editor at the *Aurora*, Whitman wrote for a number of Democratic papers like John O'Sullivan's *Democratic Review* and John Neal's *Brother Jonathan*; both of which created a space for democratic discourse on politics and culture. O'Sullivan's paper, for example, attempted to foster an American literature devoid of European pretense and advocated untrammeled expansion to the Pacific Ocean. In writing for these papers, Whitman positioned himself as a "respectable" journalist for the masses and avoided publishing in the "sporting press" of titillating exposés and lurid tales.³ The *Aurora* prided itself on staying above these subjects and celebrated the arrest for libel of the flash press proprietor and editor, William Snelling, and the subsequent trial where his former partner, George Wooldridge, testified against him.⁴

Whitman edited the *New York Aurora* from March through April 1842.⁵ A highly politicized, Democratic city paper with a circulation of about 5,000, the *Aurora* was one among many other political journals of similar stripe and had to position itself accordingly. To do so, the owners consistently defined their newspaper against Levi Slamm's *New Era*, the local Tammany organ. This anti-Tammany Democratic stance was a good fit for Whitman's loco-focoism.

Previously, the *Aurora* employed the radical Mike Walsh who, by 1840, represented the cause of labor reform against entrenched stalwarts in the New York Democratic Party. Walsh's Spartan Association started as a radical fringe of the Party that sought to unseat Tammany politicians in the name of labor rights and the "Bowery B'hoys."⁶ After a pilgrimage to Brook Farm in 1844 and an immersion in Fourierist theory, Walsh published anti-capitalist tracts in his own newspaper, *Subterranean*, and sought to expose the wretched working conditions of the city's major industries. By 1843, Walsh declared that "no man can be a good political democrat without he's a good social democrat" and when accused of being a "leveler," Walsh claimed to "glory in the name."⁷ The *Aurora* provided the first forum where Walsh established his legitimacy as a Democratic critic of Tammany Hall. Like Walsh, Whitman actively engaged the political and social issues of the moment and often commented on the political wrangling within the Democratic Party itself. His earlier persona of the Schoolmaster, the wise outsider, was therefore untenable. The Editor had to be an insider to establish his credibility on a paper that spoke to the inner workings of the Party. Whitman only managed to maintain elements of his outsider's perspective by changing his persona.

In his Editor persona, Whitman constructed an objective style that incorporated the tone of both an eyewitness and unbiased correspondent. Whereas the Schoolmaster's egalitarian ethos gave him license to attack consumerism in didactic little lessons, the Editor's objective tone allowed him acute critiques of society that had immediate relevance to the Democratic readers of the *Aurora*. In one important way, the Schoolmaster and the Editor mimicked each other: both judged individual choice rather than over-reaching forces as the cause of dislocation and depression in the new market economy.

To credit Whitman with journalistic objectivity seems anachronistic. Historians of journalism traditionally note the proud partisanship of newspapers before the Civil War. According to Gerald Baldasty, an editor of a paper like the *Aurora* played the roles of political party spokesman, disseminator or party philosophy, and voice of candidates loath to publicly promote their own ambitions. The *U.S. Telegraph*, founded in 1826 by supporters of Andrew Jackson to rival the pro-Adams *National Intelligencer* and *National Journal*, was a good example of the type of newspaper whose ends reflected this open partisanship. The editor of the *Telegraph*, Duff Green, even helped organize pro-Jackson rallies as part of his editorial duties. [8]

Historians usually cite the ideal of journalistic objectivity as growing out of the Civil War. David Mindich argues that editors like Charles Dana at the *New York Tribune* utilized the "inverted pyramid" style with a descending order of facts from the most important to the least in reaction to the official reports from Secretary of War Edwin M. Stanton. Stanton, in the hope of controlling information from the front, turned the War Department into the national repository of accurate information and, thereby, forced editors to rely on government sources. To encourage editors to accept these government-sanctioned reports, Stanton broke open the narrative style of reporting common to newspapers before the war and constructed a method of purveying information that gave the reader the impression of reading only the facts. These reports, however, implicitly invited readers to construct their own narrative based on this "objectively" presented information. [9] The inverted pyramid style in American journalism shifted the process of narrative construction from the writer to the reader.

In the 1840s, the decade during which Whitman began his fifteen-year career as a journalist, the narrative style in journalism was itself novel and, according to its practitioners, a means by which to present information truthfully. In her study of the gothic in American prose, Karen Halttunen notes a cultural turn in the late-18th century from the ethics of original sin, where a crime was only an exacerbated form of the evil to which all humans were prone, to the ethics of Enlightenment liberalism where all people were "essentially good, rational, and capable of self-government." This turn from a religious to a secular understanding of human nature affected truth telling itself as the penny press began to rival sermons for the authority to distill chaotic society into consumable meaning. This liberal understanding of human nature, however, created a new problem of evil. Without original sin, how could crime be explained? According to Halttunen, by the 1840s, the criminal became the "other" who represented a divergence from normal humanity. Charles Dickens, a writer and journalist who Whitman admired, called the criminal intellect "a horrible wonder apart." [10]

If original sin no longer explained the origin of evil in people, perhaps certain experiences could. In this regard, Locke's theory of the *tabula rasa* filtered into the cultural psyche. To truthfully understand an individual, one located the origins of individuality in past experiences. This theory could be applied to societies, political systems, and economies. The present marked a culmination of the "chain of circumstances" which created it and, therefore, depended upon a narrative to explain it.[11] Walt Whitman, like most journalists in the 1840s, assumed that narratives and truth went hand-in-hand. In fact, truth telling without a narrative required a biased observer who removed what was intrinsically true of all events: the story. In this regard, an objective report necessarily invoked a narrative, but, different from the objective style of the inverted pyramid, placed the onus on the reporter to determine the sequence that gave events meaning.

Whitman incorporated this editorial role into his new persona. Like the Schoolmaster, Whitman-the-Editor defined himself rhetorically for his readers. Throughout the life of this persona, he self-referentially described his work, related his thought processes in the midst of creation, and compared his position to that of other professionals deemed (by him) to be essential to the Republic. Like the Schoolmaster, the Editor improved the nation from his unique vantage point.

Whitman returned to a New York in the midst of becoming the premier American metropolis. The population of the city grew from 123,706 in 1820 to 515,000 around twenty-five years later. Brooklyn also saw equivalent growth in the same period from a hamlet of 5,210 to a metropolis in its own right with 200,000 inhabitants by 1860.[12] The infrastructure of the greater New York area could not sustain this growth comfortably and, as late as the 1840s, many streets were unpaved and unlit, hogs wandered the alleys and infiltrated piles of uncollected garbage, and cows were commonly herded through the streets to graze on the outskirts of the city.[13]

The city's boom economy suffered painful busts. The Panic of 1837 began symbolically on March 15 with the collapse of the granite office building of J.L. and S.I. Joseph and Co. on Wall Street. Two days later, the firm financially imploded after a number of New Orleans merchants, to whom the company issued loans, defaulted on their debts. By April 11, one hundred twenty-eight firms declared bankruptcy. According to the diary of George Templeton Strong, "The merchants are going to the devil *en masse.*"[14]

The Panic and ensuing depression affected both Whitman and his persona. The bust devastated the real estate market and construction trades which frustrated Walter Whitman, Sr.'s hope of cashing in on the strong economy in Brooklyn and New York. Until the economy revived in 1843, unemployment reached nearly 33 percent. When an advertisement for twenty laborers was posted in City Hall in August 1837, five hundred workers applied.[15] The Panic also temporarily stymied the New York union movement. Between 1833 and 1836, the General Trades Union (GTU) sought to create "one great phalanx against the common enemy of workingmen, which is *overgrown capital* supported by AVARICE [emphasis original]." On the eve of the Panic, two-thirds of New York workers belonged to fifty-two confederated unions. After 1837, ensuing unemployment cut union bargaining power to nothing. A state Supreme Court ruling that defined unions as illegal monopolies added insult to already serious injury.[16] In reaction to this situation, many workers turned to religion and politics in lieu of union activism.[17] Whitman's writings in this period reflected this change; they hardly mentioned labor collectivism at all.

In conjunction with the collapse of the economy, upper and lower class congregations, Episcopalians and Anglicans, Baptists and Methodists, turned inward and looked to personal salvation as remedy for economic and social dislocation. During this period, William Miller predicted the coming Armageddon down to the day (April 23, 1843) and convinced over 50,000 "Millerites" to prepare for the end times.[18] Seeking to cash in on apocalyptic fears, bowery dry-goods merchants advertised "White Muslin for Ascension Robes."[19] In 1838, Bishop "Dagger John" Hughes arrived in New York City to help the Catholic immigrant population maintain its faith and survive the economic downturn.[20] Hughes eventually became a lightening rod for Tammany Hall politics and a target for Whitman's scurrilous nativist attacks on the Irish in the spring 1842.

Whitman embraced the rhetoric of self-improvement and moral persuasion, but like much of the Democratic press, rejected overt religiosity. In this way, he used contemporary discourses to uphold traditional republicanism and transform it for modern use. The people did not need a religious crutch to overcome their problems, just as in the "Sun-Down Papers" they needed no new-fangled device to observe God's glory. People needed only to see clearly and use their elemental common sense. The Editor showed them the truth. Thereafter, he expected they would fix themselves.

Charles Dickens and the Objective Style

Whitman's arrival at the *Aurora* coincided with Charles Dickens' visit to New York City in 1842. On February 14, a little over one month before

Whitman became editor of the newspaper, the *Aurora* reported on the "Great Boz Ball" at the Park Theater.[21] In this article, the editor of the *Aurora*, Thomas Low Nichols, celebrated Dickens who "danced...with thousands of his admirers around him.... [T]he author of the Pickwick Papers...balance[d] his partner with the most graceful and Pickwickian manner."[22] This began a love affair between the *Aurora* and Dickens (which Whitman was happy to continue when he took over from Nichols)[23] and was the first of many cases where the New York press, in regards to the Englishman, easily mixed the fictional and the non-fictional. According Nichols, Dickens created characters so realistic that the observer could seek signs of his fiction in the real world. Dickens, himself, began his writing career as a journalist and his first bound publication, *Sketches by Boz* (1836), started as a series of newspaper articles. These "sketches" included both descriptions of individuals: "The beadle," "The schoolmaster," "The curate," and scenes that detailed "The streets," the "Doctors' commons," and "Greenwich fair," etc.[24]

Throughout March 1842, the *Aurora* noted Dickens' keen eye for the truth. In an article published on March 1, the paper described the author's strut of a "lion," but found it "fortunate...that Boz was not always a lion; else had we never had those...life like [sic] sketches which prove him to have walked abroad into the great theater of human life with his eyes open."[25] The Englishman's seeming truthfulness and unadulterated observations justified a conflation of the real and the realistic. Unfortunately, Dickens' fame made it impossible for him to see the real America, "if his wish to visit the alms house should be known, the Mister Bumble of this hemisphere must have on his best coat... and the Oliver Twists get extra allowances of prog."[26] Later, on March 16, the *Aurora* noted that Dickens proved himself the most talented novelist of his times because one could observe examples of "poor Oliver, and crazed Barnaby, and pathetic Nell" everyday on the streets of New York.[27]

Not all of the New York press celebrated Boz's visit. Whitman's editorials began with a debate over whether the Englishman's portrayals of humanity, in all its disgraceful forms, posed a danger to democracy and a faith in the people to rule for themselves. According to these critics, Dickens' characters were so convincing that he threatened to undermine democracy with his grim portrayals of individuals. This represented a certain anxiety toward the wisdom of democracy on the part of the Democratic press in the mid-1840s. Dickens' stories did not properly portray the best (and only the best) of the common people; his characters were occasionally so despicable that they threatened to call into question the wisdom of universal male suffrage itself. Whitman wrote three editorials in defense of Dickens in 1842. He published the first of these immediately preceding his tenure at the *Aurora*, the second less than a month later while editor of the *Auror*, and the third in the *Evening Tattler* after Dickens' famous critique of the United States in the summer of that year. Instead of traditional reviews, these editorials meditated on the value of Dickens' style and its merit as social commentary.

The Editor's first essay on Dickens set this tone. Entitled "Boz and Democracy," Whitman called Dickens a "glorious writer of his well-deserved fame" and defended Dickens' "graphically drawn and deeply colored picture[s]." After a brief introduction, Whitman quoted extensively from a negative review of Dickens' work in the *Washington Globe*. The *Globe* blamed the Englishman for aiding "the course and progress of vice among us, by placing before the already degraded, examples of new modes of wickedness." According to this critique, a portrayal of the downtrodden in this state threatened the Republic. The critic did not deny the realism of Dickens' portrayal. Instead, he decried the author's unwillingness to rhetorically uplift readers and present ideal types. This *Globe* critic could not "comprehend how a writer can be fairly entitled to the credit of being the champion of that class of mankind which he pictures in colors so revolting to our feelings and sympathies." Dickens, then, in his realistic portrayal of the lowest common denominator, weakened the government of the common man.

Whitman rejected this interpretation. The portrayal of human beings "in [their] lowest stages of degradation" did not establish an author as a friend of democracy or not. A true portrayal of humanity only asked the reader to vicariously experience examples of virtue and vice without the pretense of abstract moralizing. According to Whitman, Dickens asked the reader to observe "that although social distinctions place others far higher or far lower..., [we]...are human beings alike, as links of the same chain." When Dickens described humanity in this way, and not in the "abstract style of the essayist, or the lofty dreams of the poet," he "[taught] his readers to abhor vice."[28]

Here, Whitman experimented with a new editorial tone. Whereas in the "Sun-Down Papers" he openly moralized and wrote diatribes against the evils of tobacco and coffee, he now celebrated Dickens for putting "before those whom he would reform, the strong, naked, hideous truth." An objective look at society provided the means to social improvement. Because the "rich cannot taste the distresses of want from their own experience," Dickens reformed "through the power of the pen."[29] This reflected the Enlightenment liberal and Lockean understanding of humanity that conceived morality as "not only natural but pleasureable."[30] Instead of being coldly clinical, Dickens' objective portrayal sought to produce the warm emotions of sympathy and the burning desire for reform. Whitman concluded this editorial with a personal paean to

Dickens: "I cannot lose the opportunity of saying how much I love and esteem him for what he has taught me through his writing—and for the genial influence that these writings spread around them where they go." He also defended Dickens for personal reasons, "...I cannot tamely hear one whom I have long considered as a personal friend and as a friend to his species, thus falsely and uncharitably, and groundlessly attacked."[31]

The April edition of John O'Sullivan's *Democratic Review* also attacked Dickens "with a fierceness" that shocked Whitman. The *Review* blamed the Englishman for exaggerating the negative elements of humanity and endangering the nation's morals. According to the critic, "there are no such characters in human nature, and the moral effect of exhibiting such to the imagination is very bad."[32] In response, Whitman claimed that Dickens held "up villainy to public scorn" as "the physician cures no cankers except by cutting with a sharp blade." In citing the physician, Whitman tried to convince his audience that this objective look at humanity exposed self-evident social evils in a scientific manner. He also accused the *Review* editor of living in an sheltered fantasy, "Is the *Review* sure that 'no such characters exist in the world, or in nature,' as Dickens' villains?"[33] Here, Whitman equated the real world with Dickens' fiction and implied that he and Dickens shared a common charge: to edify the community by holding its own "glaring reality" before it. This offered a compelling method for Whitman's own socio-political critique.[34]

Whitman's final editorial about Dickens appeared in the *Evening Tattler* four months after his dismissal from the *New York Aurora*. Scholars question whether the letter Whitman quoted in the editorial, purportedly by Charles Dickens, was in fact authentic. [35] Dickens himself, in response to the maelstrom caused by the letter, denied its authenticity. In fact, some scholars imply that Whitman may have forged it himself.[36] Whatever the case, Whitman applauded Dickens' ability to cut "into the flimsiness of our American aristocracy" and recognize the danger of the "worship of pelf"[37] where "every refined wish" succumbed to "the great whirlpool of avarice." Conveniently, Dickens made Whitman's case in his letter, "I have always thought that much good might be done by selecting out characters from the lower walks of life, and embodying in their stories, how often it is that the beauty of innocence and integrity might be seen among the poor...."[38] For Whitman, Dickens' realistic fiction inspired moral improvement. Eyewitness editorials served the same purpose.

Egalitarian and Judge

By adapting Dickens' objective style to the New York streets, Whitman's Editor played both egalitarian and judge. Assuming the elemental equality of humanity provided him with a claim to objectivity where all verdicts were self-evident, the reader only had to tabulate the facts to understand the truth. The Editor, then, maintained his status as one of the people. His conclusions were theirs because the facts spoke for themselves.

Laborers and wage-earning journeymen faced many unpleasant facts in the spring of 1842. In addition to the temporary breakdown of unionism and rising unemployment, the artisan occupations that had disappeared during the depression were unlikely to reappear when prosperity returned. The shift from an apprentice-artisan economy to one of semi-skilled industrial workers caused an identity crisis in young New York laborers who "proclaimed they were freemen who knew no master, but worried they were slaves to their employers."[39]

The rise of gang activity in New York in this period symbolized both economic dislocation and a loss of self-definition among young workingmen. According to Philip Hone, "The city is infested by gangs of hardened wretches...[who] patrol the streets making the night hideous and insulting all who are not strong enough to defend themselves."[40] These turf-based gangs took colorful names and "uniforms" to identify themselves: Forty Thieves, Kerryonians, Shirt Tails (because they left their shirts un-tucked), Plug Uglies, Roach Guards, Dead Rabbits, etc.[41] Some of these gangs translated their street credibility into connections to volunteer fire brigades or political muscle. Mike Walsh's "Spartan Band," for example, went from gang to wing of Tammany Hall in the space of ten years. Walsh was mid-way through this transformation when he wrote for the *Aurora* in the early 1840s.

By the time Whitman began his tenure at the *Aurora*, the young working-class artisan and gang member was culturally distilled into the image of the "Bowery b'hoy." Some scholars have interpreted the b'hoy, a cigar smoking ruffian, with soap locks and flippant use of the word "hoss," as an inspiration for Whitman's celebration of the urban proletariat.[42] This would indeed be a strange transformation since Whitman had so maligned a similar cigar-smoking character in the "Sun-Down Papers." However, a careful look at worker imagery in the *Aurora*, as presented "objectively" by the Editor, shows an idealized laborer closer to the ideal of his father's generation than that of the Bowery b'hoys. In an *Aurora* article entitled "About Boy-Men," Whitman decried a new kind of boy "...between the ages of eleven and sixteen, ...smoking a cigar or tossing off a glass of liquor with the utmost nonchalance.

He assumes all the airs and attitudes of a grown man.... Nothing so ill becomes a youngster as the...effrontery which mark boy-men."[43] This was the Schoolmaster's last explicit diatribe against pretentious young mechanics.

An article published in February 1842 entitled "Can This Be Justice?" represented the Editor's new and more narrative style of critique. In it, Whitman related the story of three criminals, two rich and one poor, who pay for their crimes according to their wealth. The poor and starving drunkard, arrested for stealing a loaf of bread, languished with a "deep disgust with himself in his soul." In prison, the "jailbird...went from bad to worse, and was soon in a dying condition." Two other criminals, both "rascals of rank," plotted a financial scheme where "the bubble burst" and both walked away from the ruins richer than before. At a dinner after their malfeasance, the two toasted "even handed laws...which in our glorious republic, dispense to all impartially their due" while, according to the Editor "widows [were] left with narrow competence, young children, sick people, whose cases were hopeless...were sufferers by...bankruptcy...." [44]

This morality tale implied that misplaced wealth caused vice. The rich forced the poor to steal and called them criminals. Rich speculators stole and toasted just laws while their schemes further debased the poor. Standing alone, this editorial marked Whitman as an advocate of economic leveling; the criminal rich were evil schemers, the criminal poor were victims of circumstance.

However, other editorials of this spring showed a more nuanced understanding of the origins of social injustice. For example, a little less than one month later, in an editorial entitled "The Last of Lively Frank," the Editor presented a different story of human degradation. Using the narrative approach, Whitman recounted the story of a visit to the house of young Frank who, according to the Editor, lived a charmed boyhood, "his good temper, his vivacity, and his exuberance of animal spirits, his common appellation...and his extraordinary intelligence raised him up many friends." To his surprise, however, Whitman found Frank in a "blackish, grimy, miserable looking house" with "filthy stairs" in an "attic room." Frank lived in "bleak poverty," dying on what the Editor "suppose[d] must be called a bed." Frank's figure was "ghastly" and told a tale of "chances thrown away...[and] extravagances indulged in." Frank told the Editor of his "negligence, his idleness, his letting his talents run to waste, and, at last, his reduction to the state in which we found him."[45]

The sight of poor Frank inspired the Editor's rumination on "similar events that are daily going on in this great city." These events included "delicate women" working themselves to illness, boys forced to be "familiar with vice," girls whom "absolute starvation" drove to "ruin," men, bereft of hope, "ready to meet death with a welcome."[46] This flight of fancy is difficult to justify. Frank clearly authored his own degradation; the Editor said as much. However, Frank brought to mind the suffering of innocents who, as seen in the Editor's piece of February, suffered because of wealth's greed. Whitman classified poverty brought on by personal vice and that brought on by the vice of others in the same category. One inspired meditation on the other. Both shared common cause and common results.

Whitman here reflected popular reform literature common to the penny press and cheap exposés in the first half of the 19th century. For example, in James McCabe's *The Secrets of the Great City*, a young man is degraded by degrees. After leaving home for the city he happens into a "fashionable" saloon with "waiter girls" and "fancy men" who turn out to be gamblers and confidence men. Later, the innocent newcomer's new "friends" murder him and dump him in the harbor.[47] The moral of the story is clear; good behavior is a matter of self-interest. Frank's trajectory follows a similar descent; however, Whitman turned this tale from one focused solely on the lost individual to a fable of personal degradation that had social ramifications. Frank's story reminded the Editor of starving street urchins and ruined women. In this way, Whitman connected the morality of self-preservation to social duty and, therefore, maintained an imperative of individual responsibility. For the Editor, wealth was not the problem. Though wealth could inspire certain immoral acts, so, as in the case of Frank, could personal attributes like "intelligence" and "vivacity." Both Frank and those that oppressed the working poor committed the same crime. Both assumed their inherent superiority (based on wealth or just good luck) and bred avarice, degradation and injustice in their wake.

This was likewise clear in a short editorial of April 1842 entitled "Playing in the Park." In this piece, the Editor described the common sight of young, poor children playing in public during sunny weather. According to the Editor, these children took part in games like "running races, trundling hoops, playing marbles." Unfortunately, "one or two understrappers" who had charge of the park, often rushed into the midst of the youngsters and "beat them with rattans...[to] disperse them." The Editor called this "useless and brutal." Though poor, the children had a right to "their little amusements." In fact, "on the Battery, and in other public grounds, any quantity of offspring of the rich and fashionable may be daily seen playing, and no objection is made." Here, Whitman drew a parallel between the essential qualities of rich and poor: they loved to play. Chasing poor children out of the park taught a lesson contrary to "the proper moral [guidance of] *young republicans* [Whitman's emphasis]."[48] A citizen's duty was to instruct future republicans in the truth that individuals had equal access to public space regardless of economic status. Let the poor play in the park. Let the rich play on the Battery. The desire to play and the right to do so in their respective public spaces marked the beginning and end of the Editor's argument. In this context, the seeming contradiction between Frank and the drunkard and the widow and the poor children came together. Equality existed *in spite* of wealth. Whitman aimed at reform through an acknowledgment of an essential equality that manifested itself everyday across the social hierarchy. The recognition of this kind of equality inspired mutual benevolence between the rich and poor for the good of the whole.

An idea of equal rights across classes had a long pedigree by this period. Since the American Revolution, artisans interpreted their rights as springing from the Tree of Liberty that "pushed up through the dead weight of Imperial tax collectors, overbearing Royal governors, and aristocratic corruption."[49] A select group shared this heritage. As diverse authors note, white, male property holders conceived of themselves as equals among a mass of dependents.[50] Traditionally, artisans assumed that they formed part of this economically diverse republic of freemen. However, the widening social gap between wage earners and employers made the equal rights rhetoric for all white males less and less realistic. Whitman grounded his morality tale of young republicans unjustly deemed a public nuisance in these contemporary class anxieties. In this regard, unions thought more progressively than the Editor. The General Trades Union, before its dissolution, called for higher wages and greater equality between the skilled and industrialized trades and, in doing so, critiqued oppressive social structures and institutions.[51] On the other hand, the Editor criticized bad individual choices on the part of wage earners *and* capitalists in his attempt to maintain the ideal of free and equal citizens of different wealth.

Little Republics

Whitman used the objective style to trump the public's method of defining itself in an attempt to frame public discourse in ways convenient to his own reform ideology. Jürgen Habermas cites three institutional criteria common to the public sphere that are significant to these editorial forays into public life. According to Habermas, first, realms of public discourse (salons, coffee houses, pubs), "preserved a kind of social intercourse that...disregarded status altogether." Second, the public used discussion in specific locations to create areas of "common concern." And, third, these locations remained, in principle, "inclusive" and open-ended so as to preserve their status as "public" and, therein, maintained the power to define what was and what was not proper for public discourse.[52] Whitman sought to outdo this process in his *Aurora* editorials. Instead of allowing the public to define itself and its beliefs in reaction to events, he used his objective style to expose the public to his interpretation of its true image.

For example, in "Life in a New York Market," the Editor recounted a visit to meat-sellers row. Here, he celebrated the nation's bounty and proclaimed, perhaps in reference to the economic doldrums in the aftermath of the Panic of 1837, that "we cannot be on the verge of despair, when such spectacles as these may be witnessed in the land!" The marketplace represented the Republic in miniature "for a man who loves to see the workings of human nature." Whitman lauded the confident mason and the boarding house owner who offered "good solid accommodation" by "foraging for her Sunday dinner." There were "old maids...careful housewives of grades high and low, as well as all sorts, and sizes, kinds, ages, and descriptions... wending... pricing... examining" and "purchasing." The butchers also appeared in a humorous, but favorable light, "they gesticulate with the grace, the affected bendings and twistings of a French dancing master." In this tabulation, one not only senses the future Bard of *Leaves of Grass* who celebrated humanity in a flowing series of snapshots, but also the Schoolmaster of the clam excursion who found a picture of the entire nation in very particular circumstances. He embraced the mason, boarding-house owner, widow, son, housewife and butchers. These individuals fulfilled their roles appropriately; wives and artisans shopped at the market for goods to maintain their place as wives and artisans; butchers acted liked butchers. These many roles maintained their integrity in the new market economy and, therefore, met with Whitman's approval.

The little republic also included outlaws. The Editor observed a flirtatious young woman who "carries out the foible of her sex, and apes her superiors," a wage earner who belonged to "one of those trades which require a man to stay cooped up in the house in some constrained bodily position," and "a man whose pressure of business has caused him to go without his supper." The flirtatious girl, in the market for something other than the goods for sale, had no appropriate place; she fell prey to a "foible" of her gender. As neither wife nor daughter, she became an archetypical jezebel whose sexuality destabilized the market's good order. In this regard, Whitman alluded to an explosion of prostitution in New York City in the face of high rents, few adequate employment opportunities, and an industrial economy that replaced young, female workers with low-paid male immigrants.[53] Likewise, the over-worked businessman, there because his work forced him to skip his dinner, inspired pity, but also a rejection of whatever selfishness (either his own or his employer's) brought him to this state. The stooped-shouldered wage earner represented an unnatural force in the Republic; he was the flush mason's opposite and warning.

The marketplace contained threatened innocents as well. When he saw a group of poor youths, the Editor opened "the flood gates of our charity..." and gave the children some candy. In this altruistic act, Whitman placed himself actively in the scene, "we feel more satisfaction from having bestowed on those...boys a ten minutes joy, than if we had...heard that 'our party' had gained the...contest."[54] Here, he found his better self and invited the reader to do likewise. The boys in this little republic, like a gaggle of Oliver Twists, turn our sympathy into action; by entering the moment, the Editor turned from observer to actor and took the reader along with him for a moment of vicarious moral persuasion. His charity toward these youngsters hearkened back to his celebration of the innocence of youth in the "Sun-Down Papers." The young were still pure and had no role except as future citizens. Whitman utilized the traditional passion play of innocents threatened and presented these young people with two options: embrace the role that will define you (mason, butcher, mother, widow), or drift in ill-defined limbo and personal degradation (broken laborer, over-worked businessman, sexualized girl). According to the Editor, a little kindness in this regard went a long way toward leading these children down the right path. Instead of sentimentality, this benevolence demonstrated fraternity toward young republicans.

Two days after his visit to the market, on March 18, 1842, Whitman published an editorial entitled "New York Boarding Houses" where he again found equality and ethical consumption in the doings of the Republic. In this piece, the Editor claimed that New Yorkers were "a boarding people" and that "this notion holds good, to a certain degree, for every section of the republic [sic]." After describing different types of boarding houses, Whitman came to that of Mrs. C and made the rounds of the breakfast table.[55] The landlady was a "fleshy, red cheeked, good looking woman;" Mr. K was a "good humored" New Englander; W was in "dry goods keeping in Greenwich Street;" A was a "Jewish gentleman of Chatham Street;" Mr. B was a jeweler and a "gentleman;" Y was from Saratoga Springs; Dr. H was a dentist, and Mrs. H was his wife. As at the market, the Editor made a miniature picture of the nation in the seemingly mundane scenes around him.[56]

Many cultures lived in this little republic; men and women, Jews and gentiles sat together, each a citizen of the breakfast table. By playing their role appropriately, all received the Editor's stamp of approval. Some passed through or were resident aliens (New Englander and Jew), some stayed as permanent residents (dry goods keeper, clothing store owner, land lady), but the Editor justified all in this place of convivial transaction. Instead of the highly competitive world of winners and losers, Whitman's America of markets and breakfast tables contained both individuality and equality without hierarchy or leveling.

In his Editor's voice, Whitman portrayed citizens as distinct and, by necessity, unequal in the particular. Different backgrounds, economic status, and personal inclination defined them. However, when they came together, their differences bred mutual benefit. Unhappiness or physical degradation marked those who acted selfishly or unduly haughty. Punishment, unfortunately, did not always fall on the criminal; oftentimes the poor and weak suffered for the injustice of the rich and powerful. Nevertheless, the evidence always pointed to the crime. All of Whitman's degraded characters, the desperate thief, dispossessed widows, despicable Frank, the poor children in the park, the flirtatious girl and the underfed businessman provided evidence of crimes against the Republic. The Editor exposed these crimes and, through moral persuasion, prevented their perpetuation. Whether he described the American public sphere as a "chain" (echoing the Whig politician, Daniel Webster) or a marketplace (reflecting both the Whig and Jacksonian celebration of opportunity) or a boarding house, Whitman rooted his egalitarianism in diverse interests functioning mutually in public. This required the morality of persuasion, personal charity, good manners and a sense of one's proper place. This also mirrored the common conception of the traditional artisan's workshop.[57] Many hands made the Republic, and justice grew from equal parts functioning in their prescribed role.

"Insidious Traitors From Abroad"

Whitman's short tenure at the *Aurora* coincided with a crisis in the New York Democratic Party. In 1842, Bishop John Hughes used the new political clout of the growing population of Irish-Americans to force the Democrats Party to support public funding for parochial schools. This threatened to make mutually exclusive two hallmarks of New York Democracy: natural rights and a separation of church and state.

John Higham notes that nineteenth-century nativists like the Know-Nothing Party based their anti-Irish politics on a belief that Protestantism was the bulwark against European despotism. This principle translated into the "zeal to destroy the enemies of a distinctively American way of life."[58] Anti-immigrant sentiment of this variety usually found itself among the Whigs or, in the case of the xenophobic Know-Nothing Party, with the Republicans after 1856.[59]

The Democrats did not typically play nativist politics. In fact, Irish-Americans utilized the natural rights rhetoric of the Party to squelch any question of their citizenship.[60] The Party's ambivalence and occasional hostility toward religious politics appealed to minority religious populations like the Catholic Irish in Protestant America. As Jeffersonian Republicans benefited from artisan politics coupled with immigrant enfranchisement in the 1790s, so too Whitman's Democratic Party appealed to immigrant populations in the 1830s and 1840s. This coupling of natural rights theory and a strong advocacy of a separation between church and state served the Democratic Party well in the 1830s. However, the debate over public funding for religious schools threatened to subvert this coalition between the working-class Irish and native New York Democrats. In the spring 1842, Whitman saw in Bishop Hughes' political machinations a threat dire to the Republic itself.

Whitman's articles in the *Aurora* described Irish Catholics as unscrupulous, "insidious traitors" and the "lowest class of foreigners" steeped in "foreign insolence."[61] Even in this era of strong nativist sentiments, the Editor's rhetoric unnerved some readers of the *Aurora*. In the March 30 edition of the newspaper, one wrote that he noticed in Whitman "a kind of vindictiveness, a want of charity, a disposition to ultraism,"[62] and argued that to attack immigrants in the U.S. was like depriving "the tree of its sap."[63]

Scholars have tried to explain this rash of anti-Irish virulence in Whitman's editorials. Jerome Loving believes that Anson Herrick, part owner of the *Aurora*, motivated this xenophobia. For Loving, the contradiction between Whitman's nativism and his humanitarianism was too incompatible to come from the same mind; in these moments, the Editor was literally not himself.[64] However, the evidence shows otherwise. On April 19, 1842, toward the end of his tenure as editor of the *Aurora*, Whitman wrote an article explaining the necessity of a "leader" in every issue. In it, he claimed, "most of the principal articles are concocted by one Whitman" and that the owners of the *Aurora* expected these lead editorials "to be something particularly well written, and particularly worth reading." If we accept Whitman's claim to be the author of the leaders, it is worth considering how many of these leaders over the months of March and April 1842 (when Whitman was the editor) were explicitly nativistic.[65]

For each of the twenty-four days that he edited a copy of the *Aurora* (March 28 to approximately April 23, excluding Sundays), Whitman wrote the leader. Of these twenty-four leaders, eight expressed anti-Irish sentiments.[66]

This count excludes the total number of nativist articles that appeared over the seven weeks that Whitman wrote for the *Aurora* (that total is thirty-five); he probably wrote many of these articles as well.[67] It is difficult to imagine that Whitman, as editor, had so light a hand especially since the only article that mentions Whitman by name also cited him as the author of the lead editorials. It is fair to say that he penned at least a substantial number of the nativist pieces that appeared in the *Aurora*.

David Reynolds calls Whitman's xenophobia a "strange dance" and points out that though Whitman "spared no vitriol in describing Bishop Hughes," he also "resisted thoroughgoing nativism" by rejecting parties like the Native Americans and the American Republicans. For Reynolds, this seeming contradiction in Whitman's reaction to immigrants foreshadowed the "odd coupling of intense Americanism and sincere internationalism" in his later poetry.[68] Reynolds' view remains a common interpretation of the supposed incongruities in Whitman's vision. He finds a "strange" and "odd" relationship between Whitman and contemporary xenophobia. Reynolds places Whitman's nativism and his humanitarianism as one of many paradoxes at the center of his ideology and accepts it as part of his style.

A close look at the editorials, however, exposes a more coherent explanation. Of the sixteen nativist editorials Whitman wrote during March 1842 (these included articles written both before and during his tenure as editor), fourteen regarded the attempt by Bishop Hughes to obtain public funding for Catholic private schools through the Maclay Bill. The remaining two railed against Hughes' attempt to, as Whitman saw it, politically blackmail Tammany Hall into support for this resolution.[69] Conversely, of the nineteen anti-Irish editorials Whitman wrote over the next month, twelve treated the political effect of this perceived political blackmail and the remaining seven referred to the school debate whose origins lay in the Maclay Bill. This places Whitman's "nativism" in a different light.

Over these two months (March and April 1842), Whitman's nativism revolved around a single issue, the New York public school system and, as part of that issue, the influence of Roman Catholic leaders on the New York Democratic Party.[70] What Reynolds sees as a paradox in Whitman was, instead, a paradox in Tammany Hall. How could the Party balance its natural rights rhetoric and its traditional suspicion of religious politics in the face of Irish-Catholic demands? As long as the Irish were an ethnic and religious minority, the Party's pro-Irish and secular platform worked. However, when the Irish argued that they had a natural right to a publicly supported Catholic education and used their political muscle to procure these ends, cohesive Democratic ideology broke down.

Whitman's bosses at the *Aurora* probably put some pressure on Whitman to fight the Maclay Bill and the rise of Irish influence in the Party. Down the street from the *Aurora* offices, Levi Slamm's *New Era* took the Hughes' side of the issue and the *Aurora* aimed to capitalize on the debate. Even if directed, Whitman put his own spin on the public school argument. In this way, he promoted the views of unaffected citizenship that he first put forward as the Schoolmaster. For example, in an editorial entitled "The Penny Press," Whitman clarified his understanding of the role of the American school: "the penny press is the same as common schools among seminaries of education." The press, like the schools, "makes the great body of people intelligent, capable, and worthy of performing the duties of republican freemen."[71] The penny press and the schools functioned like the breakfast table and the meat market; both were places where individuals learned how to be citizens. Even though the press and public schools catered mostly to the needs of "the lower and middling classes...[e]verywhere is their influence felt."[72] The Editor's comparison of the penny press and the public schools reflected his idea of egalitarian reform; there needed to be a place where citizens of different status came together to learn the workings of democracy.

Whitman's view represented a contemporary ideal of the New York public school system, but not its reality. Since the Free School Society's (FSS) founding in 1805 by philanthropists like Thomas Eddy, it provided eleven charity schools for poor children "who do not belong to or are not provided for by any religious society." By 1825, philanthropist John Griscom boasted that some twenty thousand children "taken from the most indigent classes" went to FSS schools.[73] In this same year, the FSS initiated the creation of a single, public school system (though still under private management) open to all children "not as a charity, but as a matter of common right."[74]

Though egalitarian in theory, the New York public school system of the 1840s reflected its Protestant origins. The curriculum embraced contemporary evangelism, using, for example, the King James Bible in its lessons and preaching the civilizing effects of Protestantism and personal conversion over redemption through the Catholic Church. Most of the teachers saw themselves in both missionary and pedagogical terms and created an implicitly anti-Catholic curriculum that characterized the so-called tyranny of the Catholic hierarchy and underhandedness of the priesthood and the papacy.[75] This forced many New York Catholics to equate public education with religious indoctrination.

In this context, Whig governor William Seward saw a political opportunity and proposed that Catholic parochial schools have access to public funds equal to those of the public schools.[76] In 1841, Bishop John

Hughes, in order to compel the Democrats to support this piece of Whig legislation originating in Albany, created a separate Carroll Hall ticket to push Tammany Hall to either support the bill or split the party and face a Whig victory in the municipal elections of April 1842.[77]

"The System Must Stand"

Hughes and his allies argued that a Protestant curriculum in the New York public school system pedagogically excluded large portions of New York's working poor.[78] Whitman dismissed this claim with his objective style. In the first of his editorials on the subject, he related a visit to a public school in which he saw "nearly four hundred boys, bright eyed, healthy, fine looking fellows, engaged in their various avocations and studies." Whitman used this empirical evidence to reject the charge of exclusivity of the New York public schools: "We are told that the school society is a monopoly.... Is that a monopoly which opens its arms to every inhabitant of the city, without regard to rank, trade, or creed...?" In response to his rhetorical question, Whitman noted that in four public schools the population of students was four-fifths Catholic.[79] When one gentleman visited a school on Hudson Street and found it thinly attended the teacher explained that, on the day of his visit, most students helped their mothers with the washing. For the Editor this proved that the schools "give...education to the poorer classes" because so many working-class students had gone home for washing day.[80] The absence of children in this case proved their existence.

According to Whitman, Bishop Hughes' charge of Protestant one-sidedness was part of a scheme to besmirch the reputation of New York public education and, for the sake of political gain, undermine its popularity with the Irish. Whitman argued that the bishop "sent orders in all directions to have the Catholic children taken from their accustomed situation..." to make municipal inspectors think that Catholics rejected the public schools. Hughes used this tactic, according to Whitman, to provide "evidence that a large mass were prevented by conscience from patronizing the society's establishments." If four-fifths of public schoolchildren were Catholic (as Whitman noted four days before), and Catholic schoolchildren suddenly disappeared from the schools, something sinister must be afoot.[81]

In this regard, Whitman ignored the fact that American republican ideology, with its emphasis on a Protestant legacy, represented a belief system that many Irish-Catholics found threatening to their own cultural cohesion. The Editor claimed no ill will toward poor immigrants who "could not write for themselves." Instead, Catholic leaders had tricked their hapless parishioners into signing the pro-Maclay petition and forced Irish parents to keep their children away from the schools; "this cunning, flexible, serpent tongued priest...has the insolence to appear in the public forum, and pour vials of discord amid us...." In this way, the Editor positioned himself as a friend to future Irish citizens and a defender of republican consensus. According to Whitman, Hughes threatened the secular nature of the public forum through a plot to sequester the Irish in sectarian homogeneity.[82] He wanted their political clout all to himself. The bishop and his cause fostered what many Americans claimed to fear most in the Catholic masses: a group mind that bowed to a foreign hierarchy. A Catholicization of the public schools (or at least their funding by public dollars) would threaten an institution that Whitman understood as the cultivator of free minds for the benefit of an authoritarian religious institution.

Whitman carefully separated Hughes from the rest of Irish New York. In an editorial of March 10 he stated approvingly, "the Irish number strong in New York; their votes count as much as those of any men." According to the republican ideology of the period, American equal rights were founded upon the universal human rights cited in the Declaration of Independence. Irish Catholicism, for Whitman, did not intrinsically represent a threat to these rights, as long as it remained in its proper place outside of the public sphere. When demagogues used it for political ends, it sapped the vital independence of American citizens and created a populace under the control of "despicable politicians [who] care little through whom they rise into power...."[83]

The Editor's nativist rhetoric fit within the traditional English and American fear of plotting priests and politico-religious intrigue. Hughes' argument about cultural autonomy was "delusive logic...founded upon 'abstract' notions of antimonopoly." Here, again, the Editor rejected what he considered "abstract" arguments in favor of objective facts, "insidious Roman priests are at the bottom of this business." Hughes threatened to pull the Irish Catholic vote away from the Democrats in the April election and spread "the worst poison of sectarian spite...." This grab for power, rooted in demagogic politics, resulted in "the crushing of the most beautiful code of education that the whole United States can show."[84] For Whitman, this fight was also for the future of the Irish in America. Would they become free citizens of the Republic, or sectarian subjects of Rome? Whitman envisioned no middle ground in this case, at least in the frantic days before the local elections of 1842.

Whitman's attack on political demagoguery reflected a common anxiety toward mass politics during the 1830s and 1840s. The second two-party system made the republican ideal of a political consensus unrealistic and exposed the myth that politics were solely about the common good. Many middle-class authors, like Artemus Muzzey in *The Young Man's Friend* (1838), warned against nefarious urban characters that used charm to erode a citizen's principles and political demagogues who used "insidious attacks...to trample on law, order, property and life."[85] When, on Wednesday, March 16, pro-Maclay partisans raided an anti-Maclay meeting at Tammany Hall, the Editor suspected "sly, false, deceitful villains" in the form of "Irish priests" as the cause of the uproar. In the heat of the twenty-four hours after the meeting, he claimed to have no "prejudices against foreigners, because they are such," but also that "they are becoming altogether...under the control of that reverend villain, Hughes."[86]

During the height of the controversy in late March 1842, Whitman advocated vigilantism as the only recourse against Hughes' autocratic scheme, "In the west, where the statute book affords no remedy for outrage, the injured community takes the case into its own hands."[87] On April 13, after a raid on Hughes' residence by Mike Walsh and his "Spartan Band," Whitman quipped, "had it been the reverend hypocrite's head, instead of his windows, we could hardly find it in our soul to be sorrowful."[88] Whitman echoed the same on April 12 when he argued that a state senator who abstained from voting against the Maclay Bill "deserved a coat of tar and feathers."[89]

Scholars have strained to explain this advocacy of violence in Whitman's rhetoric.[90] However, his words fit within a broader American tradition, grounded in the Declaration of Independence, of justified political violence. Artisan republicans retained this language as a hypothetical recourse against tyranny through the 1840s and beyond.[91] Whitman's reference to tarring and feathering reached back to the activities of the Sons of Liberty who, in the heat of the taxation controversy of the 1760s, threatened pro-British tax collectors and shopkeepers with the same punishment. None of this justified vigilante activities or exculpates Whitman from the charge of advocating violence. According to his arguments, however, he did not aim his virulence at Irish Catholics, but at a would-be tyrant; he justified this call for violence with the logic of American republicanism.

"Tammany in Trouble"

During the week of March 24, 1842, the Democratic supporters of the Maclay Bill threatened to run an independent candidate in the mayoral election on April 12. That week, the *Aurora*'s rival paper, the *New Era*, came out in support of Bishop Hughes and the Maclay Bill. The Editor, by this point beside himself in self-righteous anger, began to sound like the

Schoolmaster during the 1840 campaign when local politics got the better of his all-inclusive tone. Whitman described the *New Era* as a "vulgar, anti-American newspaper funded only by corporation patronage." Hughes and the *New Era* sought to "control the ballot boxes" and make them servants to "a cabal of foreign Jesuits." Whitman called on Tammany to "scorn to curry favor with ignorant fanaticism" and to cast themselves "on the people's sense of right."[92] It is worth noting that Whitman's second editorial on Dickens appeared about a week later. In this editorial, the Editor noted, "...almost within the reach of our voice, there is a palpable counterpart to the worst embodiment of evil that the brain of Dickens ever transcribed on paper!" Whether Whitman had Levi Slamm,[93] the editor of the *New Era*, or Hughes in mind, it is clear that he saw a narrative of Dickensian proportions in the Maclay Bill controversy.[94]

On March 29, the Editor's benevolence temporarily returned when Robert H. Morris, who chaired the riotous anti-Maclay meeting at Tammany Hall earlier in the week, was nominated to run for mayor.[95] The next day, while commenting on a letter that criticized his "highly offensive" statements, Whitman clarified his position and modified his rhetoric, "our love is capacious enough, and our arms wide enough, to encircle all men, whether they have birth in our glorious republic, whatever be their origins or their native land." He then ruminated in tones that echoed both Democratic and Whig celebrations of equal opportunity, "We possess in this republic the advantages and the capacities, for evolving the Great Problem...the problem of how far Man can have his nature perfected by himself."[96] Here, perhaps inadvertently, Whitman connected the tradition of Protestant personal redemption with the contemporary rhetoric of individualism and self-improvement. Even in his celebration of the Irish potential as successful citizens, the Editor could not conceive (at least on paper) of their redemption through a religious institution that claimed superior authority to democratic politics and individual initiative.

One week later, events forced Whitman again into despair. After a meeting at St. John's Hall, the Hughes faction of the Democratic Party threatened again to run an "Independent Democratic Republican" ticket and split the Democratic vote in the mayoral election of April 12. For the Editor, "better that all should be lost, than such a precedent established. The foreign riff-raff once yielded to in this case...there will be no end to their demands."[97] This statement, one of the few in which Whitman expressed explicitly anti-immigrant sentiments, pointed to his ambivalence toward Irish immigrants in general. However, only four days before, he took an editorial "peep" at the synagogue Shearith Israel on Mill Street and wrote of it positively. Whitman's anti-immigrant statements remained tied to the fight over the Maclay Bill and, more broadly, to a power struggle within the Democratic Party. The heat of his rhetoric should not be confused with an overarching navitist ideology.

With the passage of the Maclay Bill on April 9 (which, in the end, forbade all public funding of religious education) and Morris' acceptance of this reality, Whitman asked his readers not to vote Democrat as "[e]very suffrage given by a democrat [sic] for the Tammany ticket is so much to aid the behests of the Hughes clique."[98] The debate, for Whitman, shifted completely from the school bill to Hughes' undue power in the Democratic Party. On April 12, the day of the municipal election, Whitman broke party ranks and hoped that "a defeat of the Tammany ticket might teach the Tammany leaders a wholesome lesson."[99] Finally, in the aftermath of the election, the Editor made his sentiments clear, though the Democrats retained the mayor's seat, the common council went to the Whigs. Whitman summed up his judgment of this result with the statement, "It is well."[100]

Aftermath

After the election of 1842, Whitman's editorials in the *Aurora* changed markedly in tone and dropped in number. On April 18, the Editor repudiated "such doctrines as have characterized the 'Native American' party" and claimed to want to see "no man disfranchised, because he happened to be born three thousand miles off." He ended this final editorial on the Maclay Bill controversy with the resolution that it was "unnecessary that we should draw the line of exclusiveness, and say, Stand off, I am better than thou."[101] In less than a week, Whitman left the *Aurora*.

The owners, in a quip of May 16, described Whitman as "the laziest fellow who ever undertook to edit a city paper."[102] In a short rebuttal published in the *Evening Tattler*, Whitman claimed that "during the few weeks we continued there, we saw...more mean selfishness...more disregard of all manliness and good manners...more low deceits...more attempts at levying 'black mail'...heard more gross blasphemy and prurient conversation, than ever before in our life."[103]

The Editor's final articles for the *Aurora* lacked the careful balance between his eyewitness's tone and his passion for social uplift. They included airy pieces on "Life and Love," "The Ocean," and "Dreams." It is difficult to say to what extent the election of 1842 and the passions it aroused soured the relationship between Whitman and the owners of the *Aurora*, but the Editor lost his voice in his final eleven days at the paper.[104]

CHAPTER FOUR

THE EDITOR AGAINST AFFECTATION

The few documents that show Whitman's whereabouts between the summer of 1842 and spring of 1846 portray a transient existence.[1] Still, he published widely during these years and can be found in newspapers as diverse in their politics and interests as the *Sunday Times & Noah's Weekly Magazine*, the *Democratic Review* and the Whiggish newspapers *American Review*, and *Brooklyn Evening Star*. Whitman also edited the *Tattler, Sunday Times,* and *New York Statesman* during the spring of 1843, but, unfortunately, few copies of the *Tatter* and *Sunday Times* and no remaining copies of the *Statesman* exist.[2]

Whitman's voice often changed to suit his audiences during these years. For example, his article "A Dialogue" from the *Democratic Review* of November 1845 imagined a conversation between a convicted criminal and "the people" and argued that "the very facts which render murder a frightful crime, render hanging a frightful punishment" and turned into a diatribe against the hypocrisy of a church which demanded its followers "Strangle and kill in the name of God!"[3] Here, Whitman's tone and topic reflected the Democratic Party and *Democratic Review*'s implicit suspicion of religiously justified policy. On the other hand, an article published that same month for the *American Review* lamented the destruction of St. Paul's Church for "a place whose corner-stones rest upon pride, and whose walls are built in vain-glory...who is opposed to *such* conservatism...comes from that father of restlessness, the Devil."[4] Here, Whitman took the rhetoric of the crusading evangelical to make his point. Both of these articles lacked a consistent editorial voice because Whitman lacked a specific editorial forum. While at the *Aurora*, he utilized the consistency of his position to ruminate and theorize not only on the topics of the day and their effect on the Republic, but also on the nature of the newspaper and the calling of an editor. Whitman's work for the *Democratic Review* and the *American Review*, on the other hand, proved too sparse to establish a consistently personified voice.

Steadier work came between the autumn of 1845 and spring of 1846 when Whitman wrote for the *Brooklyn Evening Star*. This position reestablished his contact with an early mentor, the owner of the *Star*, Alden Spooner, for whom Whitman worked as an apprentice. Spooner's *Evening Star* leaned Whig and supported temperance and the tariff, but Spooner also sympathized with the Owenite Fanny Wright and the abolitionist poet Lucy Hooper. An artisan's son like Whitman, Spooner embraced the new market revolution with some ambivalence.[5] At the *Star*, Whitman wrote on topics as diverse as education, fashion, music and the theater and avoided topics where his Democratic leanings ran counter to Spooner's Whig ideology.

Education and Heart

Education continued to be important to Whitman in 1845. In his articles for the *Star*, he twice mentioned the theories of Horace Mann, once to support Mann's rejection of corporal punishment in the schools and once to puff an up-coming lecture by Mann himself.[6] Whitman believed in the civilizing influence of public education, but whereas Mann's arguments centered on the economic and social benefits of uniform public education, Whitman believed the schools incubated and sustained a child's natural abilities.[7] For example, in one of Whitman's many diatribes against corporal punishment, he asked, "how many noble spirited boys are beaten into sullen and spiteful endurance of what there is no earthly need?" In turn, he demanded that teachers "Awake!...to...the young freshness wherewith God has formed them...."[8]

Whitman returned to themes he first explored in his meditations on the dangers of affectation and his attack on the sectarianism of the Maclay Bill: public schools should nurture a student's natural goodness rather than inculcate social dictums or allow pretentious self-creation. To this end, he recommended the employment of "lady-like, well educated women" as teachers who had a "natural sympathy with the feelings of children" so as to prevent the creation of "those awkward gaukeys, those blustering ill-favored juvenile rowdies, that swarm now in every street."[9] In this regard, Whitman echoed contemporary pedagogical theories regarding women and children. Whereas in the late-eighteenth century both were considered passionate and prone to sin, in the second quarter of the 19th century, with the advent of a more sentimental and naturalistic epistemology, women and children were celebrated for their inherent goodness, innocence, and transparency.[10] Accordingly, maternal love best raised children. Female teachers protected a young person's delicate goodness from the cruelties of a heartless and mercenary society. Whitman utilized these arguments to justify his own idea of the proper role played by the public school in the new market economy.

In an editorial entitled "Some Hints to Apprentices and Youth," Whitman returned to the subject of loafing, but in opposition to his Schoolmaster editorial on the subject, used it in a way familiar to his readers. "Boy," he asked, "how much of your leisure time do you give to *loafing* [Whitman's emphasis]?" By loafing in this case, the Editor meant the "vulgar habits of smoking cigars, chewing tobacco, or making frequent use of blasphemous or obscene language." This kind of consumption and pretense was "poison for a boy's energies, moral, mental and physical."[11] The working-class culture of the Bowery b'hoys and the New York gangs of the 1840s again met with his disapproval. For Whitman, these working-class toughs used cigars, alcohol, underworld argot, and fashion to make themselves a spectacle and, therefore, exhibit the dangerous pretense endemic in the consumer economy. Whereas the Schoolmaster on the clam excursion or the Editor in the meat market loafed with noble purpose, these boys carried out a dangerous masquerade. [12] Here, again, Whitman tailored his rhetoric to his audience while maintaining certain core ideals. By attacking loafers in the *Star*, he appealed to his Whig readers and their inclinations toward moral reform. However, in his celebrations of loafers in "Sun-Down Papers no. 9," he hoped to shock and ridicule his Whig audience who had supported Harrison in the election of 1840. In both cases, his antipathy toward an affected identity built through fashionable consumption remained. This explains Whitman's different loafers—one an Adam before the fall, the other an urban ruffian—and the consistent ideal of clean, unpretentious living drawn from each.

In this attack on Bowery b'hoy culture, the Editor also reflected the middle-class sentimental literature of his time. For example, *Godey's Lady's Book*, which by 1860 had 150,000 subscribers, warned women against the dangers of affectation and fashion. Living "the exterior life" ultimately forced one to live at the "expense of truth and feeling." In its European form, an oppressive aristocracy of wealthy trendsetters controlled fashion and encouraged "voluntary slavery...according to the judgment of fools and the caprice of coxcombs."[13] *Godey's Lady's Book* promised its readers a natural beauty that, when expressed through simple and plain fashion, guaranteed an individual's goodness and moral influence over others.[14] Honest fashion made honest citizens.

In the *Evening Star* articles, Whitman described successful schools as places that protected young republicans against dangerous fashion and nurtured their natural equality and unaffected identity. Within this protected environment, a child found his or her personal and authentic social role. Music was important to this ideal of unaffected education. For example, Whitman spoke admiringly about Mr. Warner, a New York teacher, "who expressed to us a firm belief, that if properly commenced with, *all children can be taught to sing.*"[15] In an article published one month later, he noted that the upper classes gave European nations their "national character" and that the music of the rich gave common Europeans "...an ease, grace, and elegance, which are not too often found in what we call good society here." As part of this argument, Whitman called for the general uplift of society through a refined taste in music, "let but the principal portion of American youth be taught music...and we shall soon have no more foundation for the criticisms of either native or foreign fault-finding, on our manners and ceremonies as a people."[16] This seemed to counter Whitman's entire pedagogical program; how could music based on the European model benefit a republic of unaffected American citizens?

On Wednesday, November 5, 1845, Whitman published the first of four articles that offered an answer to this question.[17] The previous Monday, he heard the singing group "The Cheney Family" at Niblo's Saloon. This New Hampshire quartet of three brothers and one sister thrilled Whitman for their "simple, fresh and beautiful" style and instilled in him the hope that this music might be "[a] starting point from which to mould something new and true in American music." The Cheneys (and later, The Hutchinsons, an ensemble of dedicated abolitionists) specialized in popular music like "The Irish Mother's Lament" and "Vermonters' Song." Whitman admired these groups for their "utmost simplicity" and their ability to "infuse nothing but sound American feeling in their songs...."[18] For him, when the Cheneys sang in the traditional American idiom, they spoke authentically to the American Republic.

The popularity of acts like the Hutchinsons and Cheneys marked a general change in theatrical venues and tastes. Since 1837 and the recession that closed many of the traditional playhouses, Bowery taverns began to sport popular "free and easies" and "vaudevilles" to attract the drinking public. Likewise, new theaters like *The Franklin* and *The Chatham* attracted working-class audiences with "low-brow" entertainment that rivaled the patrician theaters around City Hall.[19] The audiences at these less formal venues portrayed a mixed bag of working-class citizens in the pit, middle classes and upper class denizens in the boxes, and prostitutes and their clients in the gallery. The lights were kept on so that patrons could find their way in and out of the theater. Theatergoers considered interruptions, both affirmative and negative, part of the show. Occasionally, they hurled food and drink from the pit at the actors on the stage.[20] Whitman easily found in these vaudevilles the participatory Republic writ small.

In an article entitled "Heart-Music and Art-Music," the Editor argued that the Cheneys' music represented a pure and elemental communion with the individual citizen and the American Republic. The Cheneys sang what Whitman called "heart-music" which was "better than what is merely addressed to the ear." These singers, with "elegant simplicity," sang words a listener could understand rather than the "mass of unintelligible stuff..." common at the opera. The Editor celebrated Miss Cheney's performance of "The Irish Mother's Lament" because of her "unaffected, simple manner...her awkwardness, we may almost call it" and named it something she should "cherish...and take no pains to get rid of."[21] According to Whitman, one saw the Cheney brothers, "brown-faced, stout-shouldered fellows[,]...in almost any American church, in a country village." The sight of these singers "puts one in mind of health and fresh air in the country at sunrise."[22] In the Cheneys, Whitman saw republican aristocrats.

Whitman's celebration of unaffected art reflected a broader shift in American culture from a rational to a visceral search for a sublime truth that drew upon the emotional and darkly passionate. David Reynolds cites this transformation in American letters and noted that Whitman's years as an editor coincided with a distinctive turn to what he calls "subversive literature."[23] This literature of the passions had a scientific stamp of approval. Throughout 1840s, phrenologist Andrew Combe argued for the primacy of the portion of the brain that he claimed controlled "amativeness" (or attraction) between the sexes. Combe's "discovery," not so different from that of Alfred Kinsey a century later, allowed for the passions to enter polite conversation as discussion of them could be couched in naturalistic and quasi-scientific terms. For example, Reynolds cites the craze for "model artists" in this period that co-mingled classical art, the pursuit of the sublime, and voyeurism in public exhibits and private parlors. These exhibitions presented "Venus in a Shell," "Lady Godiva," and "Eve in Eden" with live models for public consumption.[24] Whitman embraced this new comfort with the body and approvingly called the human form "Nature's cunningest work." Any attempt to hide the natural human form also hid the truth.[25] In his music of the "heart," Whitman intermingled his usual suspicion of pretense with a twist on the ideas of the moment. Denuded of all affectation, true American music spoke directly to the senses.

In this way, Whitman combined elements of Quaker simplicity, individualism, anti-consumerism and contemporary pseudo-science to justify his "heart" music. One body communicated with another in a language elemental and self-evident because "children of nature" could not help but speak in a way as eternal as nature itself. In this regard, music spoke both on a deeply personal and also universally social level. As a listener, the individual reacted physically in a manner that defied rational explanation and easy definition. A musician made this visceral moment because she felt the emotions she expressed; the cause and effect were elemental. The performance made this an inherently social event; citizens could not have this deeply personal moment without others around them. This explains Whitman's ecstatic reactions to the Cheneys and Hutchinsons; "heart" music exemplified unaffected republicanism in action.[26]

Few scholars who have explored Whitman's theories of music have noted the subtle connections between Whitman's "heart" music and his advocacy of public education.[27] When considering them in the context of his writings in the summer and fall of 1845, it is clear that Whitman formulated a consistent and novel approach to public education and the arts that utilized his theories of the unaffected and true. Whig reformers like Horace Mann supported public education (as probably did the reform-minded Alden Spooner). Furthermore, the National Trades Union advocated public education as a means to improve the lot of the laboring classes. However, Whitman's ideal school did not transform the student into a *useful* citizen or a *successful* citizen, but into a *free* citizen able to resist the pretense of the sycophant or social climber.

In this regard, it makes sense that Whitman believed music and public education went hand in hand. A music teacher's lessons nurtured a student's "heart." The music of the "unaffected" and "simple" Cheneys and Hutchinsons, presented through the medium of a nurturing and "sympathetic" woman, allowed a student to play in a collective that appealed directly to his or her nature and ability. A child singing in the chorus, unfettered by narrow training, practiced for his or her place in the nation. Unfortunately, Whitman's position at the Whig *Star* limited his options for economic and social critique; he had to keep his interest in Democratic issues in check. After 1846, Whitman incorporated the pedagogical and aesthetic ideas he generated at the *Star* into his new role as the Editor at the Democratic *Brooklyn Daily Eagle*.

Brooklyn provided a burgeoning forum for Whitman to reestablish his Editor persona; between 1845 and 1855 the city grew six fold.[28] The *Daily Eagle* also gave Whitman a clean start. He was out of Democratic politics in New York City proper, but close enough to comment on its goings-on. From Brooklyn, the Editor reestablished a consistent voice. Journalism itself was in flux. Traditionally, newspaper articles served commentary on the issues of the day, usually with a political slant. However, after 1846, when independently owned telegraph lines converged from Washington, Boston, and Albany on New York City, two kinds of newspapers emerged: those that reported the "scoops" and those that commented on them. During the Mexican-American War (1846-1848), the *Tribune, Herald, Journal of Commerce, Courier, Enquirer,* and *Express* agreed to share telegraphed reports from the front.[29] This national news, carried via monopolized telegraph cables, forced smaller newspapers to editorialize on the news as directed by the larger newspapers.[30] Isaac Van Anden hired Whitman in 1846 as editor of the *Daily Eagle* in the midst of this shift to turn the *Eagle* from a local newspaper with a political bent into a journal of commentary on news and culture.

Van Anden was a "Hunker" (or conservative) Democrat. Called "Hunkers" for their ability to "hunker after" office or to "hunker down" in the face of change, this wing of the Party advocated the pragmatic politics of moderation in the face of growing anti-slavery sentiment in the aftermath of the Mexican-American War. The Hunkers in the Democratic Party opposed anti-slavery Democrats like Silas Wright (of whom Whitman had written a supportive article in 1844) and called them "Barnburners" for their supposed willingness to destroy the entire party in an effort to rid it of a few unsavory policy positions. Whitman's new job at the *Eagle* represented a quiet return to Democratic editorship after three years in exile in the aftermath of the Maclay Bill controversy and the 1842 election. However, working for Van Anden meant that Whitman had to uphold party ideology. His anti-Tammany politics had to be kept in check.

Nevertheless, Hunkerism generally fit with Whitman's own politics in 1846. He supported public education (as long as he did not alienate Irish Democrats) and explored his growing interest in the arts. Van Anden also expected his editor to engage in the economic and social debates of importance to Brooklyn Democrats, namely, the tariff and the rights of the economically disaffected. Whitman's editorials show that he took his ideas about education and the arts from his days as a free-lance editorialist at the *Evening Star* and coupled them with a new (and requisite) interest in economics and class politics.

Whitman brought immediate changes to the *Eagle*. In his capacity as editor, he rearranged the format of the paper to devote two columns to literary criticism (over the course of two years he reviewed 425 books, five pamphlets, and twenty-two poetic works) and wrote short observations of Brooklyn society and culture featuring education, the arts, working-class life and economics. These editorials reflected Whitman's vision of the Editor as of the people and for the people's edification. In this capacity, he rested upon what he called the "Immutable Truth." This "truth" proved that "persuasion and education were the only valid means by which to ameliorate the actions of men in matters other than those concerning the preservation of life, liberty, and property."[31]

Unaffected Education

As at the *Aurora*, Whitman equated the public schools with the daily press. Quoting Oliver Goldsmith, Whitman noted that schoolteachers and printers were both poorly regarded by their fellow citizens.[32] For the Editor, "education and refinement are not necessary to mere animal life" and most people wanted "to live the sensuous reign of a day...." As proof of this, Whitman told the story of a failed printer who made a fortune in brewing beer because "every body had stomachs, whereas very few were blessed with heads."[33]

For Whitman, bad pedagogy was a product of an unnatural understanding of children. In an article entitled "Learning &c.," he told the story of a recent Yale graduate who, after having arrived on the first day of classes from a distance of one hundred miles on foot and with only three dollars in his pocket, worked his way through university in only three years. Through his efforts, he graduated with distinguished honors and, in the course of his research on electricity, pushed his mathematical studies beyond those of his classmates. As a reward for his efforts, he published "on the law of electrical conduction in metals" in the *Journal of Science*, a journal which, according to the Editor, was unmatched "in that department of science...." Though to modern ears this sounds like a typical American success story, Whitman described this student's education and effort as "a sign of disease." In another example, a "friend" turned his son into "an accomplished musician..." who knew "several languages, and the sciences," but, alas, died at age twenty because "nature, whose laws were violated, refused to sustain the draughts made upon her weakened energy." This "folly...made [students] miserable by too great and close an application to book studies;" true education studied "LIFE" which contained the "seeds of every moral and meaning." The "true" intellectual life, then, involved "a wise consideration of *all* claims which Life has upon a man, and not the hiding of all the rest by the unnatural expansion of nearness to one."[34]

Whitman's editorials on classroom discipline give some hint of his ideal education. For him, whipping represented "the wretched government of the rod and ferule" and the teacher "who has *no other* means of making his pupils obey him" proved himself nothing more than a "petty tyrant."[35] Accordingly, the "foibles" of children exposed their most noble and unaffected attributes "which, in truth, [were] the overflowing goodness or spirit of their nature...."[36] Echoing his *Star* editorials, the heart of Whitman's reform ideology included the theory that a child's natural grace was his surest path to educational success. When an ideal democratic citizen presented himself, unaffected, to the broader republic, his childhood particularities, though nominally the missteps of youth, also represented the individual characteristics that defined him as a citizen. Squelching the child's particularities created a citizen at war with his nature. Whitman opposed education transferring information for its own sake and instead advocated ongoing lessons by which citizens learned their better natures.

The Unaffected Arts

Ideally, the arts, like the school and the newspaper, communicated native truth to the citizenry itself. Many artists and critics called for a particularly American art during this period,[37] but Whitman keenly interpreted art in pedagogical terms. In this, he exhibited a particular anxiety in an age of anxious nationalism; citizens needed to be periodically taught how to be citizens or the Republic was lost. This begged the question, how could free citizens be *taught* to be free? The Editor found his answers in the empathy that unaffected art produced in the audience. For Whitman, the theater was practice for civic life. American art produced "true" emotions in the viewer and reached the audience on a visceral level. Rather than accomplished through careful method, good art communicated through an out-pouring of authentic sentiment. Any sign of effete formalism or intellectual abstraction detracted from the egalitarian language of the heart. American arts exhibited this natural sensibility and held up an aesthetic mirror that showed citizens their own democratic nature.

Good acting, grounded "entirely in the feelings," could be achieved in the "usual way...[,] boisterous, stormy, physical, and repugnant to truth and taste[,]" or the superior way with "an invariable adherence to Nature...and work[ing] from within to the outward."[38] Though he claimed no experience with acting, Whitman knew which method he preferred "from the analogy of things." Positioning, rather than method, determined the spaces between art and life. An actor did not *act* remorseful or loving when he or she communicated this emotion to the audience. Instead, actors expressed emotions best when they "feel them at the time, and throw the feeling as far as possible into the word and act."[39] Acting, then, only entailed an actor feeling in plain view with the intention that others will feel likewise. By these means the actor and viewer communicated by "analogy." The viewer knew superior art by the way she felt, and the actor knew the quality of her performance by the way she felt. The audience brought no special knowledge or taste to the moment. Likewise, the actor had no special knowledge of how one "played" a character. Instead, the actor utilized the very humanity that his or her audience brought to the performance.[40]

Expert-critics, because of their expertise, *lost* their sense of quality as they had been "schooled artificially, till their brains have often made the same false tone as the palate of habitual user of stimulants...." Like the tobacco, caffeine, or alcohol user, the expert-critic made pretensions to a false sensibility. Citizen-critics, on the other hand, knew true quality, "[i]f a picture, a sculpture, a play or an actor, don't impress you highly, don't *affect* to be impressed highly [Whitman's emphasis]." For the Editor, art appreciation began with a communion of equals.[41] This communion had reform potential. In an article entitled "Why do Theaters Languish? And How Shall the American Stage Be Resuscitated?" he presented his vision of authentic American performance in a crisis-laden tone, "the drama of this country *can* be the mouth-piece of freedom, refinement, liberal philanthropy, beautiful love for all our brethren, polished manners and an elevated good taste." Whitman mixed the traditional rhetoric of "high culture" with that of American political idealism and thereby redefined aesthetic concepts while leaving social definitions in place:

> [American drama] can wield potent sway to destroy any attempts at despotism—it can attack and hold up to scorn bigotry, fashionable affectation, avarice, and all unmanly follies. Youth may be warned by its fictitious portraits of the evil of unbridled passions. All...every age and every condition in life...may with profit visit a well regulated dramatic establishment, and go away better than when they came.[42]

In this argument, the Editor took terms usually reserved for aesthetic and quasi-aristocratic use ("polished manners," "elevated good taste," "refinement") and redefined them in ways convenient to the proper function of a healthy republic (self-restraint, simplicity, tolerance). According to the Editor, "with all our servility to foreign fashion, there is at the heart of the intelligent masses...a lurking propensity toward what is original, and has a stamped American character."[43] Good theater honed Americans' naturally republican sensibilities.

As in his anti-immigrant diatribes at the *Aurora*, Whitman employed nativist rhetoric when analyzing a republican institution, in this case the theater, he perceived under threat from foreign despotism. The British

Shakespearean, Edmund Kean, for example, raised nativist scorn as early as 1821[44] and his son, Charles, met with a similar reaction from Whitman, "his manner, gait, and gestures are all unnatural." According to the Editor, nepotism, rather than natural-born talent, made Kean's fame. In responding to a critic who called his comments "barbarous," "unmanly" and "unmannerly," Whitman, two days after his review of Kean's performance, agreed that perhaps his words centered unduly on one actor and that he could cast an even wider net to catch examples of the European pretense that infected American drama. Three years later, in 1849, working-class nativism of this kind inspired a riot at the Astor Place Theater.[45] The riot's origins lay in an incident where the American actor, Edwin Forrest, supposedly hissed the British Shakespearean, William Macready, during a performance of *Hamlet* in Edinburgh. In New York, the rivalry between the two actors fed class-based antagonism; before the riot, Tammany Hall operative Isaiah Rynders distributed pamphlets at working class pubs that asked "Shall Americans or English rule this city?" and demanded that readers "express their opinions this night at the English Aristocratic Opera House!"[46] On May 10, ten thousand working-class protesters gathered outside the Astor Place Theater to protest Macready's portrayal of Macbeth. After a citizen militia fired a volley into the air, they shot into the crowd of protestors and killed twenty-two.[47]

Many actors, however, lived up to Whitman's vision of unaffected art, "Miss Clarke at the Olympic is better, and truer.... Jamison can give Kean any odds, and play better. John R. Scott is better."[48] In her role as Nancy Sykes at the Park Theater, Charlotte Cushman managed to "identify herself...completely with the character she [was] playing." In the character of Evadne, Cushman managed to portray "the total revolution of a mighty and guilty mind" from pride, defiance, and anger to fear, remorse, and self-conscious vileness. Cushman's "natural" style could not be "superceded by the fifth rate artistic trash that comes over to us from the old world...." Whitman equated Cushman's talent with her appeal to the unaffected grace of the common people. European actors "afforded many an intellectual man and woman...a rich treat...." However, "Miss Cushman assuredly bears away the palm from them all."[49]

Whitman's openly disdainful remark towards the "intellectual" is worth noting here. He did not explicitly equate refined "taste" with wealth. Rather, over-intellectualization produced European airs. Pretentious art might do well for the aristocratic decadence of Europe where individuals, both rich and poor, repressed their identities to satisfy the whims of the autocrat. In monarchies, everyone pretended to be something he was not. Cushman's visceral acting, on the other hand, spoke to an American sensibility that celebrated simple truth and defied European mendacity.[50] Europe and America expressed different cultures, one aristocratic and one republican. Both, in their proper place, worked. Either, out of place, threatened the surrounding social order. Though Whitman spoke to a working class, male audience here, his critique was not explicitly class-based. Instead, the Editor's criticism of aristocratic manners in the arts implicitly accused European actors and their American admirers of limp-wristed sycophancy. European sensibility, with its affected style and professional airs, was a kind of fraud that posed for foppish patrons and expert admirers. In this regard, affected actors undermined the idea of true and essential personhood. Kean's staged masculinities challenged republican sensibility by positing that identity, itself, was a put-on for another's sake.

In his attacks on Kean and expert-critics, Whitman utilized nationalistic language common in the Democratic press. This rhetoric channeled New York class politics and the fear that upper-class European sensibilities translated into cultural tyranny. As at the *Aurora*, Whitman catered to his audience's tastes and interests while implicitly incorporating his own ideals into the mix. In the case of the theater, Whitman's critique of European acting was largely rhetorical. Throughout 1846, the Editor spoke highly of William Macready, the same British actor whose work inspired the Astor Place Riots three years later. In fact, Whitman compared Macready to the American actress Charlotte Cushman for his ability to portray unaffected emotions. For the Editor, Macready "in his best days" exemplified the empathetic acting that proved essentially republican, "he touched the heart, the soul, the feelings, the inner blood and nerves of his audience." This authentic style opposed the "ordinary actor" who "struts and rants away, and his furious declamation begets a kind of reciprocal excitement among those who hear him." The difference between this type of acting and the authentic kind seen in Macready proved the difference between hammering "away...at the ear" and touching "the heart."[51]

Whitman probably referred to Edwin Forrest, the hero of the working class at the Astor Place Riot, in his negative appraisal of the strutting and ranting actor. Though the Editor carefully separated Forrest's "American style" from imitators who with "unnatural and violent jerks, swings, screwing of the nerves of the face, [and] rolling of the eyes..." undermined the idea of true acting, he also noted that Forrest, himself, played Spartacus (a part written for him) in *The Gladiator* only "passing well." In fact, even the "rough boys in the pit" reacted to poor imitators of Forrest's style "with expression[s] of...contempt," but let forth "spontaneous bursts of approbation...toward acting of the most...simple, truthful, and natural" kind.[52] This expressed the nuance of the Editor's ideal American theater; authentic emotions played in plain view made acting truly republican, but the local hero of an American/British theatrical rivalry, Edwin Forrest, personified the kind of affectation Whitman critiqued. Ironically, the British actor, William Macready, represented the unaffected acting style he celebrated.

For the Editor, Forrest's overblown acting represented the flip side of an effete European style; both were patently false. Macready, on the other hand, like Cushman, received justification (at least to Whitman's eyes) from the audience itself. Whereas citizens experienced "excitement" while viewing Forrest, Macready and Cushman inspired "spontaneous...approbation;" the overblown kind of acting elicited a spectator's awe, the empathetic and natural kind inspired a citizen's unadulterated acclaim. One proved a false stimulant, the other a natural nostrum. The national origins of the actors proved secondary to this argument; the audience's reaction confirmed this. Whitman carefully split the difference between a critic's honed sensibility and a patriot's simple nativism by citing Macready's natural style as the truly republican. In doing so he implied that a republican sensibility transcended national lines and thereby gave implicit support to the universalist rhetoric of the Declaration of Independence, the Democratic Party, and, later, the world-embracing language of *Leaves of Grass*. The Editor made this argument while the rivalry between Forrest and Macready remained largely aesthetic.[53] However, as Forrest and Macready came to symbolize class differences exclusively after 1847, both disappeared from Whitman's editorials all together.[54] By the time of the Astor Place Riot in 1849, Whitman no longer worked at the *Brooklyn Daily Eagle*, but it is a fair guess that he would have reacted to the violence of that day with some ambivalence.[55]

The Editor also presented a subtle critique of American literature. In an era where international copyright did not exist in the United States, books by popular authors could be reproduced cheaply for mass consumption. Harper and Brothers, for example, published the *Harper's Illuminated and new Pictorial Bible* (1846) (which Whitman reviewed) as well as unlicensed versions of Dickens, Thackeray, and the Brontë sisters. Authors, themselves, became commodities. As Horace Greeley remarked to Henry David Thoreau, "you may write with an angel's pen, yet your writings have no...money value until you are known and talked of as an author."[56] The explosion in the book trade created ancillary genres that catered to "high-brow" and "low-brow" literary tastes. For example, Lewis Gaylord Clark's *Knickerbocker* magazine (1834), a literary monthly, did not pay its authors (the editors expected their authors to be financially stable amateurs) and saw its reviews republished in numerous Whig newspapers.[57] The *Knickerbocker* sought to be the voice of stability and high literary culture. Conversely, John O'Sullivan's *Democratic Review* tried, as part of the "Young America" movement, to foster American authors who could overcome the "the anti-democratic character of our literature."[58] George Palmer Putnam's publishing house bolstered this effort by rivaling Harpers' dependence on the classics and offering the populace "American literature."[59] Whitman took these aesthetic debates and worked them into a revised persona of the Editor: the social critic who sought, like a blue-blood at the *Knickerbocker,* to discern quality from trash, but, in the spirit of the *Democratic Review,* to do so for a democratic audience.

Though the Editor's criticism of European stage manners reflected the tastes of many theater patrons of the period, a rejection of English literature out of hand was ill advised. Classics and contemporary authors like Shakespeare, Bunyan and Dickens enjoyed a wide readership and influenced Whitman himself. In fact, the Editor acknowledged the American debt to Britain's "spirit of progress and independence" and called authors like Milton, Bunyan, and Defoe "god-like." Whitman catered to his audience's tastes through his differing analyses of British theater and literature. While he harshly attacked European acting, regarding literature he gently asked his readers "have we in this country nothing to add to the store of their manifold genius?"[60]

Like drama, good literature portrayed an objective reality via subjective emotions, but with an important difference. Whereas ideal drama expressed intense emotions to an audience of collected citizens and, through their empathetic sensibility, communicated both individually and communally, the novel spoke to the solitary citizen. As such, it encouraged anti-social and undemocratic behavior. Many nineteenth-century critics of the novel agreed with Whitman when he advised "parents and guardians [to] exclude works of fiction from their houses, and enjoin their young charges to abstain altogether from the perusal of them."[61] The novel was risky business because the act of reading required a citizen to be disconnected from his peers and (unlike the school and the theater) beyond their immediate gaze. The best books instructed the private citizen in public citizenship.[62] Frederika Bremer's didacticism attracted the Editor to her novels. They educated the reader on "the mild virtues...how charity and forbearance and love are potent in the domestic circle." This type of fiction proved safer than the "affected sentimentality of [Edward] Bulwer, and the verbose weakness of [Henry] James [Sr.]." As when he searched the streets for Dickens' characters, Whitman noted many of Bremer's characters "around us" and celebrated the novel's moral impact, " [the] pure moonlight beauty of Elise [that] attracts the desire of every mother-reader to be likewise beautiful in her nature!"[63]

Poetry and non-fiction functioned in a similarly didactic fashion in the Editor's reviews for the *Brooklyn Daily Eagle*. William Cullen Bryant's poetry exulted "in the issues of freedom for nobler ends and larger interests." Bryant's poetry made "all men participators in [the great arguments by] seeking and developing the universality that lies at the core."[64] Ross Brown's *Brown's Whaling Cruise, and History of the Whale Fishery* avoided "flummery" and taught the virtues of hard work.[65] The Harper's edition of the illustrated Bible "provok[ed] thought and pleasure in the mind...."[66] To modern readers, Whitman's approval seems occasionally off. He described Melville's *Omoo* as entertaining but "all books have their office...and this a very side one."[67] On the other hand, Henry Howe's *Memoirs of the Most Eminent American Mechanics* received a positive review as "good reading for the young workingmen of this republic."[68] Many of Whitman's reviews seem surprisingly pedestrian when considering the later literary fame of their author. However, Whitman's Editor made few critical analyses in pursuit of the sublime; instead, he critiqued the influence of literature to the extent that it benefited the Republic. In this regard, good literature, like good theater, served didactic ends.

"Have We No Consumers?"

Many scholars have interpreted Whitman's ideology to be that of an artisan producer on the cusp of the new-market, consumer economy.[69] This is not an inaccurate reading, but a partial one. In light of his theories of free trade and the tariff, the Editor of the *Eagle* identified the working class as modern consumers rather than as victims of industrialization. Instead of interpreting the consumer economy as the cause of affectation, protective tariffs created an affected economy that undermined the natural consuming power of laborers. At the *Eagle*, Whitman redefined the free artisan who owned his shop into a free wage earner and consumer who maintained his artisan integrity. In this way, Whitman's wage-earning worker still upheld the republican ideal of Jeffersonian independent farmers and artisans. For the Editor, tariffs, unreasonably low wages, and slavery stood in the way of this unaffected economy of free consumers

The tariff divided American political parties as early as the so-called "Tariff of Abominations" of 1828. For the Whigs, the tariff on textiles gave the United States a necessary edge against the superior producing power of Great Britain. This edge, in the form of a tax on imports, insulated domestic products against foreign competition. Conservative Whig politicians argued that this provided universal benefit as it protected both capitalists and laborers from foreign competition. This mirrored the argument for an "organic" economy so often advocated by conservatives: what is good for the head is good for the rest of the economic body. Democrats generally fought the tariff. However, because of their diverse interests, they did so for varied reasons. For labor activists, the tariff undermined the American working class by falsely raising prices and perpetuating a parasitic "owning" class. The tariff also exacerbated British dominance in the world market by taking for granted that American industry could not compete on an even playing field. Southern Democrats, moreover, argued that the tariff levied a national tax that only benefited the Northeast and limited the purchasing power of the British (who, by the 1840s, bought most of their raw cotton from the South), thereby adversely affecting the Southern economy. Finally, many Southern Democrats questioned a national economic policy that had only regional effects. Underpinning this argument were fears that the federal government could abolish slavery itself; this fueled the Nullification Crisis between South Carolina and the Jackson Administration.[70] New York Democrats also felt acutely the existence of this import tax; much of the domestic profit generated from it went into the hands of Whig business leaders. Whitman argued on safe ground when he used Democrats' distaste for the tariff to present his theory of an unaffected economy.

Whitman's arrival at the *Daily Eagle* in March 1846 coincided with the Polk administration's introduction of the low Walker Tariff to Congress; he entered the dialogue as the debate itself came to a close. In a short article that supported further cuts in import taxes, the Editor noted that everyone talked "as though the direct profit of those directly engaged in great manufactures were the *only* thing worth consideration! Have we no *consumers* [Whitman's emphasis]? Are not four-fifths of the people interested in getting things cheaply?"[71] On August 5, 1846, he called unpatriotic those who criticized the lower tariff, "Have not the American people as staunch hearts, as stout nerves, as nimble figures, as much physical power, as the men of Europe?" When the Whigs talked of protecting both employees and employers with the tariff, it was "an insult to the noble American workingman to speak of 'protecting' him in this way!"[72] In fact, the lower duties that made up the Walker Tariff needed to be cut even further, but "we must creep before we can walk."[73] To prove his point, Whitman equated free trade with physical health and self-reliance. Upon a visit to the Castle Garden Fair in October 1846, he noted the quality and affordability of the American products for sale and mocked Whigs for "protecting" the working class with their support of the tariff, "Poor youth! He is running over with health; he must therefore be nursed and medicined a bit."[74] For Whitman, a healthiest economy had the least encumbrances, "the freer you leave the whole matter from any hampering restrictions, the more boundlessly will the energies and workmanship of the American people be expanded."[75] A free market showed respect for laborers because it allowed them to naturally compete and consume.

Not all workers agreed. In the early 1840s the union movement reemerged and incorporated the rhetoric of moral persuasion and traditional radicalism into its vocabulary. The Order of United American Mechanics and the Mechanics' Mutual Protection Association established themselves in New York City in 1845 and 1846 respectively and emulated the Christian workingmen's organizations prominent in Europe in the 1840s that looked to Christ as "the Reformer of Judah who laboured himself as a carpenter." In this way, the union movement incorporated the religious rhetoric of the Second Great Awakening and the religiosity of New York reformers after the Panic of 1837. Likewise, women from six trades organized the Ladies' Industrial Association and modeled it on the General Trades Union that had been defunct for nearly ten years. Describing themselves as "daughters of the Patriots of '76," these women organized a strike in 1846 that sparked Whitman's interest in wage issues. Also, in 1847, the New York Protective Union created a series of cooperative shops where all workers received their due according to the labor theory of value. No wages were paid according to hours worked. No managers oversaw production exclusively.[76]

For the Editor, however, unions barely existed because they were unnecessary for Whitman's idea of the workingman's republic. For example, during a strike of Irish laborers who were building a dock for a local company, Whitman called the union's attempt to "regulate the prices of labor...contrary to the dictates of that clear, high, immutable truth, the freer and the more without restrictions of any kind you leave trade and prices to regulate themselves, the better for all parties."[77] Remedies for workers came through moral persuasion and the free market because "[w]e, ourselves, bring our destiny upon us, for good or for evil, and we alone are the main cause of the effect."[78]

The only union activity of ongoing interest to Whitman during his two years at the *Eagle* was the "sewing girls" strike of 1846-47. Instead of interpreting it as a labor fight, however, he framed it in the language of womanhood in peril, "...if anyone will watch the movements of these patient and gentle...girls..., and tell why they prefer the crust of bread and palette of straw to silks and satins, luxury and fine living, they will be wise indeed."[79] The arguments Whitman made on behalf of these working women defined their economic degradation as particular to their gender, "No wonder the pest houses and brothels in that city are increasing in number every day: no wonder that so many are seeking refuge from poverty and distress in those places...." Low wages, then, in "that" city across the river, increased the preponderance of a crime particular to women.[80] Here, Whitman echoed similar sentiments he made at the *Aurora*; feminine crime (primarily prostitution) could be traced directly to wages kept near starvation by "the old clo' merchants" in their pursuit of undue profit. Moral persuasion, then, could solve this problem. Low wages reduced women to an "unnatural" state: the prostitute.[81] If management paid workingwomen their due, they would not be reduced to unnatural acts. Unlike young mechanics (who he defined by their work), Whitman defined young women by their dependence. His appeal for higher wages for workingwomen (and, significantly, a general absence of similar appeals for workingmen) made this plain.

Whitman made similar arguments throughout the strike.[82] In December 1846, he claimed that wage-earning women faced one of two unpleasant choices, "on one side is virtue, but accompanied by stern and gaunt attendants—wearying labor, stinted food, mean dress, and the cool regard of the world." And on the other side, "vice, but smiling and buxom—offering pleasure, an easy life, comfort, and fine apparel. Is not the temptation great?" He ended this editorial with a very simple social equation: "open the eyes of men to the *fact* of the intimate connexion between *poor pay* for women, and *crime among women*, and the greatest difficulty is overcome {Whitman's emphasis}." A life of comfort *and* virtue could not be found in the world of working women. For the Editor, free trade meant benefits, overall, for the worker, but by worker he meant working men and, by default, their families. His ideal laborer headed a household where women did not have to work at all.[83] For Whitman, the workingwomen were "girls" and, by implication, unmarried. Their low pay and youth left them in danger of slipping into the underworld of prostitution. The Editor imagined these women, not unlike the youngsters whom he sought to protect in the marketplace and the park, as still unformed and in need of benevolent protection. They walked a tight rope between a safe matronly status and a life of degradation; he had no concept of them as having a vocation or trade upon which they would build a life. Therefore, he presented the reader with an obvious choice: pay these girls more money until they can find a husband and make a family, or they will become whores.[84] The choice, then, became one of concern to the future of the Republic. Would they fill the city with working families or impoverished, immoral individuals?

During this same period, Whitman found examples of the free market functioning to his approval. These examples modeled the potential of a well-functioning community of worker-consumers. In an article on the growing suburb of Bedford, he noted with approval the "eligible lots [that] are procurable in that portion of our city at a very cheap rate, the owners take plenty of breathing space for their residences, and the enjoyments of semi-rural life are attainable...." Bedford combined the "conveniences" of the city with the "advantages" of country life and the Editor noted the "agreeable picture of domestic life": a pretty wife "upon the piazza" awaiting the return of her husband, the children ready to run at the approach of their father, the furniture, the pure white china, and the spotless table linen "[made] life rationally agreeable." Whitman noted that people "out there do not, as in the dense and selfish city, take delight in alleging that they are unacquainted with their next door neighbor!"[85]

This celebration of domestic life came in the same issue as an article in support of the sewing girls' strike, but the Editor never equated the wealth of Bedford with the industrial production of consumable goods in the city; one did not cause reflection on the other and Whitman expressed no sense of larger socio-economic forces at work (even to the extent that cheap textiles made for inexpensive table linens). In this light, the tariff's origins were personal; a few selfish Whigs taxed the very things that made life in Bedford possible for everyone. However, the powers of moral persuasion could convince the people of its adverse effects and inspire them to vote appropriately. According to the Editor, "it appears that besides the thirty millions a year, paid into the National Treasury by us consumers, we actually pay other sixty millions, to the 'protected' classes." This "infamous extortion...out of the pockets of the working people" forced a blacksmith to pay a 52 percent tax on his hammers, a carpenter to pay 42 percent on his, and "wives...to pay 75 percent more on their common ingrain carpets." For male laborers, the tariff unduly taxed their tools (and, therefore, their means to profit); for women, the tariff unjustly taxed household goods. No grand economic system oppressed workers; the supporters of the tariff and the greedy unmanliness of the "old clo'" merchants did.[86] Workers freed themselves by simply supporting a lower tariff (and the political party that advocated it). Thereafter, they would have the potential to make their unencumbered way to domestic comfort in nearby Bedford.

The Free-Soil Fiasco

As in his personas of "Schoolmaster" and "Editor" at the *Aurora*, Whitman sought to create a persona that maintained a balance between "knowing" the people (a position of superior objectivity) and being "one of" the people (and their equal). This allowed him to promote a reform ideology that required children to naturally develop in a benevolent environment, adults to hone their citizenship with peers through the arts, and consumers, through a free economy, to establish households of domestic comfort and tranquility. By the late 1840s, Whitman incorporated slavery into his arguments about affectations that threatened the nation. Ideologically, he sympathized with the free-soil insurgency in the Democratic Party and, by 1848, once again found himself on the wrong side of Tammany Hall.

Free-soil politics are often confused with a moderate form of abolitionism; they were, however, in many ways abolitionism's political opposite. Abolitionism, as pursued by reformers like William Lloyd Garrison, Henry Ward Beecher, and John Brown, offrered a reform program that assumed the moral necessity of slaves to enjoy freedom and, in this regard, had many of the trappings of the conservative labor reform movement; it sought to "uplift" a segment of the population through moral justification (and evangelical rhetoric). It is no surprise that the majority of prominent abolitionists in New York state politics (William Seward best known among them) were Whigs who became active in the Republican Party in the 1850s. Free-soilism, on the other hand, had its origins in the Democratic Party and labor issues. As such, it united the mainstream Democratic program of individual freedom and expansion with the radical labor ideology of egalitarianism through government fiat.

The free-soil movement originated with a proposal by Pennsylvania Congressman David Wilmot that a proviso be added to the Polk administration's request for $2 million in war funding. Though Wilmot supported the expansion of the United States to the West, he proposed that the government close these territories to slavery. He supported this proposal with arguments about labor and race. According to Wilmot, the expansion of slavery and the establishment of future slave states undermined the dignity and economic security of the free white laboring classes. To artisans attuned to the perceived decline in their labor value, the prophecies of Wilmot charted a process already evident in the free-market economy. According to this logic, labor already had its value undermined by the advent of industry and an employer class; the spread of slavery would finally reduce it to a permanent, abject underclass. Echoing this fear, in 1849, a New York free-soil newspaper reprinted an ominous slave advertisement from a southern newspaper: "Mechanics for sale."[87]

Wilmot's arguments unleashed the latent antagonism between rank-and-file New York Democrats and the leadership of the Party. Free-soilers framed their attacks on Tammany Hall as the common people against monopolistic interests that benefited from slave labor (both in the South, and among business leaders in the North). The ensuing debate divided the New York Party into so-called Hunkers and Barnburners and, in 1846, when a Whig defeated the free-soil Democratic governor of New York, Silas Wright, the poet and editor William Cullen Bryant blamed it on the "treachery of the Hunkers."[88] When Silas Wright died in 1847, the Barnburners in the New York Democratic Party planned a ceremony at the state convention in Syracuse and urged fellow Democrats to nominate candidates who supported free-soil ideals in honor of Wright's memory. When one Hunker quipped that "It is too late, he is dead," James B. Wadsworth, a free-soil advocate, jumped onto a table and shouted, "It is not too late to do justice to his assassins."[89] After Democrats voted down nearly all of Wright's proposals in the name of party unity, the Barnburners walked out of the proceedings. In 1847, when Democrats lost overwhelmingly to Whigs in state elections and in the ward elections that same year in New York, party stalwarts blamed the Barnburner faction for the loss. In response, free-soil Democrats joined the short-lived "Free-soil Party" and sent delegates to its national convention in Buffalo.[90]

At first, Whitman hedged slowly toward anti-slavery politics. Like most free-soilers, the Editor expressed ambivalence toward African-Americans and especially abolitionists. In an article from April 1846 written four months before Wilmot made his proposal, he railed against "pharisaic philanthropists" who "go into paroxysms of distress for the slave at the south...but give no day, no hour, nor cent to the scores of sick, sinful, and starving ones to be found in any of our great American cities."[91] On August 7, one day before Wilmot proposed his proviso in Congress, Whitman called on abolitionists to "hold their tongues, and let the slow but sure and steady spread of political and moral truth do its work among the people."[92] In January 1847, while still publishing editorials decrying the "ultraism" of abolitionists, Whitman also wrestled with the human propensity to oppress others, "what an incomprehensible machine is man! [W]ho can endure toil for his own liberty...and the next moment...inflict on his fellow men...bondage...?"[93] However, as late as March 1847, he still interpreted the defeat of the Wilmot Proviso philosophically, "it is by no means vitally important. [W]e have more faith in public opinion than law...let all hands smooth down and become calmer."[94]

Through the spring and fall of 1847, in the run up to the local elections and in the face of growing dissent between New York Hunkers and Barnburners, however, Whitman began to openly equate slavery with the degradation of labor by a slave-holding class,[95] and in November he blamed the defeat of the Democrats at the polls on the party's rejection of the

"Jeffersonian" Wilmot Proviso.[96] Whitman's inflammatory rhetoric further exacerbated the divided Democrats when he asked rhetorically, "have the ages rolled backward...that we went to war to *stop*, seventy years ago, [what] we shall now keep up a war to *advance?*" By December 1847, not so unlike five-years previous at the *Aurora*, the Editor found himself at odds with his own party and, by default, his newspaper. In the aftermath of the November state election, Democrats sought to regroup by bringing Barnburners back into the party fold and evicting those who refused to put aside the free-soil debate. Whitman, as seen in his editorials of these final months, chose the latter.[97]

What explains Whitman's change of mind between 1847 and 1848? The first and clearest answer is Whitman's disgust with the Democratic convention of 1847 during which the Hunker bloc expunged Barnburner policies from the Party. Whitman, like many younger Democrats, saw in governor Silas Wright another William Leggett. Wright's loss of the governor's mansion, his death soon thereafter, and the blame he received (post mortem) for the loss of the recent election left Whitman, and other Party rebels, with the impression that the Hunker faction of the Party committed treason against Wright's memory. This inner-party squabble divided along ideological lines cut by the Wilmot Proviso one year earlier. In September 1847, Whitman wrote an editorial entitled "American Workingmen, versus Slavery" where he argued that "[a]n honest poor mechanic, in a slave state, is put on par with the negro slave mechanic" and "the *workingmen* of the free United States...are not willing to be put on the level of negro slaves...in territory which, if got at all, must be got by taxes sifted eventually through...them, and by their hard work and blood."[98] Here Whitman echoed the sentiments of free-soil Democrats nationally and Barnburners locally.

However, by late 1847, Whitman incorporated these national and party debates into his own ideology. In December 1847, in his capacity as editor of the *Eagle*, Whitman heard a lecture at the Brooklyn Institute by Henry Giles, a Unitarian minister and abolitionist advocate. Whereas he previously critiqued what he saw as the hypocritical radicalism of abolitionists like William Lloyd Garrison, he now expressed his engagement with Giles' thesis.[99] The theologian gave voice to Whitman's growing conviction: slavery was part of laborer's plight. In an editorial published on December 10, 1847, Whitman claimed that "[Giles'] picture of a slave, the *thing* without feelings of a man, *not* a husband, *not* a parent, *not* a patriot, and impossible to be either...was burningly fearful and true. It will long live upon our memory...."[100] Giles echoed Whitman's argument against pretense in the new market economy: it reduced the free artisan by rejecting his essential equality to other men. If masters dehumanized slaves in a similar fashion, then slavery presented only an exacerbated form of the problem. Giles spoke Whitman's language of equality and dignity. Whereas Abraham Lincoln, over ten years later, justified African-American freedom economically, Whitman understood equality in much more existential terms.[101] The new market economy proved potentially dangerous to the worker because it encouraged self-making rather than self-respect; the worker had to be taught to avoid pretense. Slavery allowed a slaveholder to define a worker as a slave rather than as a man; the slaveholder had to be taught about this impossible contradiction. Both threatened "the foundation of our republican government and the rights of all human beings" because within both lay the possibility of oppressing a person's essential nature.[102] Once set, this precedent killed republics.

Whitman portrayed righteous consumers as free, working, white and, after 1847, black. They deserved the freedom to seek living wages because a living wage allowed them to live naturally as a spouse, parent, and patriot. Anything that sought to squelch these elemental qualities (slavery, tariffs, cigars, affected manners) was oppression. For Whitman, a free republic recognized what individuals were naturally; it did not impart roles onto them (whether to lift up or reduce). Similar to the rising wages he expected as the result of free trade, the end of slavery would come through the spread of the free market to the West. Like most free-soilers, Whitman saw the existence of slavery as a threat to the nobility and economic viability of the worker. Unlike most free-soilers, Whitman recognized the slave as holding the same essential characteristics as white workers.

Unfortunately, this attitude left him without a job and, after 1848, without a political party. In early 1848, Whitman's publisher, the Hunker Isaac Van Anden, accused Whitman of being a Barnburner who sought to divide the Democratic Party over the issue of slavery. David Wilmot himself received a similar tongue-lashing from the conservative wing of his own party. When, against his publishers' wishes, Whitman wrote an article opposed to the pro-slavery Democratic candidate Lewis Cass, he put his job in jeopardy.[103] That year, he served as a delegate to the short-lived Free-Soil Party convention in Buffalo, New York and sealed his reputation as a party apostate.

Whitman's last editorial for the *Brooklyn Daily Eagle* appeared on January 14, 1848. In this short piece on broken lamps in Brooklyn, the Editor recounted the miraculous story of a broken city light that burned all night and ended with, "We begin to believe in Miller's theory, that the end of the world is at hand."[104]

PART THREE

BARD

1848–1855

CHAPTER FIVE

PERSONA NON GRATA

Between 1848 and 1855 Whitman's Editor persona suffered dislocation and underwent philosophical transformation. The nation itself experienced similar turmoil. Democrat David Wilmot's proviso of 1846 reopened the slavery debate and solidified free-soil politics in the North. This debate smoldered in the aftermath of the Mexican-American War (1846-1848) and the so-called Compromise of 1850 and rekindled with ferocious energy in the years following the Kansas-Nebraska Act (1854). By 1856, the two national parties split along sectional lines and the Kansas territory exploded in violence that reached the Senate floor when South Carolina Representative Preston Brooks clubbed the abolitionist senator Charles Sumner for his remarks on "the harlot, Slavery."[1] Whitman, caught up in the unraveling of the nation, was fired from the *Brooklyn Daily Eagle* for his Barnburning politics.

Whitman's Editor sought a public voice that could instruct citizens outside of the boundaries of partisan politics. This is not to say that the Editor avoided politics; in the Maclay Bill and free-soil controversies Whitman engaged in contemporary debates. He attempted to justify his arguments, however, with rhetoric that transcended party lines and hewed close to the natural rights ideology of the American Founding. In the case of the Maclay Bill, the Editor sided with nativism in the name of public schools and the unaffected, non-sectarian education of future citizens. Regarding the Wilmot Proviso, Whitman judged slavery as an institution that both threatened the natural dignity of the average worker and created a clique of slaveholders whose status and self-definition depended upon the illegitimate labor of others. In both cases, he spoke to an essential identity in all Americans that deserved recognition and respect in the public sphere. Unfortunately, in the heat of partisan fights within the Democratic Party itself, the Editor found his ideals at odds with the dominant position of his party. In an attempt to speak for all, Whitman found himself speaking to no one.

Whitman described his years after 1848 and before writing *Leaves of Grass* as "simmering" and claimed, "Emerson brought me to a boil."[2] During these boiling years, the Editor underwent a transformation that ended in a new public identity. This transformation, however, was publicly slow and intermittent. Its culmination, after seven years, saw the melding of Whitman's aesthetic theory and labor reform ideology in the new persona of the Bard.

Whitman is often grouped with transcendentalists like Emerson and Thoreau.[3] Whitman, himself, made the connection. After publishing the first edition of *Leaves of Grass*, he sent a complimentary copy to Ralph Waldo Emerson and received, in return, the famous greeting "upon the beginning of a great career."[4] The story, however, is more complicated. Before 1848, Emerson was almost absent from Whitman's editorials. Though he wrote one approving review of an Emerson lecture in 1842,[5] when compared with the corpus of Whitman's editorials between 1842 and 1855, the connections are meager. In fact, during Whitman's early weeks as a writer for the *Aurora*, the newspaper called transcendentalism no different than "rank deism" and offered to quote a "few specimens" of this philosophy, but "the *Aurora* is of...a serious cast [and] it would be laughable to induce laughter in the reader."[6] In a quip for the *Eagle* in 1847, Whitman quoted approvingly from the first paragraph of Emerson's 1841 lecture "Spiritual Laws," but commented on it in only one sentence (where he called it "truthful" and "beautiful"). Neither of these examples point to a close reading of Emerson or having been influenced greatly by him when he worked steadily as a journalist. Perhaps the Editor felt an affinity for the popular notions of Emerson, but there is little hard evidence of any deep reading of the Concord sage before 1848 in his public statements.

Reform, for Emerson, was a mind-set through which one could subvert staid social institutions and traditional ways of thinking; reform thinking fertilized the ground for a conversion into a whole person, independent and self-defined. As a "keener scrutiny of institutions and domestic life than any one we had known," reform bred progress.[7] In Emerson's hands, temperance, evangelicalism, and abolitionism worked like training exercises for a holistic reconfiguration of the fractured person into an authentic individual. "Nature" (1836) denounced customs and traditions and celebrated authenticity and natural language. "The American Scholar" (1837) presented "right reading" as a means to overcome a fractured society. The "Divinity School Address" (1838) attacked organized religion in the name of individual revelation. "The Poet" (1844) dismissed formal verse in support of democratic engagement with contemporary speech and rhythms. These works, in cursory terms, echoed

Whitman's reform program. They sought something essential and transcendent in the individual. Emerson's reform, however, looked forward to a better way of being outside of social structures, "In the wilderness, I find something more dear and connate than in streets or villages. In the tranquil landscape...man beholds somewhat as beautiful as his own nature."[8] In these essays, Emerson sought to push through to an authentic sensibility beyond society. Whitman's Editor, on the other hand, drew inspiration from an idealized republican commonwealth and a tradition of self-fulfillment in the public sphere.

Henry David Thoreau's advocacy of the simple life and critique of the new market economy in *Walden* (1854) echoed many of Whitman's editorials (all the way back to the Schoolmaster series), but Thoreau, like Emerson, was connected to the Boston liberals socially and ideologically. His "deliberate" living played upon the middle-class masculine fantasy of meditative privacy popular in the 1850s.[9] It is not surprising, then, that the 1854 edition of *Walden* sold 2,000 copies (compared to the 795 *printed* of Whitman's first edition).[10] In this light, Thoreau's dictum "Old deeds for old people, and new deeds for new" opposed Whitman's celebration of an "agreeable picture of domestic life."[11] Whitman's notion of the daily press as the educator of the masses challenged Thoreau's description of the modern reading public as "tit-men...[who] soar but little higher in our intellectual flights than the columns of the daily paper."[12]

Though he sought the notoriety and influence of Emerson and Thoreau, Whitman, contrary to the Boston Romantics, typically hewed to the conventional. After attending the addresses of such prominent abolitionists and free-soilers as Cassius Clay, John Parker Hale and Charles C. Burleigh, Whitman gave them little mention in the *Eagle* editorials. His reticence originated in his profession and persona. Too intimately involved in the political fracas that the likes of Emerson and Thoreau sought to transcend, the Editor could not be a "rebel" in the Transcendentalist sense. When Whitman ran afoul of his contemporaries, he lost his job and, by default, the platform from which to launch his public identities and reform ideology. Superficially, Whitman and the Boston transcendentalists both promoted the recovery of "true" identity. Emerson and Thoreau understood this identity, however, in a way similar to the modern solution to an existential crisis; to unify a fractured identity, one eschewed convention and reconnected with the subjective self. Whitman, on the other hand, demanded his readers find their identities with each other. This represented a much more conservative assessment of the possibilities of self-improvement and an egalitarian's suspicion of individuality. Whereas Emerson and Thoreau rejected the public sphere as a place for authentic identities, Whitman told his readers that in public they became whole.

New Orleans Simmer

In March 1848, Whitman took a job as an essayist at the *New Orleans Crescent* and held this position for only three months.[13] He claimed that he took the job after an impromptu offer from one of the newspaper's owners whom he met in the lobby of an old Broadway theatre near Pearl Street.[14] J.E. McClure and A.A. Hayes, two New Orleans journalists who recently started the *Crescent,* probably valued Whitman for his connections to northern newspapers, his experience and his need for employment. Whitman may have even heard that McClure was visiting New York to purchase supplies and sought him out.[15] Whatever the case, upon accepting a position as staff, and with full knowledge that his readership would not be sympathetic to his free-soil leanings, Whitman severely curtailed his professional and political inclinations in return for a job.

The editorials published in the *Crescent* portray an essayist in search of a voice. The "Excerpts From A Traveler's Note Book" (published in early March 1848) offered flat and distant descriptions of geography and towns on the river during his two-week journey by rail and riverboat. From Louisville south Whitman described "a long stretch of monotonous country;" the river town of Cairo, Illinois could never be "any 'great shakes,' except in the way of ague."[16] He commented on the essential nature of humanity by only noting that travelers got used to drinking and washing in the "mass of yellowish brown liquid" of the Mississippi River.[17] Though he celebrated "the men of the West" for their lack of "frippery and artificial fashion," he did so at a distance and without the intimate style common to his work at the *Aurora* and the *Eagle.*

As a contributing editor at the *Crescent,* Whitman experimented with a new voice that avoided the immediate politics of his days at the *Eagle* but, nonetheless, presented a coherent ideology that echoed ideas he had been formulating since 1845 while writing for the *Evening Star.* In a series entitled "Sketches Of The Sidewalks and Levees; with Glimpses into the New Orleans Bar (Rooms)," Whitman also returned to something like his objective tone from his days at the *Aurora,* only in this case, for a humorous effect. Jerome Loving compares these sketches to "the antebellum tradition of the Humor of the Old Southwest."[18] An example of this style is Johnson J. Hooper's character Simon Suggs who commented on southwestern culture with a jaundiced eye.

His description of a camp revival and crooked preacher from *The Adventures of Captain Simon Suggs* provides a good example:

> "Bless my poor old soul!" screamed the preacher in the pulpit; "ef yonder aint a squad in that corner that we aint got one outen yet! It'll never do"...raising his voice... "you must come outen that! Brother Fant, fetch up that youngster in the blue coat! I see the Lord's a-workin' upon him! Fetch him along... glory...yes!...hold to him !"[19]

Whitman's character, "Peter Funk, Esq," a "by-bidder" employed in a "Mock Auction," might have been familiar to his readers from Asa Green's *The Perils of Pearl Street* (1834). This "picturesque narrative" of New York City presented Funk as an archetypal grifter who, playing the shill, encouraged unsuspecting passers-by to purchase the cheap goods (at inflated prices) that his partner auctioned. Co-mingling Hooper's humorous topics with a stock character from the New York streets, Whitman struggled to find a new style for his prose. Like Hooper, Whitman employed the tone of a knowing observer to bring the reader into a winking collusion with the writer; both knew the ruse and, therefore, could admire the way Peter Funk pulled off the scam.

> You're a gentlemen of leisure about New Orleans, may be, stranger, and lounging about——street. You hear the musical sound of the "human voice divine" crying out "fivenaff, five-n-aff—only going at twenty-five dollars and-n-aff for this elegant gold watch and chain, in prime running order, just sent in by a *gentleman leaving town*, and only five-n-aff! Did I hear you say six, sir?"[20]

Unlike Hooper, Whitman also used comical literary references in these pieces, echoing the Shakespearean burlesques popular in New York throughout the 1840s.[21] For example, he ended his essay on Peter Funk with a quote from Act III of *Hamlet*, "conscience makes cowards of us all," and added that "Peter's conscience makes no coward of him..., Peter'll be rich one of these days." Accordingly, Peter avoided "the native hue of resolution thus sicklied o'er with the pale cast of thought" because he held "none of these sickly thoughts, or other consideration 'for the morrow,' except it be what coat or what colored whiskers he shall put on."[22] Whitman used irony to elicit humor here, but connected high literature with the mundane to produce this humorous effect. In "Miss Dusky Grisette," he quoted Byron's "Don Juan" to describe the particular beauty of an octaroon street vendor.[23] In "Daggerdraw Bowieknife, Esq," he loosely quoted Byron's "The Corsair" to give credence to the cutthroat nature of his subject.[24] In "John J. Jinglebrain," Whitman quoted Shakespeare's *King Lear* to give evidence of the pretensions of an over-aged fop.[25] In "Timothy Goujon V.O.N.O. (Vender of Oysters in New Orleans)," he referenced "well favored men" with a quote from *Much Ado About Nothing*.[26] He commented upon the troubles in Ireland with a snippet from *As You Like*

It.[27] Samuel Sensitive's romantic yearnings took their cue from Thomas Moore's "Love's Young Dream."[28] In all seven of the "Sketches" written for the *Crescent* between March and May 1848, Whitman connected his observations of New Orleans to literary references.

Whitman's "Sketches" read like a careful attempt to salvage some elements of his Editor persona and reform ideology from his time at the *Eagle* and *Evening Star* while maintaining a tone and subject that would not offend his Southern readers. He chose the safe style of humorous sketches similar to Hooper's while importing his own aesthetic theories into this genre. In this way, Whitman's literary references served a reform purpose higher than quote dropping as they upheld the idea of good art as a reflection of life unaffected; through laughter, they elicited the recognition that high aesthetics existed in the everyday. In this way, Whitman managed to degrade the affectations of high culture while simultaneously raising the reputation of the low and making social commentary from a bystander's perspective. This allowed him to put into effect his own literary theory of art: an artist's genius lay in the ability to capture the beautiful, fateful, tragic and comic of the everyday. In his *Crescent* sketches, Whitman humorously mixed the sublime and mundane and presented them as essentially the same.

The reasons for Whitman's termination from the *Crescent* are unclear. He implied that the break was over finances and letters home also indicate that his fifteen-year-old brother, Jeff, who accompanied him on the trip, became increasingly homesick throughout the spring.[29] When Whitman's employers refused him a cash advance on May 24, he severed connections with the paper and returned to New York.[30]

Brooklyn Simmer

Whitman's personified voice remained displaced between the summer of 1848 and the publication of *Leaves of Grass* in July 1855. During these seven years, he helped start a short-lived free-soil newspaper, the *Freeman*, commented on art and the countryside of Long Island in the *Evening Post*, lectured on aesthetics and was elected president of the Brooklyn Art Union, helped his father in the house-building business, opened a stationary shop, and wrote (infrequently published) poetry, some of which became part of *Leaves of Grass*. None of these positions lent Whitman the forum through which to consistently purvey a public persona. For this reason, the Bard of *Leaves of Grass* seemingly springs, fully grown, into the public eye in 1855. It is difficult to analyze a unified persona and reform ideology between 1848 and

1855 because Whitman lacked a consistent medium (as he had at the *Aurora* and *Eagle*) onto which he could project this persona. However, there are a few disparate strains in Whitman's prose and poetry in this period that give some hint of the generation of the Bard persona. Each, for different reasons, proved incongruent with the Editor persona, but worked well within the context of a self-contained collection of poetry.

Misbegotten Free-Soiler

Whitman's free-soilism, which had become politically untenable by 1848, exemplified the first of these strains. In the late summer, Whitman served as one of fifteen New York delegates to the Free-Soil convention in Buffalo, New York, but this third party lost momentum after the presidential election that year and all but disappeared by the Compromise of 1850. Free-soilers who wanted to influence national politics were forced to compromise with slaveholders or exist in political exile. When he took a job as the founding editor of the *Daily Freeman* (owned by the free-soil judge Samuel B. Johnston) in June 1848, Whitman hoped to find a more politically accommodating forum in which he could continue to ply his craft.[31] The one extant edition of the *Freeman* called on "Free Soilers! Radicals! Liberty Men! all whose throats are not quite tough enough to swallow Taylor or Cass! come up and subscribe to the *Daily Freeman*."[32]

Whitman's editorials throughout this single edition reflected an interest in abolition (a term used loosely in the *Freeman*) only as a means of maintaining the dignity of white labor. Likewise, the Editor sought to pull in Southern white laborers with the argument that "some fifteenth, or at the utmost some tenth, of the white inhabitants of the South...hold bondsmen." He also claimed to know "a very respectable body of slave owners who, the same as we, condemn slavery." This, then, reflected Whitman's ongoing attempt at a universal reform program. Slavery in this context represented the misinformed assumptions of a few wealthy men who wrongly thought that the institution benefited them. Whitman hoped that an exposure of this error would solve the problem.[33]

After the offices of the *Freeman* burned down in 1848 and the second incarnation of the paper was taken over by Democratic Hunkers, editorship for Whitman in the political environment of 1849-1850 proved no longer tenable.[34] Free-soilism, the most decisive issue in Democratic politics, like slavery, the issue that divided the nation, could only be communicated universally through a medium more all-encompassing than the partisan press.

The All-Seeing "I"

In 1851, Whitman returned to the first-person eyewitness voice that had been germinating since his days as the Schoolmaster. In this period of dislocated personas, Whitman published a series of "traveling" essays where he also replayed the objective role of an everyday observer. In both "Letters from a Traveling Young Bachelor" and "Letters from Paumonok" Whitman echoed the Schoolmaster in "Sun-Down Papers no. 10" and the observer of the "little republics" in the *Aurora*. In this second strain that hints at the Bard persona, Whitman stepped away from the political tone of the Democratic editor in contentious times.

On his rambles, Whitman presented himself as proudly no one special: "Having neither the funds nor disposition to pass my little term of ruralizing at fashionable baths, or watering places, I am staying awhile down here at Greenport, the eastern point of the Long Island Railroad." Like the Schoolmaster, he turned bemused observations into ethical lessons, "the fields, the waters, the trees, the interesting species of humanity...all are, for me, ministers to entertainment."[35] The fashionable were pitiful because "they evidently preserve all the ceremoniousness of the city—dress regularly for dinner, fear to brown their faces with the sun, or wet their shoes with the dew, or let the wind derange the well sleeked precision of their hair." This affectation forced him to conclude that, "very few people...know how to enjoy the country."[36] This tone and scene echoed the "Sun-Down Papers" in another way. In the case of the Schoolmaster, Whitman used the clam-hunting excursion as a scene through which to re-establish his neutral and authoritative tone. In "Letters from Paumanok," he reinvigorated himself by escaping the city (incidentally, to a location not-so-far distant from the clam hunting excursion of 1841) and reestablished a temperate tone outside the city's confines. Likewise, Whitman recycled the eyewitness quality of his articles at the *Aurora* where the truth unveiled itself. In relating a visit with "Aunt Rebby" and "Uncle Dan'l," he noted that, "Aunt Rebby expressed it as her positive opinion that the young folks of the present day don't enjoy half as much fun as the young folks of fifty years ago did." So as not to lose any readers on his point, Whitman added that, "She was seventy years old, and remembered the days of General Washington. Those were jovial times, but now 'it was all pride, fashion and ceremony.'"[37] Upon arriving at Uncle Dan'l's house, the Editor-in-exile related, "he invited us in and treated us to good berries. And so, at sundown, we had a nice cool walk of three miles, back to our quarters."[38] Though a number of scholars have traced Whitman's poetic "I" to this period, "Letters from Paumanok" also read like return, both in style and subject, to earlier, less politicized subjects.[39]

A new and almost frenetic intimacy also appeared in these essays. In describing the joys of music, he ran through a string of rhetorical questions that berated the reader into self-examination, "have not you, too, at such a time known this thirst of the eye? Have not you, in like manner, while listening to the well-played music of some band like Maretzek's felt an overwhelming desire for measureless sound...a sublime orchestra of a myriad orchestras...a colossal volume of harmony?"[40] This grab-by-the-lapels quality of Whitman's "I" in "Letters from Paumanok" rarely appeared in the earlier essays. He also made intense and intimate promises: "Come, I will not talk to you as to one of the superficial crowd who saunter here because it is a fashion.... I will trust you with confidence; I will divulge secrets."[41] Formerly, the Editor knew his reader's essence from the *outside* because he understood the nature of humanity and the Republic. In this new tone, Whitman knew his reader's essence from the *inside* because he shared in their desires and knew their secrets. The difference between "I" and "You" broke down in this intimacy.

In these "Letters" Whitman also rediscovered (and recycled) the Hicksite belief in the regressive nature of the Good. As Aunt Rebby knew, the best things were the old and eternal things; underneath the pretense and performance, people were the same. Their common reaction to music told them this; their common reaction to nature told them this. Whitman never really abandoned this understanding of humanity's essential sameness in this regard, though during his years at the *Aurora* and the *Eagle* this vision catered to contemporary issues and debates. His trip to rural Long Island allowed Whitman to lose his partisan voice and find one that could again make claims to eternal truth.

The Artist as Apostle

Whitman's evolving aesthetic theory made up the third of these strains that contributed to the Bard persona. As early as his days as the Schoolmaster, Whitman sought an unaffected aesthetic that uncovered the "true" American hiding underneath each citizen. At its core, the Schoolmaster and Editor saw the plight of the working class as a problem of the mind. Education and honest aesthetics, then, provided salvation. As Editor of the *Eagle*, Whitman acted as a citizen-critic who served the people's interests by exposing pretentious Eurocentric art. In the late winter and early spring 1851, Whitman published two articles that publicly defined an aesthetic theory that he had been formulating over a number of years. American art would do the opposite of European art where aristocratic patronage divided individuals into those who had "taste" and those who did not. In America, the expert-critic acted like an authoritative teacher among poor students; he celebrated the "best" and punished the "worst" based on his expertise. Whitman's citizen-critic, on the other hand, revealed the true nature of pretentious art and, in contrast to the expert-critic, knew intuitively the best art because he knew the authentic from the affected. In this regard, the Editor turned "taste" inside out. To have taste a citizen needed only inborn sensibility.

The New York art world by the mid-1840s was ripe for this kind of aesthetic egalitarianism. The Panic of 1837 and ensuing depression temporarily disrupted the traditional artistic patronage system in New York City where wealthy patrons utilized art as a form of highbrow conspicuous consumption. After the collapse of this patronage system, artists and art dealers used more creative methods to reach a public. For example, James Herring, a professional portraitist and engraver, created the Apollo Gallery in 1838 in hopes of taking advantage of a larger and more popular paying audience. The Apollo charged 25 cents for admission and shared all proceeds with its artist-members. When the Apollo failed to generate significant profit, Herring redesigned the gallery into the Apollo Association in 1839 (later renamed the American Art Union, or AAU, in 1844). The AAU charged subscribers $5 for a year's subscription, distributed its pieces by lottery to subscribers at the end of every year and allowed all non-subscribers to view the exhibits for free. The AAU, by the late 1840s, had 19,000 yearly subscribers and exhibited approximately 400 pieces of art each year before being ruled illegal as a form of gambling by a New York court in 1852. Before its demise, Putnam and O'Sullivan celebrated the AAU as a friend to "patriotic" American arts and artists. [42]

In "Something About Art and Brooklyn Artists" (published in February 1851), Whitman described the collection of paintings housed in the short-lived Brooklyn Art Union, whose owners modeled it on the AAU (and whose subscribers elected Whitman president). In this article, Whitman celebrated the Brooklyn Art Union's support of artists outside the "establishment" and, in this comparison, again connected the role of art with that of public education, "How would the cause of education stand now, were it not for the powerful favor which is extended to it from so many quarters, apart from those who are directly interested?" The Brooklyn Art Union, according to Whitman, played the patron to struggling artists much as the taxpayers acted as patrons of young citizens through the schools. In this regard, Whitman celebrated the art of Walter Libbey whose painting of a flute-playing boy exhibited "naive...spirit" and "grace." Echoing the aesthetics of the Editor, the picture of a boy and his flute had "a character of Americanism about it....[T]here is nothing to prevent his becoming a President, or even an editor of a leading newspaper."[43] In this case, Whitman refined his idea of the artist's role as purveyor of the nation's ideals. Whereas the Cheneys unconsciously inculcated democratic aesthetics through their very commonness, Whitman's new artists consciously made democratic art because of their native genius. In a lecture he gave to the Brooklyn Art Union, the artist became an apostle of democratic aesthetics: "To the artist, I say, has been given the command to go forth into all the world and preach the gospel of beauty." This beauty conflated the democratic and the aesthetic to avoid the "absurd error [that]...the two [are] distinct." Political figures like George Washington, Mary Stewart, and Giuseppe Mazzini, "all great rebels and innovators," reminded citizens, as artists did, "how slaves have battled against their oppressors—how the bullets of tyrants have, since the first king ruled, never been able to put down the unquenchable thirst of man for his rights."[44] In this regard, Whitman sounded very much like other European political-romantics of this period (who were still recovering from the revolutionary spasms of 1848). Whitman may even have read a copy of Henry Hedge's *Prose Writers of German* (1842) and discovered the ideas of Immanuel Kant, Friedrich von Schelling, Georg Wilhelm Friedrich Hegel and the physiologist Johann Caspar Lavater who found the holy in the seemingly insignificant.[45] Likewise, Emerson's essay, *The Poet*, which Whitman heard in lecture form in 1842, reflected this vision of the artist. In this case, poets "were liberating gods. They are free and they make free."[46]

Whitman's verse from this period began to aspire to this ideal. Much of his poetry between 1850 and 1855, while celebrating the transcendent union of nature, art, and freedom, also wrestled with political issues of the moment, specifically, slavery. Two poems from 1850, "Song for Certain Congressmen,"[47] and "The House of Friends,"[48] portrayed his anger over the Compromise of 1850 and the growing national crisis. "Song for Certain Congressmen" was both editorial and poem. In this piece, Whitman raged against his own party as much as he criticized the institution of slavery:

> We are all docile dough-faces,[49]
>   They knead us with the fist,
> They, the dashing southern lords,
>   We labor as they list;
> For them we speak—or hold our tongues,
>   For them we turn and twist.[...]
>
> To put down "agitation," now,

We think the most judicious;
To damn all "northern fanatics,"
                Those "traitors" black and vicious;
The "reg'lar party usages"
                For us, and no "new issues.[...]"

Principle—freedom!—fiddlesticks!
                We know not where they're found.
Rights of the masses—progress!—Bah!
                Words that tickle and sound;
But claiming to rule o'er "practical men"
                Is very different ground.[...]

Take heart, then sweet companions,
                Be steady, Scripture Dick!
Douglas, Cass, Walker,
                To your allegiance stick!
With Brooks, and Briggs and Phoenix,
                Stand up through thin and thick!

With thick sarcasm, Whitman spoke for the "dough-faces" and their compromise with slaveholders and attacked certain politicians (Douglas, Brooks, etc.) by name. These poems have understandably not stood the test of time in the traditional Whitman canon because they are not really poems at all; this exemplified the essence of Whitman's dilemma in the aftermath of the Wilmot Proviso. His Editor worked through moral persuasion. However, as an editor, reform and partisanship went hand-in-hand. The newspapers served Whitman well when he could use them and his position as editor at the *Daily Eagle* as a platform for his reform ideology. However, the foundation of this platform was the Democratic Party and, by 1848, this party chose to compromise on slavery rather than to face a possible division within its ranks. This reality perhaps still stung when Whitman rationalized his departure from the newspaper business nearly thirty years later, "The newspaper is so fleeting: is so like a thing gone as quick as come: has no life, so to speak: its birth and death are almost coterminous."[50] In this early verse he struggled to create a more convenient forum for his politically inexpedient ideology.

In a poem of the same period, "The House of Friends," it is not clear if Whitman meant the nation, the slave, or himself when he described a wounding by "friends:"

If thou art balk'd, O Freedom,
The victory is not to thy manlier foes;
From the house of friends comes the death stab.

Virginia, mother of greatness,
Blush not for being also mother of slaves;
You might have borne deeper slaves—
Doughfaces, crawlers, lice of humanity—
Terrific screamers of freedom,
Who roar and bawl, and get hot i' the face,
But were they not incapable of august crime,
Would quench the hopes of ages for a drink—
Muck-worms, creeping flat to the ground,
A dollar dearer to them than Christ's blessing;

These poems seemed poetic in their imagery and form, but, like editorials, spoke to immediate issues. At his best, the Editor put the immediate into universal context; at his worst, the Editor ranted and raved. Whitman wrote these poetic-editorial diatribes in the same vein as the Schoolmaster enraged at the election of 1840 or the Editor against the Maclay Bill and the expansion of slavery; these were the sounds of his prose personas self-destructing and his poetic persona, whose words had political ramifications, coming to life.

After 1852, Whitman worked as a carpenter with his father, delved into the New York art world, and wrote freelance articles for various New York publications. In his notebooks of this period, he described a poet saying to the world "Come, God and I are now here/What will you have of us...." But also in this notebook, he envisioned himself misunderstood by the forces of pretense; "It would be as though some publisher should reject the best poems ever written in the world because he who brings them to be printed has a shabby umbrella or mud on the shank of his boots."[51] During these years, Whitman began to steadily visit the opera and apply his theory of art to it. Upon seeing the Italian contralto Marietta Alboni, he commented privately that "all persons appreciated Alboni, the common crowd as well as the connoisseurs, for her the New York theaters were packed full of...young men, mechanics, 'roughs,' etc., entirely oblivious of all except Alboni."[52] Some form of this aesthetic theory had been part of Whitman's public persona for a decade. When Whitman recreated his public voice in the all-uniting Bard, the Editor continued to speak from within.

CHAPTER SIX

THE BARD AND WORK REDEFINED

By 1855, Whitman's Editor persona proved no longer tenable. Whitman himself created the paradox that ultimately led to this persona's demise. In both his incarnations as the crusader at the *Aurora* and the social critic at the *Daily Eagle*, the Editor sought to expose the unaffected grace of the democratic individual and thereby inspire personal revelation and transformation. However, the Editor could only display his persona against the backdrop of a city newspaper that catered to institutional demands and political fights.[1] Slavery represented a pernicious form of affectation in this regard because it called the work of another one's own. When Tammany Hall Democrats rejected Whitman's idealized brand of free-soil theory (along with free-soilism in general), they forced the Editor into silence. His failure (and bad luck) at the *Freeman* only underscored this point.

Whitman's Bard offered a democratic persona similar to the Editor, but in a more flexible model. Whereas the Democratic press publicly rejected and isolated the Editor because of his anti-slavery sentiments, Whitman's new apostle-poet did not need a newspaper. Whitman-as-Bard spoke to his readers the way he had formerly demanded artists speak to them. In this context, the political newspaper itself became an affectation; it stood between the Editor and the people. A book of poetry, on the other hand, transcended the merely political; it spoke to immediate issues with a timeless voice. Now, citizens only needed "heart" to "hear" the Bard's song. He communicated with them viscerally and directly, like the singing of the Cheneys or the acting of Charlotte Cushman. The Bard reminded the people of things they intrinsically already knew.

Bardic Manifesto

Whitman expected his first edition of *Leaves of Grass* to have social and political impact. In his introduction, he defined the nation, the people, and the poet as a conduit between the two, and laid out a radical formula that he intended to have moderate, concrete results. This introduction used most of Whitman's aesthetic theories from the previous ten years, but did so in a way unencumbered by the logistics and political considerations of the traditional editorial.[2] As he did with the personas of the Schoolmaster and the Editor, Whitman took hold of a profession (in this case, a poet), defined it in terms he found useful, and used this definition as a means to legitimize his arguments.

For the Bard, America represented all humankind. Its size, varied geography, and disparate populations and interests fostered a microcosm of the world itself. The poet described this nation as "action united from strings necessarily blind to particulars and details magnificently moving in vast masses."[3] Here, Whitman's metaphor served as his symbol for the seemingly discordant nation. What many interpreted as a broad land divided by sectionalism, country and city, and rich and poor, exhibited, in fact, a harmonious orchestra of "strings" which worked to create an entirely cohesive "movement." This symphonic revision of divisive politics provided an essential facet of the Bard's project. It represented Whitman's faith that as unaffected music spoke to the common people, so too each person had a role to play in the Republic. He conceived of people in the symphony as both parts and product. Whereas other nations were "indicat[ed] by their leaders," America grew from "the common people."[4] These common people included everyone in the Republic: "the coming of immigrants...the free commerce...the endless gestation of new states...the convening of Congress...the noble character of young mechanics...the factories and mercantile life and labor saving machinery...."[5] Though individual interests might seem divergent, the poet "...does not see men and women as dreams or dots," but as symbolic of the "eternity in men and women."[6] The Bard celebrated all of America and, in his wide arms, enclosed and exposed as whole what appeared separate and conflicting.

The Bard served a purpose higher than patriotic reflection; he was the nation's "referee."[7] With the popularity of professional sports in the last century, this term raises images of a striped whistle-blower who enforces rules in a timed competition. Whitman's use of the term harkened back to an earlier meaning. Between the early-eighteenth century and the rise of organized sports in the 1870s, a referee often meant one to whom "the management or superintendence of something is entrusted."[8] This describes Whitman's personified voice from his days as the Schoolmaster. Nature entrusted him (and, therefore, the people entrusted him) to convey a unified vision of the Republic to the people. This position eschewed authority and status. In fact, "the others are as good as he, only he sees it and they do not."[9] The poet's only claim to authority lay in his knowledge that he was no better than anyone else; he therefore spoke confidently to every citizen's unadulterated nature. For the frontispiece of the first edition, Whitman dressed like a mechanic with a work shirt unbuttoned over his chest, a "wide-awake" hat cocked to one side, and his hand placed confidently on his hip. In this way, Whitman made his persona visible.[10]

Whitman also adapted an editorial practice in this new format that helped define the Bard persona as both individual and universal. He left his name off the title page and binding, a custom common in editorials before the advent of the by-line, and buried self-referential statements in the text of the poem itself:

> Walt Whitman, an American, one of the roughs, a kosmos,
> Disorderly fleshy and sensual....eating drinking and breeding,
> No sentimentalist....no stander above men and women or apart from them....no more modest than immodest.[11]

This egalitarian, yet apostolic persona, coupled with a symphonic vision of the cohesive nation, allowed Whitman to propose a reformist program that celebrated individuality and called for unity. These reform ideas showed a certain ideological consistency as Whitman moved from forum to forum, persona to persona, over fifteen years. Both Schoolmaster and Editor sought to settle the anxiety caused by the early consumer economy with the notion that all people shared inherent nobility and equality. Both also accepted the existence of difference as part of the natural order of things. Instead of the Schoolmaster's didactic lessons, Whitman-as-Bard revitalized the objective tone of the Editor who observed, related, and let the facts speak for themselves. This objective style maintained that value and meaning were intrinsic to the objects observed. Once things were seen in a proper light, the truth revealed itself. Like the Schoolmaster and the Editor, the Bard sought to reform America without a revolution. When Americans acknowledged the Republic's organic and mutually beneficial nature, salvation would be automatic:

> if the savage or felon is wise it is well...if the President or chief justice is wise it is the same...if the young mechanic or framer is wise it is no more or less...if the prostitute is wise it is not more or less. The interest will come round...all will come round.[12]

Wise individuals, in their place and complete in themselves, acknowledged the symphonic nature of the nation. Whitman refused to force the melting away of distinction while eroding arrogance, illusionary status, and divisive jealousy.

The Bard required a democratic medium as all encompassing as his message. There are some clues as to the gestation and justification of Whitman's "free verse" that began with the jarring statement:

> I CELEBRATE myself,
> And what I assume you shall assume,
> For every atom belonging to me as good belongs to you.[13]

Whitman read and pondered the nature of aesthetic genius for ten years. His ideas in this regard found occasional space in his editorials for the *Eagle* and during his time at the Brooklyn Art Union and reflected the idea of "natural genius" popular with romantics in the early 19th century. This ideal posited that certain graced individuals had an in-born ability to capture the essence of the cosmos and, through art and literature, put these truths before their fellow citizens. In *Leaves of Grass*, the Bard proved one such genius and spoke, to modern ears, in a seemingly authoritarian tone at the beginning of the book. The demand that the reader assume what the Bard assumed, however, provided a statement of natural fact. As both Bard and reader shared the essential building blocks of the cosmos, both were singular *and* universal. The reader and the Bard assumed the same things, whether the reader knew it or not.

An early sign of Whitman's thinking about genius along these lines came from an article he clipped and saved from the *American Whig Review* in May 1845 by H.N. Hudson entitled, "Thoughts on Reading." At the top of the page, Whitman wrote "Good article" in pencil and carried on a written commentary with the author throughout. Next to the statement, "...in Greek mythology, Hercules was the impersonation of moral energy..." Whitman scrawled, "no, of obedience and the divine lustiness of labor."[14] He viewed labor as a divine human attribute, not an ancillary by-product of human need. In the same article, he underlined the following passage, "One important distinction between talent and genius is, that talent gives us information of the objects...that exist; genius calls up and draws out what is within us...."[15] Whitman must have found this standard of genius difficult to achieve as an editor where talent was about the highest goal to which he could aspire; only artists like Walter Libbey exhibited genius. The Bard, on the other hand, exemplified the ultimate genius; he collapsed the space between individuals and the masses, between the present and the past, and between the people and himself and spoke directly to their essential identities. The Editor harangued an audience from the outside. The Bard seduced them from the inside.

Whitman was not alone in envisioning a particularly American poetry before 1855. As early as 1825, novelist John Neal called for "a great revolution [where] *prose will take precedence of poetry*: or rather *poetry* will disencumber itself of rhyme and measure, and talk in prose—with a sort of rhythm, I admit."[16] Emerson claimed that, "it is not metres, but a metre-making argument, that makes a poem, a thought so passionate and alive, that, like the spirit of a plant or an animal, it has an architecture of its own, and adorns nature with a new thing."[17] Likewise, Martin Tupper wrote *Proverbial Philosophy* (1838) in free verse stylistically similar to Whitman's.[18] The poetry that Emerson and Tupper called for resonated viscerally and spoke to the conventions of the inner self. As Tupper's work sold one million copies over the course of the 19th century and one reviewer, in 1856, called Whitman "a wild Tupper of the West" it is likely that Whitman had some experience with these ideas of free verse before 1855.[19]

Whitman's well known "tallying" of creation also had precedents in the literary milieu of the time. For example, four years before *Leaves of Grass*, George Lippard's *Adonai* (1851) achieved an all-encompassing verse similar to Whitman's four years later.[20] Compare Lippard:

> And as they passed on along they behold the faces of all nations.
> They saw the faces of all men that people the earth of God.
>   Irishmen were there, raising their famine-wasted
>   hands above their blasted foreheads.
> Frenchmen were there, kneeling on the earth, with
>   their faces buried against the sand.
> Englishmen were there, carrying burdens on their backs, which bowed them to dust.
> Russians were there in chains, with their eyes veiled
>   even from the dim light.
> Hungarians were there with their wasted faces covered
>   with the blood of their murdered kindred.
> Romans were there, with the arms of everyone tied behind
>   his back to an Iron Cross which, sharp at the edges, cut the hands which it manacled.
> Negroes, Caffirs, Hindoos, Indians, the men of China,
>   Japan, and the Islands of the sea–the men of Europe and the New World–these all
> were there, with their wives, their mothers, their sisters and little ones.[21]

to Whitman:

> One of the great nation, the nation of many nations— the smallest the same and the
>   largest the same,
> A southerner soon as a northerner, a planter nonchalant and hospitable,

> A Yankee bound my own way....ready for trade....my joints the limberest
>   joints on earth and the sternest joints on earth,
> A Kentuckian walking the vale of the Elkhorn in my deerskin leggings,
> A boatman over the lakes or bays or along coasts....a Hoosier, a Badger, a
>   Buckeye,
> A Louisianian or Georgian, a poke-easy from sandhills and pines,
> At home on Canadian snowshoes or up in the bush, or with fishermen off New-
>   foundland...,[22]

or to Whitman's tabulation of nationalities:

> The poor Irishman lives in the simple house of his childhood, with the well known
>   neighbors and faces,
> They warmly welcome him....he is barefoot again....he forgets he is well off;
> The Dutchman voyages home, and the Scotchman and Welchman voyage home...
> and the native of the Mediterranean voyages home;
> To every port of England and France and Spain enter well filled ships;
> The Swiss foots it toward his hills....the Prussian goes his way, and the
>   Hungarian his way, and the Pole goes his way,
> The Swede returns, and the Dane and Norwegian return...[23]

Though similar in style and construction, the tones here are different. In a review of Lippard's earlier work, *The Nazarene* (1845), Whitman called Lippard's fiction "unmitigated trash—There is too much of this wild unmeaning stuff spread on good white paper that might be better employed."[24] Though critical of Lippard's melodramatic style, Whitman embraced the all-encompassing quality of Lippard's tallying and coupled it with the Editor's objective sensibility; this allowed the Bard to express in words the convergence of the writer, reader, and the natural order. Formerly, the Editor found examples of Dickens' characters in the world. Now, someone reading his poetry could recognize the world in Whitman's words.

The Merge Thesis and the New Work Nexus

Many scholars have noted that, for Whitman, the soul manifested itself physically; this explains his interest in creating poetry that had physical resonances.[25] He also defined the nature of the human body (and therefore, the soul) through a redefinition of the labor theory of value. The Bard sought to reconcile competing interpretations of this theory through a merge thesis that proposed the essential unity of all things. His argument began with a question: "Who need be afraid of the merge?" and provided an answer in an egalitarian program that redefined, yet maintained, hierarchical structures in the new market economy.[26]

The poet presented his merge thesis in the first sections of "Song of Myself" and, in doing so, sounded like a booster for free market economics. For the Bard, "urge and urge and urge" provided the "procreant" of the world. He was "satisfied" with this organic cosmos, "Always substance and increase/ Always a knit of identity....always distinction....always a breed of life," but tenuously so.[27] Little things, common in the consumer economy, troubled him, "trippers, askers, people I meet, dinner, dress, looks, business, dues." However, Whitman saw no cause and effect between the cosmic "urge" and the troubling fashions, finances, and appearances. These worries could be overcome; they were secondary to the primal urge that created the world. They grew from the individual's perspective and resolved themselves through a change of mind. The Bard chose to "witness and wait."[28]

Revelation came when his soul "parted the shirt from my bosom-bone and plunged your tongue to my barestript heart." In this moment, the Bard realized that "all men ever born are my brothers...and the women my sisters and lovers."[29] The commingling of the physical and the spiritual led Whitman to further revelations: "all goes onward and outward...and nothing collapses,/And to die is different from what any one supposed, and luckier."[30] Here the Bard reconciled the harmony of the cosmos with the unpleasant particulars in the world. He elevated himself (via an intimate moment with his soul) into transcendent singularity. However, to say that hierarchy does not exist does not necessarily to make it so. To call us all *essentially* equal avoids the particular problems (trippers, askers, business, dues) that brought about the inspired witnessing and waiting in the first place. Whitman, through much of the remainder of *Leaves of Grass*, sought to level hierarchy while maintaining the status quo that proved, by the Bard's own celebration, inherently good.

Evidence of the merge came in the poem later entitled "The Sleepers." Here, Whitman tallied the seeming contradiction of unity and individuality:

> Elements merge in the night . . . . ships make tacks in the dreams . . . . the sailor
> sails . . . . the exile returns home,[...]
>
> The beautiful lost swimmer, the ennuyee, the onanist, the female that loves unre-
> quited, the moneymaker,
> The actor and actress . . those through with their parts and those waiting to
> commence,
> The affectionate boy, the husband and wife, the voter, the nominee that is chosen
> and the nominee that has failed,
> The great already known, and the great anytime after to day,
> The stammerer, the sick, the perfectformed, the homely,

> The criminal that stood in the box, the judge that sat and sentenced him, the fluent
>   lawyers, the jury, the audience,
> The laugher and weeper, the dancer, the midnight widow, the red squaw,
> The consumptive, the erysipalite, the idiot, he that is wronged,
> The antipodes, and every one between this and them in the dark,
> I swear they are averaged now . . . . one is no better than the other,
> The night and sleep have likened them and restored them.

This dream-like unity also existed in the wakeful world. Even though all were "averaged" in sleep, sleep merely made apparent what was actual, but often unseen, in the everyday. According to the Bard "one is no better than the other" in the hurly-burly daytime as well.

To prove this empirically, Whitman revised the idea of work. The word "work" carries within it a confluence of two meanings. The first relates to the work one does. I am a blacksmith. That is my work. The second meaning represents the product of one's occupation; horseshoes, tools, and the like are the blacksmith's work. In this simultaneous sense, one is what one produces. This allows an inanimate object to define an occupation and an individual; a worker is classed into a social hierarchy by the "importance" of what he or she produces. The radicals of New York's labor movement avoided revising this nexus of meaning; in fact, their rhetoric rested entirely within its parameters. When Robert Owen or Mike Walsh defined capitalists as "parasites," they redefined the value of industrialists by implying that capitalists' work made no valuable product at all. An industrialist benefited from works generated by someone else's labor; therefore, capitalists, like parasites, lived off the work of others. If this defined industrialists' "work" (their product), it also defined their "work" (their occupation). Therefore, society wrongly perceived capitalists as the "top" of a production process; they were, in fact, no better than bottom feeders. Within this nexus, Mike Walsh proudly proclaimed himself a "leveler."

By his own poetic standards, the Bard could not disregard or dismiss one element of America in favor of another. Some critics imply that Whitman paid lip service to all American classes while, in fact, envisioning an artisan utopia devoid of the changes wrought by the Industrial Revolution.[31] If so, Whitman was unaware of the contradiction between his merge thesis and the extant America he celebrated, or he wrote in bad faith. On the other hand, if we accept that Whitman sought to compromise the competing ideologies around him with his own nostalgia for an unaffected past, a certain consistency appears in his ideology. To foster this compromise, Whitman redefined work.

For the Bard, work established identity, but not status. In short, passing vignettes, he identified Americans by their contribution to the Republic and, in identifying them in this way, placed occupation at the center of self. In this tallying of the American people, many sections of "Song of Myself" read like an inventory of occupations at mid-century:

> The pure contralto sings in the organloft,
> The carpenter dresses his plank....the tongue of his foreplane whistles its wild
>   ascending lisp,
> The married and unmarried children ride home to their thanksgiving dinner,
> The pilot seizes the king-pin, he heaves down with a strong arm,
> The mate stands braced in the whaleboat, lance and harpoon are ready,
> The duck-shooter walks by silent and cautious stretches,
> The deacons are ordained with crossed hands at the altar,
> The spinning-girl retreats and advances to the hum of the big wheel,
> The farmer stops by the bars of a Sunday and looks at the oats and rye,
> The lunatic is carried at last to the asylum a confirmed case,
> He will never sleep any more as he did in the cot in his mother's bedroom;
> The jour printer with gray head and gaunt jaws works at his case,
> He turns his quid of tobacco, his eyes get blurred with the manuscript;[...]
>
> The canal-boy trots on the towpath—the bookkeeper counts at his desk—the
>   shoemaker waxes his thread,
> The conductor beats time for the band and all the performers follow him,
> The child is baptised—the convert is making the first professions,
> The regatta is spread on the bay....how the white sails sparkle!
> The drover watches his drove, he sings out to them that would stray,
> The pedlar sweats with his pack on his back—the purchaser higgles about the odd
>   cent,
> The camera and plate are prepared, the lady must sit for her daguerreotype,
> The bride unrumples her white dress, the minutehand of the clock moves slowly,
> The opium eater reclines with rigid head and just-opened lips,
> The prostitute draggles her shawl, her bonnet bobs on her tipsy and pimpled neck,
> The crowd laugh at her blackguard oaths, the men jeer and wink to each other,
> (Miserable! I do not laugh at your oaths nor jeer you,)
> The President holds a cabinet council, he is surrounded by the great secretaries,[32]

An analysis of a single example exposes a consistency in this tabulation:

> The jour printer with gray head and gaunt jaws works at his case,
> He turns his quid of tobacco, his eyes get blurred with the manuscript;

Whitman identified an individual character by his work, in this case, a "jour" or "journeyman" printer. However, the *object* of his work, the printed book, is absent from the sentence. The Bard accentuated the subject and verb of the work: "...printer...works;" but, in the end, the jour printer's eyes were "blurred with" the manuscript. The product is absent. In this tallying, Whitman redefined the value of work by redefining the nexus of meanings in the word. Whereas the traditional nexus united subject and object—The *blacksmith* makes the *nails*—this new nexus concentrated on the subject and verb—"The...printer works at his case." The Bard removed the product from the process and, to leave no question as to this new nexus, he blurred the printer's eyes with the manuscript and left the result unsaid. Were his eyes and the manuscript one and the same? Was he fatigued in his efforts? Had it become impossible to tell the vision from the visionary? Whitman gave no answers to these questions, but unambiguously removed the object from the subject's work. Process was all. The Bard captured the worker working.

In this new work nexus, the worker became his work without being identified by a product. "The carpenter dresses...The pilot seizes...The mate stands... The duck-shooter walks... The spinning-girl retreats and advances... The farmer stops... The connoisseur peers... The deckhand makes... The pavingman leans... The conductor beats... The pedlar sweats... The prostitute draggles... The President holds... The crew...pack..." This created a dynamic process where the goal was activity itself. As the worker worked, he defined himself by his occupation but was not defined by the worth of that occupation's product. In this light, to value an individual by a product was absurd. An object could not exist without a worker working. Whitman placed the worker at the center of the definition of work and removed the means to hierarchy from the process. By removing products of labor from his celebration, Whitman made it impossible to value the worker by anything but labor itself.

Whitman reinforced this point in the second poem of *Leaves of Grass*, eventually entitled "A Song for Occupations." Here, the Bard inventoried many of the tools of the trades: money, manufactures, commerce, anvil, tongs, hammer, rifles, awl, shopwindows, houses, etc., and ended with the statement that "you and your soul enclose all things, regardless of estimation/In them your themes and hints and provokers."[33] Here Whitman placed the actor (you) squarely behind the act (working) by piling up objects worthless without human motivation. The origin of value lay in individuals. To enforce the point, Whitman ended this poem with an absurd tabulation of products *acting*:

> When the psalm sings instead of the singer,
> When the script preaches instead of the preacher,
> When the pulpit descends and goes instead of the carver that carved the supporting
>   desk,

When the sacred vessels or the bits of the eucharist, or the lath and plast, procreate
as effectually as the young silversmiths or bakers, or the masons in their
overalls,
When a university course convinces like a slumbering woman and child convince,
When the minted gold in the vault smiles like the nightwatchman's daughter,
When warrantee deeds loafe in chairs opposite and are my friendly companions,
I intend to reach them my hand and make as much of them as I do of men and
women.[34]

In this way, Whitman exposed the absurdity of the traditional nexus. The subject allowed the verb to be; all work depended on the existence of people. Therefore, the Bard elevated people above all (and mocked the value of products in their absence). Anyone capable of unaffected work, in whatever its form, proved holy for the Bard. Value came from the producer; conductors, sailors, mothers, ministers, presidents and prostitutes all existed with their *objects* in question, but their *subjects* and *verbs* intact. This revision of the work nexus, which exposed the secondary nature of the object produced, allowed the poet to seek egalitarian reform without the wishful thinking of a revolutionary social leveler.[35] The Bard undercut hierarchy without rejecting difference.

In the fifth poem of *Leaves of Grass*, eventually title "I Sing the Body Electric," Whitman mixed the new work nexus with a stylistically similar tallying of idealized everyday activities across the social spectrum:

The sprawl and fulness of babes .... the bosoms and heads of women .... the
folds of their dress .... their style as we pass in the street .... the contour of
their shape downwards;
The swimmer naked in the swimmingbath .. seen as he swims through the salt
transparent greenshine, or lies on his back and rolls silently with the heave of
the water;
Framers bare-armed framing a house .. hoisting the beams in their places .. or
using the mallet and mortising- chisel,
The bending forward and backward of rowers in rowboats .... the horseman in his
saddle;
Girls and mothers and housekeepers in all their exquisite offices,
The group of laborers seated at noontime with their open dinnerkettles, and their
wives waiting,
The female soothing a child .... the farmer's daughter in the garden or cowyard,
The woodman rapidly swinging his axe in the woods .... the young fellow hoeing
corn .... the sleighdriver guiding his six horses through the crowd,
The wrestle of wrestlers .. two apprentice-boys, quite grown, lusty, goodnatured,
nativeborn, out on the vacant lot at sundown after work,
The coats vests and caps thrown down .. the embrace of love and resistance,
The upperhold and underhold—the hair rumpled over and blinding the eyes;
The march of firemen in their own costumes—the play of the masculine muscle

> through cleansetting trowsers and waistbands,
> The slow return from the fire . . . . the pause when the bell strikes suddenly again—
> the listening on the alert,
> The natural perfect and varied attitudes . . . . the bent head, the curved neck, the
> counting:
> Suchlike I love . . . . I loosen myself and pass freely . . . . and am at the mother's
> breast with the little child,
> And swim with the swimmer, and wrestle with wrestlers, and march in line with the
> firemen, and pause and listen and count.[36]

The Bard merged with individuals in motion and, by catching them in the state of movement, marked them as both distinct and universal. He thereby maintained their individuality while simultaneously equalizing their actions. As referee, he held people in an animated state and preserved them alive and active for the reader. Through the Bard's words, we celebrate people intimately engaged in the day-to-day.

Whitman's arguments in these cases echo those found in the early philosophical writings of Karl Marx. In the *Economic and Philosophic Manuscripts of 1844* Marx wrote, "...the product is but the summary of the activity of production. If, then, the product of labor is alienation, production itself must be active alienation...."[37] Whitman sought to foster a mental shift in his readers that, by justifying process, reconnected them with work. However, unlike Marx, Whitman's reform ideology ended here. People did not materially improve their lot with the revelation of their labor value. Instead, they accepted and embraced their position in a well-functioning cosmic order.[38] Marx, on the other hand, envisioned a revolution that would wipe away alienation by liquidating private property.[39] In this regard, Whitman's ideas reflected the reform-through-moral-persuasion of contemporary conservatives rather than the revolutionary egalitarianism of Marx and American labor radicals. Whitman offered a recalibration of artisan ideology; Marx viewed this ideology as moribund as the economy that produced it.

The Slavery Dilemma

A number of scholars find Whitman's anti-slavery sentiments authentic and admirable, while others see him as largely ambivalent to the plight of slaves.[40] However, in *Leaves of Grass* at least, Whitman portrayed African-Americans in concrete terms related to his labor ideology.[41] For example, in "Song of Myself," the Bard described an African-American driver of a set of four horses as neither free nor enslaved, but instead with an "ample neck," "commanding" glance and "steady" driving skills. Whitman made race apparent, but not essential; the driver *worked*. Work defined and justified him, process and potential fostered self-evident equality. For the Bard, the sin of slavery lay in its effects on the idea of work. Unlike Wilmot Democrats, for whom slavery threatened white, free labor, Whitman portrayed slavery as a threat to the nature of labor itself. This placed him somewhere between free-soilers in the Democratic Party and abolitionists in the burgeoning Republican Party. When Whitman's Bard became a runaway slave in *Leaves of Grass*, the process of escape defined him.[42] Potential (and therefore, identity) lay in freedom; in bondage, the slaveholder forced a slave to act like property. Slave holding represented a kind of pretense or grand illusion. In the poem eventually titled "I Sing the Body Electric," the Bard called the slave auctioneer a "sloven [who] does not half know his business." The Bard "help[ed]" the auctioneer by singing the slave's "all abaffling brain," his "exquisite senses," his "pliant backbone and neck....goodsized arms and legs." Once again, Whitman celebrated the slave for his *potential* to work; this "help" betrayed the ignorance of the slaveholder who imagined that he could legitimately own another's *potential* to work. When Whitman described the slaves' limbs as "red, black or white," he meant it as a warning to everyone.[43]

The Bard avoided a call for outright revolt or revolution, however. Though an admirer of the American Revolution from a distance, Whitman typically shied away from an advocacy of revolutionary violence in his editorials; in his poetry, an acceptance of the cosmos as essentially good was the foundation upon which he built *Leaves of Grass*. Support for political violence would imply that the process celebrated at the beginning of "Song of Myself" had gone awry and that Americans needed to take matters into their own hands to set the world right again. Regarding slavery, in the poem, "The Sleepers," the Bard took on the persona of the slave "Lucifer" who, after seeing his owner "laugh when I look down the bend after the steamboat that carries away my woman," warned that "the vast dusk bulk that is the whale's bulk....it seems mine..., Warily, sportsman!... my tap is death."[44] Whitman here muted his justification of violence with metaphor and innuendo. Rather than calling for outright revolt, he made this instance intimately personal and individual, a matter of sympathy rather than revolution. Likewise, Whitman's poem, (eventually titled) "A Boston Ballad," argued that slavery undermined the legacy of the American Revolution and, in this regard, reflected the free-soil argument that slavery was dangerous to all laborers. This poem, written during the waning days of Whitman's editor/poet years in the early 1850s and included later in *Leaves of Grass*, raged against the Fugitive Slave Law of 1850 and the forced return of the runaway slave Anthony Burns who federal soldiers marched through the streets of Boston on his way back to slavery in

Virginia. This event confirmed the existence of a Southern conspiracy to spread the institution throughout the nation for many anti-slavery activists. When federal marshals came to take Burns away, Whitman imagined the ghosts of the revolution retreating before the "parade" of Burns and his captors. In response, the Bard called for the digging up of George III's corpse, returning it to America, and placing a crown on the skeleton's head.[45] The Bard found the epicenter of a counter-revolution in the Boston of 1854; however, for him, the narrative that ran from the Stamp Act crisis to the Boston Tea Party remained the story of Americans' investment in the American Revolution. The arrest of a runaway slave in Boston by federal officials marked a direct attack on freedom in the birthplace of the Republic, but inspired a rhetorical, rather than revolutionary, reaction.

Whitman's anti-slavery ideology begs the question as to whether he saw capitalists, as well as slaveholders, as a threat to free labor. This would require him to understand workers as "wage slaves," an idea used by both labor radicals and slavery apologists.[46] Throughout his writing career, Whitman tacitly justified the existence of capitalists and, especially after 1847, wage-earning work. He implied that a laborer, by realizing the dignity of work, could still define himself as free. The slave represented another case altogether. A slaveholder owned a slave's process and potential. This threatened the identity of all workers because it implied that someone could own another's potential. Free workers in the new market economy still owned their potential, at least according to Whitman. They no longer needed to own the tools or products of their trade because their work was the object of value. Whitman's celebration of free labor reflected his affirmation of this new understanding of value in the new market economy. In attacking the institution of slavery for the pretense of owning another's labor, Whitman embraced the contemporary argument that workers had a right to their ability to work freely. For Whitman, this was enough to establish their inherent worth, value, and equality.

Whitman's poems about enslaved African-Americans in the first edition of *Leaves of Grass* symbolized his complicated stand against slavery. Though he rejected the institution, he did so through his revised work nexus and practiced the tactic of moral persuasion over direct action. This placed Whitman near the center of Northern politics and makes his solutions seem rather tepid. In context, however, the Bard managed to lift free-soilism from a program of white laborers' rights to a critique of oppressive labor attitudes across the American economy.[45]

"THEY ALL COUNT"

Late in life, Whitman's friend Horace Traubel asked him which of the many editions of *Leaves of Grass* he thought the best. "They all count," Whitman replied, "I don't know if I like any one more than the other."[1] Any study of *Leaves of Grass* must take into account which *Leaves of Grass* is being studied.[2] Likewise, in a book like this one, there might be some benefit from a forward-looking analysis of Whitman's changing public persona from 1855 until the Civil War. Anything after the Civil War requires another study all its own. The Civil War redefined both the nation and Walt Whitman.

Theorist-Bard of the 1856 Edition

The critical reception of the first edition was mixed. Clearly, Whitman found encouragement from the complimentary letter he received from Ralph Waldo Emerson who greeted him "at the beginning of a great career,"[3] but, overwhelmingly, the public reception of this strange book of untitled poems, without clear rhythm or rhyme ranged from confusion to outright derision. For example, Charles A. Dana, writing in the *New York Daily Tribune* noted that *Leaves of Grass* seemed "shaped on no pre-existent model out of the author's own brain" and that Whitman wrote in a manner "too frequently reckless and indecent though this appears to arise from a naive unconsciousness rather than an impure mind...."[4] Dana also noted that the first edition was "not destitute of particular poetic merits" and included "bold, stirring thoughts," but the review also exposed an acute dilemma faced by Whitman in his first edition, namely, that he wanted his book to be a novel collection of poems that were essentially American in a medium (poetry) that already had established norms. Rufus Griswold in *Criterion* wrote a less subtle critique:

> [I]t is impossible to imagine how any man's fancy could have conceived such a mass of stupid filth, unless he were possessed of the soul of a sentimental donkey that had

died of disappointed love. This poet (?) without wit, but with a certain vagrant wildness, just serves to show the energy which natural imbecility is occasionally capable of under strong excitement. [5]

Whitman did not necessarily mind this type of highbrow criticism. As the Editor, he harshly criticized the expert-critic's pretensions of knowing art better than those who engaged aesthetics viscerally without training or affectation. Whitman tried to present this new style of democratic criticism by anonymously reviewing the first edition himself and completing the nice trick of utilizing his Editor's tone from his days at the *Eagle* while reviewing his new persona's work, "An American bard at last! We shall cease shamming and be what we really are."[6]

A look at the second edition of *Leaves of Grass* (1856) shows that Whitman tried to have it two ways. On the one hand, he sought popular acclaim and critical respect. On the other, he tried to overturn old standards of aesthetic decorum and respectability. In the second edition, Whitman played a conventionally unconventional theorist in the form of a poet named "Walt Whitman." The second edition of *Leaves of Grass* was physically a very different book; one scholar describes it as a "fat hymn book" in comparison to the high, thin, quatro-sized first edition.[7] This may have been Whitman's attempt to fulfill an ideal he expressed later in life, "I have long teased my brain with visions of a handsome little book at last—like the Epictetus—a dear, strong, aromatic volume, like the *Encheiridion*, as it is called, for the pocket."[8] The physical similarity of this new edition to popular publications by Longfellow and Whittier and Whitman's statement about portability imply a revised persona. Whereas the first edition's large and thin format worked perfectly for Whitman's prose-poetry style, allowing his extended thoughts to spill across the page, this new volume's portability trumped the aesthetic novelty of the first edition's free-verse form.[9] Whitman also used conventional punctuation in the second edition instead of the novel use of ellipses in the first. The verse of this new edition consequently looked less expansive on the page than it did in the first:

> I CELEBRATE myself,
> And what I assume you shall assume,
> For every atom belonging to me as good belongs to you.
>
> I loafe and invite my soul,
> I lean and loafe at my ease . . . . observing a spear of summer grass.
>
> Houses and rooms are full of perfumes . . . . the shelves are crowded with perfumes,

I breathe the fragrance myself, and know it and like it,
The distillation would intoxicate me also, but I shall not let it.
(1855)

I CELEBRATE myself,
 And what I assume you shall assume,
For every atom belonging to me, as good belongs
 to you.

 I loafe and invite my Soul,
I lean and loafe at my ease, observing a spear of
 summer grass.

Houses and rooms are full of perfumes—the
 shelves are crowded with perfumes,
I breathe the fragrance myself, and know it and
 like it,
The distillation would intoxicate me also, but I
 shall not let it. (1856)

Other pieces of evidence indicate the transformation of the Bard from "one of the roughs" who happened, almost anonymously, to capture hints of the cosmos into someone akin to a moral philosopher whose name could be used to summarize a school of thought. Whitman printed his name along the spine of this second edition so as to be found easily upon the bookshelf (and, perhaps, alongside other well-known authors). He also printed Emerson's famous quote in gilt lettering on the spine, "'I Greet You at the Beginning of a Great Career!' R W Emerson." Here, then, the Bard gave a name to himself, which, in the first edition, he buried in the first poem, and placed this name above a complimentary and hopefully visionary quote by a well-known public intellectual. The first edition of *Leaves of Grass* purveyed an "I" whose individual identity existed ever-present and capable of transformation into other identities so as to prove the rule that "every atom belonging to me as good belongs to you." The Theorist-Bard of the second edition lent a name to this idea and made it something like a personal theory.

There are other signs of this new Bard. In addition to the thirty-two poems added to the text, Whitman also added titles to each and a table of contents. To aid in comprehension, Whitman attached the word "poem" to the title of each poem: "Poem of Walt Whitman, an American," "Poem of the Body," "Poem for Women," "Sun-Down Poem," "Poem of You, Whoever You

Are" and left no question that though this was poetry of a new type, it was poetry nonetheless.

Whitman also added a prose annex to the end of the collection entitled "Leaves-Droppings" (implying some after-effects of the first edition). He divided this annex into two sections: "Correspondence" (which included Emerson's private letter of thanks and Whitman's nearly ten-page response which began "Dear Friend and Master") and "Opinions" which printed nearly every review written about the first edition, positive and negative, including two that Whitman himself wrote anonymously. By placing reviews in the back of his second edition, he hoped to give the impression of some furious theoretical debate about this new poet. In his open letter to Emerson, the Bard, now "Walt Whitman," claimed that the first edition "really sold" and that he predicted sales of 20,000 per annum of the second edition. Even the publishing house for the second edition spoke to this attempt to place this edition on the *avant-garde*. Fowlers and Wells previously published books on new "sciences" like phrenology and healthy living.[10] *Leaves of Grass*, then, proved part of a cutting-edge intellectual community that hoped to overturn staid ideological and aesthetic conventions in a manner common to the period.

In this cursory analysis, it appears that Whitman tried to change the public persona of the Bard in two ways. First, he repackaged *Leaves of Grass* in a portable and familiar framework and imagined that this new edition, with his name and Emerson's on the spine, represented an aesthetic-social model for others to reference and follow. A reader could now cite Walt Whitman as part of an intellectual movement. Second, Whitman framed this edition as part of a broader theoretical debate about proper aesthetic form that had been ongoing since the 1840s. In this regard, readers could interpret the negative reviews Whitman published as the voice of the "other side" incapable of appreciating the vision of "Walt Whitman" and his "Master," Ralph Waldo Emerson. Whitman engaged in these debates during his days as editor of the *Daily Eagle*; he now played the unaffected artist that he had defended before.

Prophet-Bard of the 1860 Edition

Though Ralph Waldo Emerson and Henry David Thoreau visited Whitman after the publication of the second edition and he received some local notice from New York *literati*, he did not establish himself as the voice of an aesthetic revolution and, more importantly, he did not become the bard of the masses he claimed to be. Approximately 1,000 copies of the second edition were printed, nowhere near the 20,000 per year the poet hoped for. In fact, between 1857 and 1860, Whitman experienced difficulty finding a publisher for his next edition.

A turn in luck came in February 1860 when the Boston publishing house Thayer and Eldridge offered to publish the third edition. Thayer and Eldridge published abolitionist tracts, including the firm's bestseller, *The Public Life of Captain John Brown*, written by James Redpath. The "Black Strings," an abolitionist society, met at the offices of Thayer and Eldridge. This put Whitman's third edition in the nexus of transcendentalist theory and politics (Emerson admired and supported John Brown) and brought recognition from radical social reformers.[11] The poet, however, never fit comfortably with radical politics and throughout his life reacted suspiciously toward labor radicalism and utopian idealism.[12]

The third edition felt like a bible.[13] Whitman added one hundred and forty-six new poems to the thirty-two that comprised the second edition (which, itself, represented more than a doubling of the first edition). The book's thickness matched a double-column printing of the King James Bible and Whitman divided it into "clusters" that functioned much like the separate books of the Bible. Additionally, he numbered the poems within each cluster rather than titling them; likewise he numbered each stanza within each poem. This, then, allowed for a reference akin to that of Biblical concordance: "Walt Whitman 1-3" refered to the stanzas:

1. I CELEBRATE myself,
And what I assume you shall assume,
For every atom belonging to me, as good belongs
    to you.

2. I loafe and invite my Soul,
I lean and loafe at my ease, observing a spear of
    summer grass.

3. Houses and rooms are full of perfumes—the shelves
    are crowded with perfumes,
I breathe the fragrance myself, and know it and
    like it,
The distillation would intoxicate me also, but I shall
    not let it.[14]

and "Enfans D'Adam 3:3" refered the reader to:

> 3.The love of the body of man or woman balks account
>   —the body itself balks account,
> That of the male is perfect, and that of the female is
>   perfect.[15]

Whitman arranged these clusters around themes that functioned like religious books within a larger theological tome. For example, "Chants Democratic and Native American" contained a nearly frenzied celebration of democracy on the eve of the Civil War and sounded not-so unlike the warnings of Biblical prophets:

> Underneath all are individuals
> I swear nothing is good to me now that ignores
>   individuals!
> The American compact is altogether with individuals,
> The only government is that which makes minute with
>   individuals,
> The whole theory of the universe is directed to one
>   single individual—namely, to You.[16]

The series "Chants Democratic" contained twenty-one poems on the nature of the American republic. "Enfans d'Adam" included fifteen poems on "amative" love between men and women. "Calamus" contained forty-five poems on fraternal, or "adhesive," love. In these two kinds of love, Whitman found the erotic and fraternal passions that held the Republic together. The themes of unity, democracy, and spirituality, organized as they were in a quasi-Biblical manner, point to a Prophet-Bard persona in the third edition.

The Bard had again transformed himself. Whereas the frontispiece of the 1855 edition showed Whitman as a jaunty "rough" in tilted hat, with open collar and right arm akimbo, the 1860 edition frontispiece presented a genteel, well-coiffured Whitman, staring wisely just behind the reader's shoulder. Whitman, the rebel theorist of democratic visions, transformed his Bard into the prophet of spiritual democracy on the eve of the Civil War.[17]

The third edition achieved the greatest acclaim and popularity to date. Of the thirty-two known reviews of the 1860 edition, only eight were negative. Likewise, around two thousand copies were printed and one thousand sold before Thayer and Eldridge went bankrupt in December 1860.[18] In these years, Whitman began to cultivate the popular persona that became the "Good Grey Poet" after the Civil War.[19]

Whitman never used this final persona in a mercenary fashion; he was never particularly annoyed when others used it either. When shown his image as a logo for the "Walt Whitman Cigar" he laughed, "This is fame!" Upon closer consideration of the image, he remarked, one would like to think with a hint of irony given his earlier stance regarding the affectations of cigar smoking, "It is...not as bad as it might be: give the hat a little more height and it would not be such an offence."[20]

In the fourteen years before the publication of Leaves of Grass, Walt Whitman's public personas maintained certain consistencies that reflected his vision of economic and social reform. As Schoolmaster, Editor, and Bard, Whitman saw the means to working-class reform as personal rather than social. This explains his diatribes against affectation. Whether the Schoolmaster railed against the dangers of tobacco, or the Editor against the threat of Eurocentric art, or the Bard in the name of working rather than works produced, Whitman portrayed the degraded status of the artisan as an attitudinal problem rather than a social or institutional one. Workers oppressed themselves when they tried to be something that they were not. In opposition to institutional reformers, Whitman argued that a citizen's essential value hid under pretentious affectation. This allowed him to place reform in the hands of individuals and maintain the traditional artisan location of value. For Whitman, reform required a change of mind (on the part of workers, on the part of manufacturers, on the part of slave-holders) rather than a revolutionary change of society. This change of mind told Americans that their value was portable and resilient in the midst economic and social flux.

Whitman's demand for a new mindset explains both the diversity of his interests and the consistency of his arguments. In pursuit of authenticity, Whitman tackled such contemporary issues as education, the arts, and tariffs with a central argument: all ills in these cases were a product of pretense. Bad education sought to impart certain values onto a child rather than cultivate internal goodness. Bad art aspired to an abstract sublime rather than speak to the elementally true in the audience. Bad economics falsely maintained certain hierarchical norms rather than allow each citizen to find his or her place in the social order. In this way, affectation was a form of injustice. Whitman therefore accepted the new market economy while celebrating the artisan of old. He could do this because identity and individual value remained static and insulated from redefinition through broad economic change. If social change undermined intrinsic identity, then the unaffected republic he believed key to social justice proved nothing more than a contingency of history. For Whitman, laborers competed for wages and inhabited a consumer's life yet remained honest artisans and good citizens. In fact, the way citizens preserved their inherent value depended upon recognition of one's immutable role in the Republic.

Whitman's public personas claimed to know the people's true nature and, from this knowledge, know what was best for them. To generate these personas, Whitman took on the voice of three professions while simultaneously defining them for his readers in ways that lent credence to his arguments. Through these self-defined professions, Whitman maintained a precarious balance between being one of the people and being above them. This gave him the authority to teach, inform, and celebrate, but also allowed him the credentials of a fellow citizen. The Schoolmaster, for example, writing at "sun down" surveyed society much as he surveyed a class of students: with intimate benevolence. This benevolence allowed the Schoolmaster to interact personally with his charges. However, it also required that he interact with them at a thoughtful distance so as to guide them to the beautiful and the good. This lent the Schoolmaster his didactic qualities. In his arguments against caffeine and false manners, he claimed to know his charges as they really were because of his close proximity to them. By uncovering this truth about affectation, the Schoolmaster exposed his readers to their better selves and cured them of the need for self-creation through consumption. Likewise, Whitman's Editor reported as an eyewitness to the goings-on about town. In this persona, he saw the Republic writ small at the dinner table, the meat market, the suburb, or the theater. The Editor's use of "I" in this case enforced his status as first-among-equals and allowed him to comment authoritatively on truth and pretentious trash. This authority stemmed not from superiority, but an enlightened equality. Everyone around the Editor, in their petty pursuits, missed their affinity for each other. Only the Editor recognized this affinity and reminded his readers of it. In the first edition of *Leaves of Grass*, Whitman refined this eyewitness persona; the Editor became an observer in private. By using verse, he transported his Editor's persona from the public sphere of the newspaper column to the intimacy of the poem. This intimacy allowed Whitman to cross the boundary between the public and the private and, from the inside, recognize essential qualities that made his readers equal and individual. Not surprisingly, Whitman never returned in earnest to newspaper editing after 1855. The medium no longer effectively served his purposes. The intimacy of the Bard, with his ability to merge with his readers and speak both publicly and privately, presented a much more compelling persona and voice.

Whitman's public personas continued to change through the ensuing years and editions. These editions varied in scope, sequence, and style. Typically, readers have ready access to the first and last editions without any sense of the transformations in between.[21] A comprehensive study of Whitman's changing Bard persona between 1855 and 1892 would be a useful contribution to the field, but is beyond the scope of this book. With the publication of the first edition of *Leaves of Grass*, Whitman created a durable public persona that allowed him to speak directly to individuals. His message to them proved deceptively simple: the best a citizen can hope to be, he or she already is.

Notes

Introduction

[1] According to M. Jimmie Killingsworth, *The Growth of Leaves of Grass: The Organic Tradition in Whitman Studies*, (Columbia, S.C.: Camden House, 1993), 103.

[2] Newton Arvin, *Whitman*, (New York: The Macmillan Company, 1938), 3.

[3] Ibid., 41.

[4] M. Wynn Thomas, *The Lunar Light of Whitman's Poetry*, (Cambridge: Harvard University Press, 1987), 22.

[5] Ibid., 77.

[6] Ibid., 78.

[7] Betsy Erkkila, *Whitman the Political Poet*, (New York: Oxford University Press, 1989), 252.

[8] Ibid., 6.

[9] Ibid., 63.

[10] Andrew Lawson, "Spending on Vast Returns: Sex, Class and Commerce in the First *Leaves of Grass*," *American Literature*, June 2003, 340. See also, Andrew Lawson, *Walt Whitman and the Class Struggle*, (Iowa City: University of Iowa Press, 2006), 85.

[11] Amy Schrager Lang, *The Syntax of Class: Writing Inequality in Nineteenth-Century America*, (Princeton: Princeton University Press, 2003), 97.

[12] Stop this day and night with me and you shall possess the origin of all poems,/You shall possess the good of the earth and sun....there are millions of suns left,/You shall no longer take things at second or third hand....nor look through the eyes of the dead....nor feed on the spectres in books,/You shall not look through my eyes either,/nor take things from me,/You shall listen to all sides and filter them from yourself, *Leaves of Grass* (1855), 14.

[13] Mary H. Blewett, *Men, Women, and Work : Class, Gender, and Protest in the New England Shoe Industry, 1780-1910*, (Urbana: University of Illinois Press, 1988) and Mary Ryan, *Civic Wars: Democracy and Public Life in the American City During the Nineteenth Century*, (Berkeley: University of California Press, 1997).

[14] Jo Burr Margadant, *The New Biography: Performing Feminity in Nineteenth-Century France*, (Berkeley: University of California Press, 2000), 7.

[15] David Reynolds, *Walt Whitman's America: A Cultural Biography*, (New York: Alfred A. Knopf, 1995).

[16] Rüdiger Safranski, *Nietzsche: A Philosophical Biography*, Trans. Shelley Frisch. (New York: W.W. Norton & Co., 2002).

[17] John Emerson Todd, *Emily Dickinson's Use of the Persona*, (The Hague: Mouton, 1968), Don Florence, *Persona and Humor in Mark Twain's Early Writings* (Columbia: University of Missouri Press, 1995), William Pannapacker, *Revised Lives: Walt Whitman, and Nineteenth-Century Authorship* (New York: Routledge, 2004).

[18] Lawrence Levine, *Highbrow/Lowbrow: the Emergence of Cultural Hierarchy in America* (Cambridge: Harvard University Press, 1988).

[19] Richard Bushman, *The Refinement of America: Persons, Houses, Cities*, (New York: Alfred A. Knopf, 1992).

[20] Sean Wilenz, *Chants Democratic: New York City & the Rise of the American Working Class, 1788-1850*, (New York: Oxford University Press, 1984) takes its title from a cluster of poems Whitman included in his 1860 edition of *Leaves of Grass* entitled "Chants Democratic and Native American."

[21] "...long foreground..." quoted from a private letter sent by Ralph Waldo Emerson to Walt Whitman upon receiving a copy of *Leaves of Grass* (1855). Whitman subsequently published this letter in the second edition (1856).

Chapter One: Artisan Undefined

[1] Jerome Loving, *Walt Whitman: The Song of Himself*, (Berkeley: University of California Press, 1999), 1-26, Reynolds, *Walt Whitman's America*, 28-51.

[2] This early dearth of factories was primarily because of a lack of a convenient source for water power; see Richard Stott, *Workers in the Metropolis: Class, Ethnicity, and Youth in Antebellum New York City* (Ithaca: Cornell University Press, 1990), 36. and Wilenz, 107 and 114.

[3] Edwin Burrows and Mike Wallace, *Gotham: A History of New York City to 1898*, (New York: Oxford University Press, 1999), 443.

[4] *The Complete Writings of Walt Whitman*, ed. Richard Maurice Bucke, et al., (New York and London, 1902), IV, 17.

[5] Loving, 30. Whitman himself typically eschewed alcohol until late in life. His brother, Andrew, was an alcoholic who died at the age of thirty.

[6] Justin Kaplan, *Walt Whitman: A Life*, (New York: Simon and Schuster, 1980), 56-57. See also Pannapacker, 23.

[7] Walt Whitman, *Complete Poetry and Collected Prose* (New York: Library of America, 1982), 694.

[8] Whitman and his mother exchanged correspondence well into her old age. These letters make clear that Louisa depended on Whitman's financial and emotional support. See, for example, *Selected Letters of Walt Whitman*, Edwin Haviland Miller, ed., (Iowa City: University of Iowa Press, 1990), especially Whitman's letters of March 27-28, 1848, 19-21.

[9] H. Larry Ingle, *Quakers in Conflict: The Hicksite Reformation* (Knoxville: The University of Tennessee Press, 1986), 184-200. Hicks, himself, was a Long Islander.

[10] Ingle, 41-42. See also Glenn N. Cummings, "Placing the Impalpable: Walt Whitman and Elias Hicks," *Modern Language Studies*, Vol. 28, No. 2. (Spring, 1998), pp. 69-86, and Thomas Hamm, *The Transformation of American Quakerism: Orthodox Friends 1800-1907*, (Bloomington, IN: The University of Indiana Press, 1988).

11   Reynolds, *Walt Whitman's America*, 37.

12   Ingle, 91-92.

13   "I can remember my father coming home toward sunset from his day's work as a carpenter and saying briefly, as he throws down his armful of kindling-blocks with a bounce on the kitchen floor, 'Come, mother, Elias preaches tonight.'" Also during this period (late-1880s) Whitman came to claim that he was "half Quaker." Whitman, *Complete Poetry and Collected Prose*, 1232-1233, also see Cummings, 73.

14   *Daily Crescent*, March 11, 1848, Emory Holloway, ed., *The Uncollected Poetry and Prose of Walt* Whitman, (Gloucester, Mass: Peter Smith, 1972), I, 197.

15   Walter Fulghum, *Quaker Influences on Whitman's Religious Thought*, Diss. (Evanston: Northwestern University, 1943), 25.

16   On the other hand, Hicksite Quakers, generally, were more approving of Whitman. See Frederick B. Tolles, "A Quaker Reaction to *Leaves of Grass*," *American Literature* 19 (May 1947), 170-171.

17   Horace Traubel, *With Walt Whitman in Camden*, (New York: Littlefield and Rowman, 1961), II, 19.

18   Whitman, "Notes (such as they are) founded on Elias Hicks" *November Boughs*, 1888, as found in *Complete Poetry and Collected Prose*, (Library of America, 1982), 1221.

19   The only extended study of Whitman and the Quakers is in Fulghum. In this work, Fulghum draws on ideological affinities between Hicksite Quakerism and Whitman's poetry after 1855.

20   See Arvin, *Whitman*, 170-175.

21   Pannapacker also notes the tension between the revolutionary and the status quo in Whitman's political ideology and cites the influence of his father's artisan republicanism, 23. Louisa Whitman's Hicksite Quakerism also contained this tension in theological terms.

22   Horace Traubel, *With Walt Whitman in Camden*, IV, 505.

23   *Brooklyn Daily Times*, June 3 1857, in Holloway, *The Uncollected Poetry and Prose of Walt Whitman*, II,3-4.

24   Whitman, *Complete Poetry and Collected Prose*, 699-700.

25   Traubel, *With Walt Whitman in Camden*, IV, 505-506.

26   *Evening Post*, November 16, 1801; *American Citizen*, April 13, 1801, quoted in Wilenz, 75.

27   Wilenz, 63, 87-91.

28   John Rodman, *An Oration Delivered before the Tammany Society, or Columbian Order, Tailors, Hibernian Provident, Columbian, Cordwainers' and George Clinton Societies*, (New York, 1813), as quoted in Wilenz, 94.

29   Alan Dawley, *Class and Community: The Industrial Revolution in Lynn*, (Cambridge: Harvard University Press, 1976), 222.

30   Adam Smith, *An Inquiry into the Nature and Causes of The Wealth of Nations*, (New York: The Modern Library, 1937, original print 1776), 30.

31   Ibid., 33.

32   George Clark, Joseph Tucker, and William Tucker, all charter members of the Mechanics Mutual Protection Association were also conservative, Whig candidates for Alderman and the New York State Assembly after the rise of the second party system, Amy Bridges, *A City*

in the Republic: Antebellum New York and the Origins of Machine Politics, (Cambridge: Cambridge University Press, 1984), 68-69.

[33] Temperance Society, "First Annual Report" *The Free Enquirer* March 25, 1829, in Wilentz, 148.

[34] Wilentz, 148.

[35] *Man*, February 20, 1830, quoted in Wilentz, 148.

[36] Temperance Society, "First Annual Report," quoted in Wilentz, 148.

[37] Wilentz, 149.

[38] Ibid., 150.

[39] Edwin P. Whipple ed., Daniel Webster, *The Great Speeches and Orations of Daniel Webster: With an Essay on Daniel Webster as a Master of English Style* (New York: Little, Brown, 1879), 26.

[40] Daniel Walker Howe, *The Political Culture of the American Whigs* (Chicago: The University of Chicago Press, 1979), 29.

[41] Whipple ed., 444.

[42] Alexander H.H. Stuart, *Anniversary Address Before the American Institute*, 1844, quoted in Wilentz, 303.

[43] Howe, 31.

[44] Whig gains recorded by Bridges, 97. Ward economic status determined by Stott, 29.

[45] Bridges, 98.

[46] Dawley, 9.

[47] Edward Pessen, *Most Uncommon Jacksonians: The Radical Leaders of the Early Labor Movement*, (Albany: State University of New York, 1967), 10-25.

[48] Pessen, 73.

[49] "Report of the National Trades' Union Convention of 1834" (New York, 1834), http://www.oberlin.edu/history/GJK/H258S2000/NationalTrades.html.

[50] Pessen, 73.

[51] Ibid., 74.

[52] Bruce Laurie, *Artisans Into Workers: Labor in Nineteen Century America*, (New York: Hill and Wang Publishing, 1989), 67.

[53] O'Sullivan as quoted by Major Wilson in Edward Pessen, ed., *The Many-faceted Jacksonian Era*, (Westport, Connecticut: Greenwood Publishers, 1977), 193.

[54] O'Sullivan, *Democratic Review*, November 1839, Ibid.

[55] Bridges, 80.

[56] For examples of pro-Loco-foco Whigs, see Wilentz, 294. Alden Spooner published Seth Luther's *An Address Delivered Before the Mechanics and Working-Men of the City of Brooklyn, on the Celebration of the Sixtieth Anniversary of American Independence, July 4, 1836*, (New York: Alden Spooner and Sons, 1836).

[57] It was probably during these years that Whitman saw Junius Booth, father of John Wilkes Booth, play the part of Richard.

[58] The piece, entitled "The Olden Time," is a retrospective on the growth of New York City. It can be found in Herbert Bergman, et al, eds., *The Collected Writings of Walt Whitman: The Journalism, vol. I, 1834-1846*, (New York: Peter Lang, 1998), 3.

59 Walt Whitman, "Starting Newspapers," *Prose Works* (Philadelphia: David McKay, 1892), I, 287.

Chapter Two: The Schoolmaster and Ethical Aesthetics

1   East Norwich (Summer 1836), Babylon (Winter 1836-37), Long Swamp (Spring 1837), Smithtown (Fall-Winter 1837-1838), Little Bay Side (Winter 1839-1840), Trimming Square (Spring 1840), Woodbury (Summer 1840), Whitestone (Winter-Spring 1841).

2   Lawrence A. Cremin, *American Education: The National Experience, 1783-1876*, (New York: Alred A. Knopf, 1980), *The American Common School* (New York: Teachers College Press, 1951), Carl Kaestle, *Pillars of the Republic: Common Schools and American Society, 1780-1860*, (New York: Hill and Wang, 1983).

3   Florence B. Freedman, *Walt Whitman Looks at Schools*, (New York: King's Crown Press), 30.

4   Walt Whitman to Abraham Leech, August 11, 1840, August 19, 1840, quoted in Arthur Golden, ed., "Nine Early Whitman Letters, 1840-1841," *American Literature* 58 (October 1986), 342-460.

5   Whitman to Leech, August 11, 1840, Ibid.

6   Whitman to Leech, July 30, 1840, Ibid.

7   Whitman to Leech, August 11,1840, Ibid.

8   Whitman to Leech, March 25, 1841, Ibid.

9   Whitman here is referring to the "Hard Cider Campaign" of the Whig presidential candidate William Henry Harrison. "Little Matty" refers to Martin Van Buren, the Democratic Party candidate and incumbent. For an interesting look at the logistics and ironies of this campaign, see Harry L. Watson, *Liberty and Power: The Politics of Jacksonian America*, (New York: Hill and Wang, 1990).

10 Whitman to Leech, August 26, 1840 in Golden.

11 William Cullen Bryant as quoted in Edward Widmer, *Young America: The Flowering of Democracy in New York City* (Oxford: Oxford University Press, 1999) 9.

12 Loving, 49.

13 For an analysis of the ways in which Whitman did so visually with the 1855 edition see Matt Miller, "The Cover of the First Edition of *Leaves of Grass*," *Walt Whitman Quarterly Review*, 24:2-3, (2006/2007) 85-97 and Ted Genoways, "The Picture of the Perfect Loafer: The Frontispiece of the 1855 Edition of *Leaves of Grass*, "Leaves of Grass: The 150th Anniversary Conference," (Lincoln: University of Nebraska, April 1, 2005).

14 The personas of "Little Girl" and "Lover-Wife-Queen" allowed Dickinson to "speak...her mind much more openly than she could otherwise do" because, according to Todd, these pat personas were familiar to her small group of readers (both of her poetry and her letters). This familiarity allowed Dickinson a low-stakes honesty as all controversy came packaged in a voice not necessarily her own. John Emerson Todd, *Emily Dickinson's Use of the Persona*, (The Hague: Mouton, 1965), 1-9, 31-52; Twain used his authorial persona to weave "fact and fiction [into] ...fictive truths, or better yet, true fictions." Don Florence, *Persona and Humor in Mark Twain's Early Writings*, (Columbia: The University of Missouri Press, 1995), 3.

[15] ...[W]ork—the occupational roles that men and women carry—is potentially and often actually a potent force in sustaining and stabilizing...the young adult's personality.... ...[T]heir work role is the chief means by which they define and know themselves." Helen Harris Perlman, *Persona: Social Role and Personality*, (Chicago: The University of Chicago Press, 1968) 61-63; see also Robert J. Weber, *The Created Self: Reinventing Body, Persona, and Spirit*, (New York: W.W. Norton, 2005).

[16] Andrew Lawson has analyzed Whitman's petite bourgeois voice in *Leaves of Grass* in his book *Walt Whitman and the Class Struggle*.

[17] Reynolds explains Whitman's role playing as "part of the participatory culture, [where he] was to a large degree an actor, and that his poetry was his grandest stage, the locus of his most creative performances," "Walt Whitman and the New York Stage," *Thesis: The Graduate School Magazine*, 9:1 (1995), 8. As I argue below, Whitman's "acting" in this sense began many years before the generation of his Bard persona.

[18] Whitman was not the first to see schoolteaching as a means to social reform. Henry David Thoreau for example, opened a grammar school in 1838 with his brother, John that eschewed corporal punishment and sought to replace the rote pedagogy of the time with practical experiences in the world (forest hikes, visits to local businesses, etc.). Ralph Waldo Emerson and Herman Melville also taught school for a time, though neither seemed to view it as a means to social reform.

[19] Gay Wilson Allen, *The Solitary Singer: A Cultural Biography of Walt Whitman* (New York: The MacMillan Company, 1955), 37.

[20] Floyd Stovall, *The Foreground of Leaves of Grass* (Charlottesville: University Press of Virginia, 1974), 29.

[21] Loving, 46.

[22] Reynolds, *Walt Whitman's America*, 74.

[23] Ralph Waldo Emerson, "Historic Notes of Life and Letters in New England," quoted by Reynolds, *Beneath the American Renaissance* (Cambridge: Harvard University Press, 1988), 61.

[24] Compare, for example, to Mason Locke Weem's *The Drunkard's Looking Glass* (1818), (New York: Reprint Services Corp, 1912).

[25] Number five of the "Sun-Down Papers" has never been found.

[26] Walt Whitman, "Sun-Down Papers: From the Desk of a School Master no. 1," from the *Hempstead Inquirer*, February 29, 1840, in Herbert Bergman, et al., eds., *The Collected Writings of Walt Whitman: The Journalism, vol. I, 1834-1846*, (New York: Peter Lang, 1998), I,13.

[27] "The girls did not seem to attract him. He did not specially go anywhere with them or show any extra fondness for their society." Former Whitman student, Charles Roe, as quoted in "Walt Whitman, Schoolmaster: Notes of a Conversation with Charles A. Roe," ed. Horace Traubel, *Walt Whitman Fellowship Papers*, no. 14 (April 1895), 81-87.

[28] Walt Whitman, "The Sun-Down Papers: From the Desk of a Schoolmaster, no. 2," *The Hempstead Inquirer*, March 14, 1840 in Bergman, et al, eds., I, 14-16.

[29] William Alcott, *The Young Man's Guide*, (New York: Lily, Wait, Colman, and Holden, 1834), Sylvester Graham, *A Lecture to Young Men*, (New York: Arno Press, 1970, first published in 1834).

[30] Bergman, et al, eds., I, 14-16.

31 Karen Halttunen, *Confidence Men and Painted Women: A Study of Middle-class Culture in America, 1830-1870*, (New Haven: Yale University Press, 1982), 56-59, 101. For examples, see James Fenimore Cooper, *The Pioneers* (1823); *The Last of the Mohicans* (1826); *The Prairie* (1827); *The Pathfinder* (1840); *The Deerslayer* (1841); Anonymous, *The Life and Adventures of Col. David Crockett* (1833), *Col. Crockett's Exploits and Adventures in Texas* (1836).

32 Eleazer Moody, *The School of Good Manners: Composed for the help of parents in teaching their children how to behave during their minority* (New York: E.P. Walton, 1818), 13, quoted in Halttunen, 99.

33 According to Halttunen, "The broadest significance of sentimental culture betweeen 1830 and 1870 lay in the powerful middle-class implule to shape all social forms into sincere expressions of inner feeling," xvii. Andrew Lawson notes that *Leaves of Grass* is marked by this middle-class impulse. The "Sun-Down Papers" imply that Whitman had been expressing these impulses fifteen years before his career as a poet.

34 David Roediger, *Wages of Whiteness: Race and the Making of the American Working Class*, (Verso: New York, 1991), 51.

35 Dawley, 20-32.

36 Roediger, 54.

37 See, for example, Barbara Welter, "The Cult of True Womanhood 1820-1860," *American Quarterly 18*, (1966), 151-74, and Mary Ryan, *The Cradle of the Middle Class: The Family in Oneida County, New York 1790-1865* (Cambridge: Cambridge University Press, 1981), 146-165, as well as Sam Bass Warner, *The Private City: Philadelphia in Three Periods of Its Growth*, and Susan Hirsch, *The Roots of the American Working Class*, (Philadelphia: University of Pennsylvania Press, 1978).

38 Walt Whitman, "The Sun-Down Papers: From the Desk of a Schoolmaster, no. 3," *The Hempstead Inquirer*, March, 28, 1840, in Bergman et al. eds, I, 16.

39 Allen, 37.

40 Sylvester Graham (1794-1851) was a prominent health reformer and Presbyterian minister who advocated temperance and sexual abstinence.

41 Walter Fulghum, "Quaker Influences on Whitman's Religious Thought," Ph.D. diss., Northwestern University, 1943; Lawrence Templin, "The Quaker Influence on Walt Whitman." *American Literature*, 42:2 (May 1970), pp. 165-180.

42 George Fox, "A General Epistle," *The Works of George Fox*, vol. VIII, (New York: AMS Press, 1975). "[B]e patterns, be examples in all countries, places, islands, nations wherever you come; that your carriage and life may preach among all sorts of people, and to them; then you will come to walk cheerfully over the world, answering that of God in everyone; whereby in them you may be a blessing, and make the witness of God in them to bless you."

43 *A Series of Extemporaneous Discourses, Delivered in the Several Meetings of the Society of Friends, in Philadelphia, Germantown, Abington, Byberry, Newtown, Falls, and Trenton, by Elias Hicks, A Minister in Said Society*. Taken in Short Hand by M.T.C. Gould. (Philadelphia: Published by Joseph & Edward Parker, 1825), 154-184.

44 Ibid.

45 By the end of the century, most monthly meetings gave up their tradition of dressing plain.

46 Walt Whitman, "Sun-Down Papers: From the Desk of a Schoolmaster no.4," *Long-Island Democrat*, April 28, 1840, in Bergman et al., eds., I, 19.

[47] "Sun-Down Papers no. 5" is missing. It was probably published in the *Long-Island Democrat* between April and August 1840. No description of the topic of this essay has been found in the author's research. One scholar has labeled Whitman's anti-tobacco essay "No. 5" (Reynolds, *Walt Whitman's America*, 74), as it is the fifth "Sun-Down Paper" of the ten in existence. However, as two "Sun-Down Papers" are labeled no. 9 (*Long-Island Democrat*, November 24, 1840 and *Long-Island Democrat* July 6, 1841) the author has preserved their original, albeit confusing, labeling.

[48] Walt Whitman, "Sun-Down Papers: From the Desk of a Schoolmaster no. 6," *Long-Island Democrat*, August 11, 1840, in Bergman et al., eds., I, 20-21.

[49] See Allen, 38, and Loving, 48.

[50] Walt Whitman, "Sun-Down Papers: From the Desk of a Schoolmaster no. 7," *Long -Island Democrat*, September 29, 1840, in Bergman et al., eds., I, 21-23.

[51] Elliott Gorn, *The Manly Art: Bare-Knuckle Prize Fighting in America* (Ithaca, New York: Cornell University Press, 1986), 99.

[52] Walt Whitman, "A Card", *Long-Island Democrat*, October 6, 1840 in Bergman et al., eds., I, 23.

[53] The *Hempstead Inquirer*.

[54] *Long-Island Democrat*.

[55] The *Long-Island Farmer and Queens County Advertiser*.

[56] Walt Whitman, "Sun-Down Papers: From the Desk of a Schoolmaster no. 8," *Long-Island Democrat*, October 20, 1840, in Bergman et al., eds., I, 25.

[57] Harrison won 53% of the popular vote to Van Buren's 47%.

[58] Probably from the German noun *Landläufer*, tramp. Merriam-Webster online dictionary, http://www.m-w.com/dictionary/loafer.

[59] The way in which Whitman uses the verb "to loaf" in this essay of 1840 only existed since 1838 according to the Oxford English Dictionary (1937). Whitman used "loafing" in an editorial published in the *Brooklyn Evening Star*, October 10, 1845, but in a more critical manner, Bergman, et al., I, 222.

[60] Walt Whitman, "Sun-Down Papers: From the Desk of a Schoolmaster, no. 9 *bis*," *Long-Island Democrat*, July 6, 1841, in Bergman et al., eds., I, 27-29.

[61] Loving, *Walt Whitman*, 49.

[62] Reynolds, 74. Reynolds, more than any other biographer of Whitman, delves extensively into these "lost" seven months.

[63] "bis" is typically used in music to mean "again" or as a direction to "repeat." Mirriam-Webster Dictionary Online: http://www.m-w.com/cgi-bin/dictionary.

[64] Walt Whitman, "Sun-Down Papers: From the Desk of a Schoolmaster, no. 9 *bis*," *Long-Island Democrat*, July 6, 1841, in Bergman et al., eds., I, 29.

[65] Halttunen, *Confidence Men and Painted Women*, 122-123.

[66] Loving, 50

[67] Walt Whitman, "Sun-Down Papers: From the Desk of a Schoolmaster no. 10," *Long -Island Democrat*, September 29, 1840, in Bergman et al., eds., I, 31-32.

[68] "The publishers of the *Aurora* would respectfully announce to their friend and public that they have secured the services of Mr. Walter Whitman, favorably known as a bold,

energetic, and original writer as their leading editor." *New York Aurora*, March 28, 1842, Paterson Free Library, Paterson, New Jersey.

Chapter Three: The Objective Editor

1   Abraham Lincoln, "Speech Before the Springfield Washington Temperance Society," February 22, 1842, *Abraham Lincoln: Speeches and Writings 1832-1858*, (New York: Library of America, 1989).

2   Whitman wrote a temperance novel, entitled *Franklin Evans* (1842), during this period which proved to be his most popular work. Over forty years after its publication, Whitman described it to his friend, Horace Traubel, as "damned rot—rot of the worst sort—not insincere, perhaps, but rot, nevertheless: it was not the business for me to be up to. I stopped right there: I never cut a chip off that kind of timber again." Traubel, *With Walt Whitman in Camden*, I, 93.

3   For extended discussion of the New York subversive press see Patricia Cline Cohen, Timothy J. Gilfoyle and Helen L. Horowitz, *The Flash Press: Sporting Men's Weeklies in the 1840s* (Chicago: University of Chicago Press, 2008); Timothy Gilfoyle, *City of Eros: New York City, Prostitution, and the Commercialization of Sex 1790-1920*, (New York: W.W. Norton, 1992); Helen Lefkowitz Horowitz, *Rereading Sex: Battles over Sexual Knowledge and Suppression in Nineteenth-Century America* (New York: Vintage Books, 2002); and Reynolds, *Beneath the American Renaissance* (Cambridge: Harvard University Press, 1988).

4   *New York Aurora*, April 20, 1842, Patterson Free Library. The report of Snelling's arrest and trial in the *Aurora* lists libel as the charge against him. However, another source states that Snelling was charged with obscenity, Stuart M. Blumin, ed., *New York By Gas-Light and Other Urban Sketches*, George G. Foster (Berkeley, CA: University of California Press, 1990, original publication 1850), 116, from Donna I. Dennis, "Obscenity Prosecution and its Consequences in Mid-Nineteenth-Century America". Available at SSRN: http://ssrn.com/abstract=813944.

5   In this capacity, Whitman replaced Thomas Low Nichols who was fired after having been threatened with libel. Whitman, a former schoolteacher with only a year of full-time journalism behind him, was a conservative replacement. Nichols, who had published widely in the sporting press, went on to write fiction with provocative titles like *The Lady in Black* (1844), *Women, in All Ages and Nations* (1849), and *Marriage: Its History, Character, and Results; Its Sanctities, and Its Profanities; Its Science and Its Facts* (1855); the latter of which he co-authored with his future wife, Mary Grove, a prominent water cure advocate and patron of literary salon life for radical thinkers, Horowitz, 287-288.

6   Burrows and Wallace, 635.

7   Mike Walsh, *Subterranean*, March 22, June 14, July 25, September 25, 1845, in Wilenz, 331.

8   Gerald J. Baldasty, "The Press and Politics in the Age of Jackson," *Journalism Monographs*, (no. 89, August 1984), 7-14, also see Michael Schudson, *Discovering The News: A Social History of American Newspapers* (New York: Basic Books, 1978).

[9]   David T.Z. Mindich, "Edwin M. Stanton, the Inverted Pyramid, and Information Control," *Journalism Monographs*, (no. 140, August 1993), 16-18. Also see Frederick Hudson, *Journalism in the United States from 1690-1872*, (New York: Routledge, 2000).

[10]   Quoted in Karen Halttunen, *Murder Most Foul: The Killer and the American Gothic Imagination*, (Cambridge, Massachusetts: Harvard University Press, 1998), 4-5. Also see John C. Hartsock, *A History of American Literary Journalism: The Emergence of a Modern Narrative Form*, (Amherst, MA: University of Massachusetts Press, 2000).

[11]   Halttunen, *Murder Most Foul*, 106.

[12]   Reynolds, *Walt Whitman's America*, 107.

[13]   Ibid., 108.

[14]   Burrows and Wallace, 611-612.

[15]   Ibid., 617-618.

[16]   Ibid., 606.

[17]   See Bridges, *A City in the Republic: Antibellum New York and the Origins of Machine Politics*, 11-14, Burrows and Wallace, 628-629.

[18]   Institute for Advanced Technology in the Humanities, The University of Virginia, "Uncle Tom's Cabin and American Culture: A Media Archive," http://www.iath.virginia.edu/utc/christn/chmillhp.html.

[19]   Burrows and Wallace, 628-630.

[20]   Ibid.

[21]   "Boz" is a pen name that Dickens took for himself as a journalist. It is taken from a character in Oliver Goldsmith's *Vicar of Wakefield* (1766) named Moses. This Dickens later changed to "Boses" which was subsequently shortened to "Boz."

[22]   This is a reference to *The Posthumous Papers of the Pickwick Club*, better known as *The Pickwick Papers* (1837) by Charles Dickens. The main character of the book is an older gentleman named Samuel Pickwick, a sympathetic character known for his natural grace, unaffected manner, and kindness. Though an older gentleman than Dickens, a comparison to Samuel Pickwick's easy grace should be understood as a compliment. It is difficult to tell from this article, however, to what extent Nichols is referring to Samuel Pickwick or to the novel of the same name in its entirety.

[23]   Whitman had already spoken glowingly of Dickens' writing that February in the newspaper *Brother Jonathan* (see below).

[24]   Titles from Charles Dickens, *Sketches by Boz* (1836).

[25]   *New York Aurora*, March 1, 1842, Paterson Free Library, Paterson, New Jersey, 2; This is not so far-fetched in a time when even positions like "reporter", and "assistant editor" were often conflated, Herbert Bergman, et al, eds., I, li.

[26]   *New York Aurora*, March 1, 1842, Paterson Free Library, Paterson, New Jersey, 2. Both characters are from Dickens' novel *Oliver Twist* (1837-1839).

[27]   *New York Aurora*, March 16, 1842, Paterson Free Library, Paterson, New Jersey, 2. These characters appear in *Oliver Twist* (1837-1839), *The Old Curiosity Shop* (1840-1841), and *Barnaby Rudge* (1841) respectively.

[28]   *Brother Jonathan* February 26, 1842 in Herbert Bergman, et al, eds., I, 35-38.

[29]   Ibid.

[30]   Halttunen, *Murder Most Foul*, 42.

31 Whitman had not met Charles Dickens by this time, *Brother Jonathan* February 26, 1842 in Herbert Bergman, et al, eds., I, 35.

32 *New York Aurora*, April 2, 1842, Bergman, et al., eds., I: 92-93.

33 *New York Aurora*, April 2, 1842, Bergman, et al., eds., I: 93. Whitman is probably referring Levi Slamm, the publisher of the *Aurora's* newspaper, the *New Era*. According to the *Aurora*, the *New Era* was the "official organ" of Tammany Hall, whereas the *Aurora* represented the true tenants of Democracy, *New York Aurora*, February 24, 1842, Paterson Free Library, Paterson, New Jersey. Whitman could also be referring to Bishop John Hughes, an ally of Levi Slamm in the Maclay Bill controversy of 1842.

34 Ibid.

35 Martin T. Buinicki, "'Boz's Opinions of Us': Whitman, Dickens, and the Forged Letter," *The Walt Whitman Quarterly Review*, 21:1 Summer, 2003. Dickens, however, wrote critically of the United States in *American Notes* (1842) and *Martin Chuzzlewit* (1843-1844).

36 Ibid.

37 Pelf here means ill-gained money, *American Heritage Dictionary*, (New York: Dell Publishing Company,1981).

38 *Evening Tattler*, August 11, 1842, Bergman, et al., eds., the last quote is taken from Dickens' "letter," I, 148 in Bergman.

39 Dawley, 63.

40 As quoted in Burrows and Wallace, 633.

41 Ibid.

42 Reynolds, *Walt Whitman's America*, 104, and *Beneath the American Renaissance*, 508-516.

43 *New York Aurora*, March 23, 1842, Paterson Free Library, Paterson New Jersey.

44 *New York Aurora*, February 28, 1842, Bergman, et al., eds., I, 39-41.

45 *New York Aurora*, March 21, 1842, Bergman, et al., eds., I, 63-64.

46 *New York Aurora*, March 21, 1842, Bergman, et al., eds., I, 63.

47 In Halttunen, *Confidence Men and Painted Women*, 38.

48 *New York Aurora*, April 12, 1842, Bergman, et al., eds., I, 112.

49 Dawley, 66.

50 Dawley, Roediger, Alexander Saxton, *The Rise and Fall of the White Republic: Race, Politics, and Mass Culture in Nineteenth Century America* (New York: Verso, 2003); Thomas West, *Vindicating the Founders: Race, Sex, Class, and Justice in the Origins of America*, (New York: Rowman and Littlefield, 1997).

51 Wilenz, 219-220.

52 Jürgen Habermas, *The Structural Transformation of the Public Sphere: An Inquiry into a Category of Bourgeois Society*, (Cambridge, Massachusetts: Harvard University Press, 1962), 36-37.

53 Fifteen years later, in 1857, Whitman noted that the problem had grown worse, "If prostitution continues so, and the main classes of young men immerse themselves more an more in it, as they appear to be doing, what will be the result?" As quoted in Gilfoyle, *City of Eros*, 29.

54 *New York Aurora*, March 16, 1842, Bergman, et al., eds., I, 55-57.

55   Which could be the same that Whitman describes in a notebook entry: "Went to New York in May 1841...boarded at Mrs. Chipman's." Mary Chipman's boarding house was at 12 Centre Street, *Notes and Unpublished Manuscripts* I, 217.

56   Other examples of "little republics" can be found in the editorials "Our City" March 8, 1842, "A Peep Behind the Scenes" March 14, 1842, "Life in New York" March 14, 1842, "An Hour in the Balcony" March 23, 1842, "A Peep at the Israelites" March 28, 1842, "Scenes of Last Night" April, 1842, "Something Worth Perusal" April 7, 1842, "The House of Refuge" April 13, 1842.

57   Stott, 37.

58   John Higham, *Strangers in the Land: Patterns of American Nativism 1960-1925* (New York: Atheneum 1955), 4.

59   There are a number of works that analyze Whitman's so-called "Anglo-Saxonism" in his poetry after 1855. See, for example, John E., Bernbrock, SJ., "Walt Whitman and Anglo-Saxonism." (Ph.D. diss., North Carolina, 1961), and Heidi Kathleen Kim, "From Language to Empire: Walt Whitman in the Context of Nineteenth-Century Popular Anglo-Saxonism," *Walt Whitman Quarterly Review*, 24:1 (2003) 1-19.

60   Roediger, 144.

61   Editorials from March 3, 1842 to March 21, 1842, Bergman, et al., eds., I, 41-62.

62   To hold extreme opinions.

63   *New York Aurora*, March 30, 1842, Bergman, et al., eds., I, 85.

64   Loving, 63-66.

65   The *Aurora* announced Whitman's new role as editor of the paper on March 28, 1842, Paterson Free Library, Paterson, New Jersey.

66   Between March and April 1842, the following "leaders" expressed nativist sentiments:, March 29, March 30, April 1, April 12, April 13, April 14, April 15, April 16, Total=8.

67   At least according to Bergman, et al., Whitman wrote the following number of nativist leaders or editorials on the following days, (1) March 7, (1) March 8, (1) March 10, (1) March 12, (1) March 15, (1) March 17, (1) March 18, (1) March 21, (1) March 22, (2) March 24, (1) March 26, (2) March 29, (1) March 30, (1) April 1, (1) April 2, (1) April 6, (1) April 7, (1) April 8, (1) April 9, (2) April 11, (4) April 12, (2) April 13, (2) April 14, (2) April 15, (1) April 16, (1) April 18, Total=35.

68   Reynolds, *Walt Whitman's America*, 99.

69   Joann P. Krieg, *Whitman and the Irish*, (Iowa City: Univeristy of Iowa Press 2000), 39.

70   Regarding other non-natives, Whitman speaks admiringly. See, for example, "A Peep at the Israelites" March 28, 1842, or "Doings at the Synagogue" March 29, 1842.

71   *New York Aurora*, March 26, 1842, Bergman, et al., I, 74.

72   Ibid., I, 75.

73   Quoted in Burrows and Wallace, 499.

74   Ibid., 500.

75   Ibid., 544-545.

76   Glyndon G. Van Deusen, "Seward and the School Question Reconsidered," *The Journal of American History*, 52:2 (Sept. 1965), 313-319, Howe, 201.

77   Krieg, 37-39. Also see Wilentz, 315.

[78] When the Free School Society was taken over by the New York government by 1840 it was renamed the Public School Society.

[79] *New York Aurora*, March 3, 1842, Bergman, et al., eds., I, 41-42.

[80] *New York Aurora*, March 22, 1842, Bergman, et al., eds., 64-65.

[81] *New York Aurora*, March 7, 1842, Bergman, et al., eds., I, 42.

[82] *New York Aurora*, March 7, 1842, Bergman, et al., eds., I, 42-43.

[83] *New York Aurora*, March 10, 1842, Bergman, et al., eds., I, 49.

[84] *New York Aurora*, March 15, 1842, Bergman, et al., eds., I, 54.

[85] Artemus Muzzey, *The Young Man's Friend* (Boston: J. Munroe, 1838), 131, quoted in Halttunen, *Confidence Men and Painted Women*, 15.

[86] *New York Aurora*, March 17, 1842, Bergman, et al., eds., I, 57-58.

[87] Ibid.

[88] *New York Aurora*, April 13, 1842, Bergman, et al., eds., I,115.

[89] *New York Aurora*, April 12, 1842, Bergman, et al., eds., I,112.

[90] David Reynolds asks in *Walt Whitman's America*, "was Whitman enjoying imaginative reprisal for the injuries against him by the Reverend Ralph Smith and his Southold congregation?" *Walt Whitman's America*, 101. For Reynolds, Whitman's virulence can only be explained as a product of a past, and largely speculative, trauma suffered during his years as a schoolteacher.

[91] Wilenz, 64-77, 102.

[92] *New York Aurora* March 24, 1842, Bergman, et al., eds., I, 1834-1846, I, 68.

[93] Whitman later wrote for Slamm's *Plebeian* in 1843, Esther Shephard, "Walt Whitman's Whereabouts in the Winter of 1842-1843," *American Literature*, Vol. 29, No. 3. (Nov., 1957), 290.66

[94] These kind of print attacks in the press were common and could inspire reactions both intense and ironic. For example, Whitman's predecessor, Thomas Nichols, was accused of libel and attacked on the street for his articles in the *Aurora* and the *Flash*. This virulence was often short-lived. After Whitman left the *Aurora* in 1842, he published in Levi Slamm's *Daily Plebian*; Lefkowitz Horowitz, 286; Reynolds, *Walt Whitman's America*, 83.

[95] *New York Aurora*, March 29, 1842, Bergman, et al., eds., I, 81.

[96] *New York Aurora*, March 30, 1842, Bergman, et al., eds., I, 84-86.

[97] *New York Aurora*, April 7, 1842, Bergman, et al., eds., 102.

[98] *New York Aurora*, April 12, 1842, Bergman, et al., eds., I, 108-109.

[99] Ibid.

[100] *New York Aurora*, April 14, 1842, Bergman, et al., eds., I, 116.

[101] *New York Aurora*, April 18, 1842, Bergman, et al., eds., I, 124.

[102] *New York Aurora*, May 16, 1842, Paterson Free Library, Paterson, New Jersey.

[103] *Evening Tattler*, August 29, 1842, Bergman, et al., eds., I, 151.

[104] *New York Aurora*, April 14-23, 1842, Bergman, et al., eds., I, 132-136.

Chapter Four: The Editor Against Affectation

[1] "Fall and winter of 1842 boarded at Mrs. R. in Spring st. Spring of 1843 board at Mrs. Bonnard's in John st. Also at Mrs. Edgarton's in Vesey. Summer of '43 at Mary's and Brown's in Duane st. October 1843 commenced with the Winants," quoted in Esther Shephard, "Walt Whitman's Whereabouts in the Winter of 1842-1843," *American Literature*, 29:3 (November 1957), 289.

[2] According to Bergman, et al., 1v-1viii.

[3] *The United States Magazine, and Democratic Review*, November, 1845 in Bergman, et al., I, 205

[4] *The American Review*, November, 1845 in Bergman, et al., I, 211.

[5] Reynolds, *Walt Whitman's America*, 84; Stovall, 41; Loving, 144.

[6] *Brooklyn Evening Star* October 22, 1845, January 22, 1846, Bergman, et al., I, 226, 244.

[7] Mann's Annual Reports provide a cohesive statement of his pedagogical vision: In his *Fifth Annual Report* (1841), Mann argued successfully that economic wealth would increase through an educated public; in the *Seventh Annual Report* (1843) he supported the Prussian school system; the *Tenth Annual Report* (1846), asserted that education was a right for every citizen; the *Twelfth Annual Report* (1848) presented an argument for the support of public education through taxation.

[8] *Brooklyn Evening Star* October 22, 1845, Bergman, et al., I, 226; Whitman had explored this topic before in when he published a short story entitled "Death in a Schoolroom, A Fact" in the *Democratic Review*, August, 1841.

[9] *Brooklyn Evening Star*, September 15, 1845, Bergman, et al., I, 217.

[10] Halttunen, *Confidence Men and Painted Women*, 57.

[11] *Brooklyn Evening Star* October 10, 1845, Bergman, et al., I, 222.

[12] A number of scholars have noted Whitman's interest in this subculture. See Reynold's *Walt Whitman's America*, Loving's *Walt Whitman*, and Andrew Lawson, "'Spending on Vast Returns': Sex, Class and Commerce in the First *Leaves of Grass*."

[13] *Godey's Lady's Book*, "Select Sentences," 10, (June 1835): 285, as quoted in Halttunen, *Confidence Men and Painted Women*, 67.

[14] Halttunen, *Confidence Men and Painted Women*, 90.

[15] *Brooklyn Evening Star*, January 7, 1846, Bergman, et al., I, 242.

[16] *Brooklyn Evening Star*, February 9, 1845, Bergman, et al., I, 252. Whitman made a similar argument after seeing a children's concert at the New York Tabernacle in "An Evening at a Children's Concert," February 20, 1846, Bergman, et al., I, 254.

[17] *Brooklyn Evening Star*, "American Music, New and True!", November 5, 1845, Bergman, et al., I, 233; *Brooklyn Evening Star*, "Heart-Music and Art Music," November 14, 1845, Bergman, et al., I, 235; *The Broadway Journal*, "Art-Singing and Heart-Singing," November 29, 1845, Bergman, et al., I, 202; *The Brooklyn Daily Eagle*, "Music that IS Music," December 4, 1846, Bergman, et al., II, 137.

[18] *Brooklyn Evening Star*, November 5, 1845, Bergman, et al., I, 235.

[19] Burrows and Wallace, 642.

[20] Horowitz, 135.

21   *Brooklyn Evening Star*, November 14, 1845, Bergman, et al., *1834-1846*, I, 235.

22   *The Broadway Journal*, November 29, 1845, Bergman, et al., I, 202.

23   Reynolds, *Beneath the American Renaissance*, 213-215.

24   Ibid.

25   *Daily Crescent*, March 6, 1848, Emory Holloway, ed., *The Uncollected Poetry and Prose of Walt Whitman*, vol. II, (Gloucester, MA: Peter Smith) 1972, I, 191.

26   For other analyses of Whitman's musical aesthetic see Robert D. Faner, *Walt Whitman and Opera*, (Carbondale, IL: Southern Illinois University Press, 1951, Loving, 81-114 and Reynolds, *Walt Whitman's America*, 154-194.

27   Thomas Brasher, *Whitman as Editor of the Brooklyn Daily Eagle*, (Detroit: Wayne State University Press, 1970), Reynolds, *Walt Whitman's America*, Faner.

28   Reynolds, *Walt Whitman's America*, 114, Loving, 103.

29   This conglomerate would become the Associated Press in 1848.

30   See Hudson.

31   Brasher, 18, 219, for Whitman's use of the phrase "immutable truth" see *Brooklyn Daily Eagle*, March 26, 1846, Bergman, et al., II, 304.

32   "Of all professions, I do not know a more useful or honorable than that of schoolmaster; at the same time, I do not see any more generally despised, or whose talents are less rewarded."

33   *Brooklyn Daily Eagle*, November 24, 1847, Bergman, et al, eds., II, 362.

34   *Brooklyn Daily Eagle*, August 21, 1846, Bergman, et al, eds., II, 26.

35   *Brooklin Daily Eagle*, April 17, 1847, Bergman, et al, eds.,II, 249.

36   *Brooklyn Daily Eagle*, July 9, 1846, Bergman, et al, eds., I, 460.

37   See Reynolds, *Beneath the American Renaissance*.

38   According to David Reynolds, Whitman here criticized the American form of the British "tempestuous style" best exemplified by George Frederick Cooke and Edmund Kean. Reynolds, "Walt Whitman and the New York Stage," 7. Whitman may also be speaking specifically about the American actor Edwin Forrest. Whitman wrote critically of Forrest in this context on December 26, 1846, *Brooklyn Daily Eagle*, Bergman, et al, eds.,II, 158-159.

39   *Brooklyn Daily Eagle*, August 20, 1846, Herbert Bergman, et al, eds., II, 24.

40   Ibid.

41   *Brooklyn Daily Eagle*, September 4, 1846, Herbert Bergman, et al, eds., II, 48-49.

42   *Brooklyn Daily Eagle*, February 12, 1847, Herbert Bergman, et al, eds., II, 195-196.

43   Ibid. For an engaging argument as to the generation of "high" and "low" culture in America, see Levine's *Highbrow/Lowbrow*.

44   Reynolds, *Walt Whitman's America*, 163.

45   British actors Edmund Kean (1821), Joshua Anderson (1831), and George Farren (1834) were all British actors who faced unruly nativist theater-goers. See Reynolds, *Walt Whitman's America*, 163 and "Walt Whitman and the New York Stage." *Thesis: The Graduate School Magazine*, [New York University] 9:1 (1995), 5-11.

46   As quoted in Burrows and Wallace, 763. Also see Nigel Cliff, *The Shakespeare Riots: Revenge, Drama, and Death in Nineteenth-Century America*, New York: Random House, 2007.

47   Reynolds, *Walt Whitman's America*, 164.

[48]   *Brooklyn Daily Eagle*, September 1, 1846, Herbert Bergman, et al, eds., II, 40.

[49]   *Brooklyn Daily Eagle*, August 14, 1846, Herbert Bergman, et al, eds., II, 17.

[50]   Whitman's critique of an "intellectual" style versus that of his more "American" aesthetic supports Richard Bushman's thesis as to the earlier generation of "high" American culture in the late-18th century. See Bushman's *The Refinement of America*.

[51]   *Brooklyn Daily Eagle*, August 10, 1846, August 14, 1846, August 20, 1846, Bergman, et al, eds., II, 10, 17, 24.

[52]   *Brooklyn Daily Eagle*, December 26, 1846, Bergman, et al, eds., II, 158.

[53]   Forrest hissed Macready's portrayal of Hamlet in Edinburgh in Marcy, 1846, Cliff, 160.

[54]   Except for a brief, positive mention of Macready on January 6, 1848, *Brooklyn Daily Eagle*, Bergman, et al, eds., II, 392.

[55]   "Walt Whitman and the New York Stage," 9. Whitman, during the Astor Place Riots was editing the daily free-soil *Freeman*. Reynolds also speculates that Whitman was ambivalent about the violence of May 10, 1849.

[56]   Quoted in Burrows and Wallace, 685.

[57]   Burrows and Wallace, 686.

[58]   *Democratic Review*, 1838, as quoted in Ibid, 685-687.

[59]   Ibid., 686.

[60]   *Brooklyn Daily Eagle*, February 10, 1847, Bergman, et al, eds., II, 191. For an extended discussion of contemporary theories of a novel American literature, see Reynolds' *Beneath the American Renaissance*.

[61]   *Brooklyn Daily Eagle*, August 18, 1846, Bergman, et al, eds., II, 20.

[62]   Halttunen, *Confidence Men and Painted Women*, 22.

[63]   *Brooklyn Daily Eagle*, August 18, 1846, Bergman, et al, eds., II, 20.

[64]   *Brooklyn Daily Eagle*, September 1, 1846, Bergman, et al, eds., II, 41-42

[65]   *Brooklyn Daily Eagle*, September 12, 1846, Bergman, et al, eds., II, 84-86.

[66]   *Brooklyn Daily Eagle*, October 21, 1846, Bergman, et al, eds., II, 94.

[67]   *Brooklyn Daily Eagle*, May 5, 1847, Bergman, et al, eds., II, 264.

[68]   *Brooklyn Daily Eagle*, February 1, 1847, Bergman, et al, eds., II, 180-181.

[69]   See, for example, M. Wynn Thomas' *The Lunar Light of Whitman's Poetry* and Andrew Lawson's "'Spending on Vast Returns': Sex, Class, and Commerce in the first *Leaves of Grass*", Andrew Lawson, *Walt Whitman and the Class Struggle*.

[70]   William Freehling, *Prelude to Civil War: The Nullification Controversy in South Carolina, 1816-1836*, (Oxford: Oxford University Press, 1965).

[71]   *Brooklyn Daily Eagle*, August 12, 1846, Bergman, et al, eds., II, 14.

[72]   *Brooklyn Daily Eagle*, August 5, 1846, Bergman, et al, eds., II, 6.

[73]   *Brooklyn Daily Eagle*, August 17, 1846, Bergman, et al, eds., II, 19.

[74]   *Brooklyn Daily Eagle*, October 10, 1846, Bergman, et al, eds., II, 83-84.

[75]   *Brooklyn Daily Eagle*, December 10, 1847, Bergman, et al, eds., II, 379-380.

[76]   Wilenz, 349-351.

[77]   *Brooklyn Daily Eagle*, March 26, 1846, Bergman, et al., I, 304.

[78]   *Brooklyn Daily Eagle*, August 19, 1846, Bergman, et al., II, 65.

[79]   *Brooklyn Daily Eagle*, August 19, 1846, Bergman, et al., II, 22.

[80]   Ibid.

[81]   Whitman's attitudes about sexuality and prostitution were not peculiar to his time. See Gilfoyle, *City of Eros.*

[82]   *Brooklyn Daily Eagle*, November 9, 1846 "Working Women," December 2, 1846 "[Values]", January 29, 1847 "The Sewing Women of Brooklyn and New York," Bergman, et al., II, 112, 136, 177-178.

[83]   Ibid.

[84]   Whitman here echoed the rhetoric of the Female Moral Reform Society and the Female Benevolent Society, Paula Baker, "The Domestication of Politics: Women and American Political Society, 1780-1920," *The American Historical Review*, 89:3 (June 1984), 632-633.

[85]   *Brooklyn Daily Eagle*, August 19, 1846, Bergman, et al., II, 22-23.

[86]   See Susan E. Hirsch, *Roots of the American Working Class: the Industrialization of Crafts in Newark, 1800-1860*, (Philadelphia : University of Pennsylvania Press, 1978) and Sam Bass Warner, *The Private City: Philadelphia in Three Periods of its Growth* (Philadelphia: University of Philadelphia Press, 1987).

[87]   Quoted in Spann, 171.

[88]   Spann, 165.

[89]   Ibid.

[90]   Ibid., 168.

[91]   *Brooklyn Daily Eagle.*, April 10, 1846, Bergman, et al., eds., I, 326-327.

[92]   *Brooklyn Daily Eagle*, August 7, 1846, Bergman, et al, eds., II, 8.

[93]   *Brooklyn Daily Eagle*, January 5, 1847, Bergman, et al, eds., II 164-165.

[94]   *Brooklyn Daily Eagle*, March 4, 1847, Bergman, et al, eds., II, 209.

[95]   *Brooklyn Daily Eagle*, April 27, 1847, September 1, 1847, Bergman, et al, eds., II, 259-260, 318-320.

[96]   *Brooklyn Daily Eagle*, November 4, 1847, Herbert Bergman, et al, eds., II, 349.

[97]   See M. Wynn Thomas, "Whitman and the Dreams of Labor," in Ed Folsom, ed., *Whitman: The Centennial Essays*, 133-153.

[98]   *Brooklyn Daily Eagle*, September 1, 1847, Bergman, et al., II, 319.

[99]   Loving also makes a case for the influence of Giles on Whitman in *Walt Whitman: The Song of Himself*, 112.

[100] *Brooklyn Daily Eagle*, December 10, 1847, from "The *Brooklyn Daily Eagle* Online" at http://brooklynpubliclibrary.org.

[101] "But in the right to eat the bread, without the leave of anybody else, which his own hand earns, *he is my equal and the equal of Judge Douglas, and the equal of every living man* [Lincoln's Emphasis]." Abraham Lincoln, debate with Stephen Douglas, August 21, 1858, Ottawa, Illinois, in Gerald Emmanuel Stern, et. al., *The Essential Lincoln*, (New York: Collier Books, 1962), 220.

[102] *Brooklyn Daily Eagle*, December 10, 1847, http://brooklynpubliclibrary.org.

[103] *Brooklyn Daily Eagle*, January 3, 1848, Herbert Bergman, et al, eds., II, 389.

[104] This is a reference to William Miller who argued that a careful reading of the Bible could predict the end of the world. *Brooklyn Daily Eagle*, January 14, 1848, Herbert Bergman, et

al, eds., II, 397. Also see Ronald Numbers, ed., et al., *Disappointed: Millerism and Millenarianism in the Nineteenth Century* (Knoxville: University of Tennessee Press, 1993).

Chapter Five: Persona Non Grata

[1]   David Donald, *Charles Sumner and the Rights of Man*, New York, Knopf, 1970.

[2]   John Townsend Trowbridge, Reminiscences of Walt Whitman," *Atlantic Monthly*, 89:166, 1902. It is not clear when this "boil" began, but it might have been as early as 1842 when Whitman heard a lecture by Emerson entitled "The Poetry of the Times." This lecture became Emerson's essay "The Poet." Whitman commented on this lecture in the *New York Aurora* where he called it "one of the most richest and most beautiful compositions, both for its matter and style, we have here, at any time," *New York Aurora*, March 7, 1842, Herbert Bergman, et al, eds., I, 44.

[3]   Reynolds, *Beneath the American Renaissance*.

[4]   Charles Eliot Norton believed this to be true, "...Walt Whitman has read the "'Dial' and 'Nature' and combines the characteristics of a Concord philosopher with those of a New York fireman," *The Letters of Charles Eliot Norton*, Sara Norton and M.A. DeWolfe, ed., (New York: Houghton Mifflin, 1913), in "Fire and Smoke: Emerson's Letter to Whitman," George Monteiro, *Modern Language Studies*, 15:2 (Spring 1985), 7. For a copy of the letter from Emerson to Whitman, see *Leaves of Grass: The 150th Anniversary Edition*, David Reynods, ed., (Oxford: Oxford University Press, 2005), 161.

[5]   *New York Aurora*, March 7, 1842, Bergman, et al, eds., I, 44.

[6]   *New York Aurora*, February 28, 1842, Patterson Free Library.

[7]   Ralph Waldo Emerson, "New England Reformers," lecture given at the Society in Armory Hall, March 3, 1844, *The Essential Writings of Ralph Waldo Emerson*, (New York: Random House, 2000), 402.

[8]   *The Essential Writings of Ralph Waldo Emerson*, from *Nature*, 6.

[9]   Milette Shamir has made a compelling case for the fundamentally middle class rebellion of Thoreau in *Walden* in *Inexpressible Privacy: The Interior Life of Antebellum American Literature* (Philadelphia: University of Pennsylvania Press, 2006), 201-202, 229-230.

[10]   Reynolds *Beneath the American Renaissance*, 99.

[11]   Henry David Thoreau, "Economy," *Walden And Other Writings* (New York: Barnes and Noble Books, 1993), and Walt Whitman, *Brooklyn Daily Eagle*, August 19, 1846, Bergman, et al, eds., II, 23.

[12]   Thoreau, "Reading," *Walden and Other Writings*, 89.

[13]   "I generally went about my work about 9 o'clock, overhauling the papers rec'd by mail, and 'making up news,' as it is called, both with pen and scissors." From an unpublished journal entry labeled "1848 New Orleans" in Holloway, ed. II, 78.

[14]   Floyd Stovall, ed., *Walt Whitman: Prose Works 1892*, 2 vols. (New York: New York University Press, 1963-64), 288, in Loving 115.

[15]   Loving, 115.

[16]   *Daily Crescent* March 10, 1848, Holloway, ed., I, 181-190.

[17]   Ibid.

[18]   Loving, 121.

[19]   Johnson Jones Hooper, *The Adventures of Captian Simon Suggs* (Philadelphia: Carey and Hart, 1845).

[20]   *Daily Crescent* March 13, 1848, Holloway, ed., I,199, Louise Pound, "Peter Funk: The Pedigree of a Westernism," *American Speech*, Vol. 4, No. 3. (Feb., 1929), pp. 183-186.

[21]   These burlesques had characters like *Julius Sneezer* and *Dars-de-Money*, Burrows and Wallace, 642.

[22]   Ibid.

[23]   "Night shows stars and women in a better light. . . " Canto II, Stanza 152.

[24]   "There was a [laughing] devil in his sneer/That raised emotions both of hate and fear."Canto I, Stanza ix.

[25]   ". . . a tailor made thee" II, 2, 50.

[26]   "To be a well-favoured man is the gift of Fortune, but to write and read comes by nature" in Whitman's hands becomes, "is the gift of nature." III, 3, 15-17.

[27]   "There's nought but care on every hand, In every hour that passes, O" II, 1, 14.

[28]   "His dream of life from morn till night, Was love—still love." Stanza I.

[29]   "Walter is trying to save up all the money he can get, and allready [sic] he has quite a sum, as soon as he gets a thousand dollars he is coming north. . . . Sometimes I get thinking about you all and feel quite lonesome, but not one fifth as much as I did when we first arrived...." Jeff Whitman, April 23, 1848, from *Dear Brother Walt: The Letters of Thomas Jefferson Whitman*, Dennis Berthold, Kenneth Price, eds. (Kent, Ohio: The Kent State University Press, 1984).

[30]   "I answered by reminding them of certain points which appeared to have been forgotten, making me not their debtor, and told them in my reply I thought it would be better to dissolve the connection." From an unpublished manuscript labeled "1848 New Orleans" in Holloway, ed., II, 77-78.

[31]   Loving, 144.

[32]   *Brooklyn Freeman*, September 9, 1848. All *Freeman* quotes taken from Loving, 144-145. A facsimile of this newpaper is housed at Duke University as part of the *Catalogue of the Whitman Collection in the Duke University Library Being Part of the Trent Collection*, Ellen Frances Frey (Durham: Duke University Press, 1945).

[33]   For the effect of "slave power" conspiracy theories see Eric Foner, *Free Soil, Free Labor, Free Men: The Ideology of the Republican Party Before the Civil War* (Oxford: Oxford University Press, 1970), 73-102.

[34]   "After the present date, I withdraw entirely from the Brooklyn *Daily Freeman*. To those who have been my friends, I take occasion to proffer the warmest thanks of a grateful heart. My enemies...and old Hunkers generally...I disdain and defy the same as ever. Walter Whitman." *Brooklyn Daily Eagle* September 11, 1849, in Loving, 146.

[35]   New York *Evening Post* June 27, 1851, Holloway, ed., I, 248 .

[36]   Ibid.

[37]   New York *Evening Post* June 28, 1851, Holloway, ed., I, 253.

[38]   Ibid.

39 See, for example, Ted Genoways, "Notes on Whitman: 'Fish, Fishermen, and Fishing, on the East End of Long Island': An Excerpt from Walt Whitman's Uncollected Serial 'Letters from a Travelling Young Bachelor.'" *Shenandoah* 50 (Winter 2000), 49-56, also Loving, 147-149.

40 Max Maretzek was the manager of the Opera House in New York, from Holloway, ed., I, 256.

41 *New York Evening Post* August 14, 1851, Holloway, ed., I, 255-256.

42 Wallace and Burrows, 687.

43 New York *Evening Post* February 1, 1851, Holloway ed., I, 236-238.

44 Brooklyn *Daily Advertizer* April 3, 1851, Holloway, ed., I, 241.

45 Whitman owned a copy of Hedge's book that was given to him in 1862 by a friend, F. S. Gray, Reynolds, *Walt Whitman's America*, 253.

46 Ralph Waldo Emerson, "The Poet," *The Essential Writings of Ralph Waldo Emerson*, (New York: The Modern Library, 2000), 301.

47 First published in the *Evening Post* on March 12, later changed to "Dough-Face Song" for *Specimen Days* (Philadelphia: David McKay, 1892).

48 Published in the *New York Tribune*, June 14, 1850, Holloway, ed., I, 25.

49 A "dough-face" was a derogatory term for Democratic politicians like Franklin Pierce and James Buchanan who, in an attempt to preserve the continuity of their party, sought compromise in the slavery debate.

50 Horace Traubel, ed., *With Walt Whitman in Camden*, IV, 2.

51 From "Manuscript Note-2" in Holloway ed., II, 83.

52 Clarence Gohdes ed., *Faint Clews and Indirections: Manuscripts of Walt Whitman and His Family*, (Durham, NC: Duke University Press, 1949), 19, Also see Faner, 229-230.

Chapter Six: The Bard and Work Redefined

1 Pannapacker, 25.

2 Whitman formulated many of the ideas that went into this introduction to the first edition of *Leaves of Grass* in a notebook from the early 1850s. These writings can be found in Holloway, II, 79-91.

3 Walt Whitman, *Leaves of Grass*, (1855), facsimilie, (New York: The Eakins Press, 1966), iii.

4 Whitman, *Leaves of Grass* (1855), iii.

5 Whitman, *Leaves of Grass* (1855), iv.

6 Whitman, *Leaves of Grass* (1855), v.

7 Whitman, *Leaves of Grass* (1855), iv.

8 *Oxford English Dictionary*, (Oxford: Oxford University Press, 1937), 1685.

9 Whitman, *Leaves of Grass* (1855), v.

[10] Ruth L. Bohan provides a compelling and exhaustive analysis of Whitman images and imagery into the 20th century in *Looking into Walt Whitman: American Art, 1850-1920*, (University Park, PA: The Pennsylvania State University Press, 2006).

[11] Whitman, *Leaves of Grass* (1855), 29.

[12] Whitman, *Leaves of Grass* (1855), x.

[13] Whitman, *Leaves of Grass* (1855), 13.

[14] Floyd Stovall, *The Foreground of Leaves of Grass*, (Charlottesville: University Press of Virginia, 1974), 268-269.

[15] Ibid.

[16] John Neal, *Randolph*, 1823, II, 190 as quoted in Reynolds, *Walt Whitman's America*, 42.

[17] Emerson, *The Poet* (1844), 290.

[18] Reynolds, *Walt Whitman's America*, 315.

[19] Paul Zweig, *Whitman: The Making of the Poet* (New York: Basic Books, 1984), 149.

[20] I am indebted to Reynolds for his analysis of Lippard's connections with Whitman, *Walt Whitman's America*, 84-95, 131-132.

[21] As quoted in David Reynolds, ed., *George Lippard: The Profit of Protest*, (New York: Peter Lang, 1986), 227.

[22] Whitman, *Leaves of Grass* (1855), 23.

[23] Whitman, *Leaves of Grass* (1855), 75.

[24] *Brooklyn Daily Eagle*, December 2, 1846, from the *Brooklyn Daily Eagle* online, http://www.eagle.brooklynpubliclibrary.org.

[25] See, for example, M. Jimmie Killingsworth's *Whitman's Poetry of the Body: Sexuality, Politics, and the Text* (Chapel Hill: The University of North Carolina Press, 1989). Killingsworth states that, for Whitman, "the exemplars of the ideal physical morality challenge those who, in revering the dead conventions of their dead forefathers, corrupt 'their own bodies.'", 3.

[26] Whitman, *Leaves of Grass* (1855), 17. For other analyses of this "merge" see Killingsworth, *Whitman's Poetry of the Body*, 1-46, and Erkkila, *Whitman the Political Poet*, 97-111.

[27] Whitman, *Leaves of Grass* (1855), 14.

[28] Whitman, *Leaves of Grass* (1855), 15.

[29] Whitman, *Leaves of Grass* (1855), 16.

[30] Whitman, *Leaves of Grass* (1855), 17.

[31] David Sprague Herreshoff, *Labor into Art: The Theme of Work in Nineteenth-Century American Literature* (Detroit: Wayne State University Press, 1991), 120. Herreshoff argues that Whitman's poems are "songs of unalienated workers in a classless utopia."

[32] Whitman, *Leaves of Grass* (1855), 21-22.

[33] Whitman, *Leaves of Grass* (1855), 63.

[34] Whitman, *Leaves of Grass* (1855), 64.

[35] Trachtenberg, likewise, sees this poem as Whitman's attempt "...to return it [work] to a living praxis, the activity of labor and production, of which the poet's own work provides the exemplary model." *Whitman: The Centennial Essays*, Ed Folsom, ed., (Iowa City: University of Iowa Press, 1994), 129. Also see Kerry Larson, *Whitman's Drama of Consensus*, (Chicago: The University of Chicago Press, 1988), 42.

36 Whitman, *Leaves of Grass* (1855), 78.

37 Karl Marx, *Economic Philosophic Manuscripts of 1844*, tran. Martin Milligan (New York: Prometheus Books, 1988), 74.

38 "I resist anything better than my own diversity,/And breathe the air and leave plenty after me,/And am not stuck up, and am in my place." Whitman, *Leaves of Grass*, 24.

39 Marx, 107.

40 Martin Klammer, *Whitman, Slavery, and the Emergence of Leaves of Grass*, (University Park: Pennsylvania State University. Press, 1995), Richard Gravil, "'The Discharged Soldier' and 'The Runaway Slave': Wordsworth and the Definition of Walt Whitman," *Symbiosis* 1 (April 1997), 48-68. For those who find an ambivalence in Whitman's view of slaves see Wai Chee Dimock, "Whitman, Syntax, and Political Theory" in Betsy Erkkila and Jay Grossman, eds., *Breaking Bounds* (New York: Oxford University Press, 1996), 62-79, D.H. Lawrence, *Studies in Classic American Literature*, (New York: Penguin, 1923), 183-84, and Pannapacker, 32.

41 In this regard, Whitman reflected many arguments that, after 1855, would come together to create a coherent Republican platform. Eric Foner, *Free Soil, Free Labor, Free Men: The Ideology of the Republican Party before the Civil War*, (Oxford: Oxford University Press, 1970).

42 Whitman, *Leaves of Grass* (1855), 39.

43 Ibid., 81.

44 For an extended discussion of this poem, see Christopher Beach, *The Politics of Distinction: Whitman and the Discourse of Nineteenth-Century America*, (Athens, GA: University of Georgia Press, 1996). 55-102. Beach explores the significance of Whitman's metaphor of the black whale with that of Melville's white whale and asks, "Was the whale, in fact, a site of interaction between a literary intertext and a larger cultural matrix?", 91-97.

45 Walt Whitman, *Leaves of Grass* (1855), 89.

46 "You are horrified at our intending to do away with private ownership of the means of production. But in your existing society, private property is already done away with for nine-tenths of the population; its existence for the few is solely due to its non-existence in the hands of those nine-tenths." Karl Marx, Friedrich Engels, *The Communist Manifesto*, Section Two; "Free laborers pay one another, for labor creates all values, and capital, after taking the lion's share by its taxing power, but pays the so-called wages of one laborer from the proceeds of the labor of another.... Capital exercises a more perfect compulsion over free laborers, than human masters over slaves: for free laborers must at all times work or starve, and slaves are supported whether they work or not. Free laborers have less liberty than slaves, are worse paid and provided for, and have no valuable rights," George Fitzhugh, *Cannibals All!*, Chapter Two, "Labor, Skill, and Capital."

47 I am indebeted to the arguments of Martin Klammer here, especially 140-157.

Conclusion: "They All Count"

1 Traubel, *With Walt Whitman in Camden*, I, 280.

2 1855, 1856, 1860, 1867, 1871-72, 1881-82, 1891-92.

3 From Emerson's letter to Whitman after having read the first edition of *Leaves of Grass*.

4   Charles Dana, *New York Daily Tribune*, July 23, 1855, 3, in David Reynolds, ed., *Leaves of Grass: 150th Anniversary Edition* (Oxford: Oxford University Press, 2005), 107.

5   Rufus Griswold, *Criterion*, 1, November 10, 1855, 24, in David Reynolds, ed., *Leaves of Grass: 150th Anniversary Edition*, 127.

6   Walt Whitman, "Walt Whitman and his Poems," *United States Review*, October 5, 1855, in David Reynolds, ed., *Leaves of Grass: 150th Anniversary Edition*, 110.

7   Gay Wilson Allen, *Leaves of Grass: Facsimile of the 1856 Edition*, (Norwood, Pa.: Norwood Editions, 1976), xiv, from Harold Apsiz, "Leaves of Grass 1856 Edition," *The Walt Whitman Archive*, Ed. Ed Folsom and Kenneth M. Price. July 2004, <http://www.whitmanarchive.org>.

8   Traubel, *With Walt Whitman in Camden*, II,175.

9   A recent theory posits that the first edition was printed on its unusually large paper because the publisher, Andrew Rome, was a publisher of legal documents (which were printed on quatro-sized pages) and that this was the paper he had on hand, Ed Folsom, Keynote Address, *150th Anniversary Conference of Leaves of Grass*, (Lincoln: University of Nebraska, March 31, 2005). Folsom expands on this argument in "The Census of the 1855 Leaves of Grass: A Preliminary Report," *Walt Whitman Quarterly Review* 24:2-3 (2006/2007), 72.

10 Reynolds, *Walt Whitman's America*, 208-210, Stovall, 159-160, Paul Zweig, *Walt Whitman: The Making of the Poet*, (New York: Basic Books, 1984), 89-90.

11 Ezra Greenspan, "An Undocumented Review of the 1860 Leaves of Grass in the Liberator," *Walt Whitman Quarterly Review*, 24:4 (Spring 2007), 201-204.

12 "Some of your vehemence is all right—will stand; some of it is impatience of youth. You must be on your guard—don't let your dislike for the conventions lead you to do the old things any injustice: lots of the old stuff is just as new as it is old.... Be radical—be radical—be not too damned radical!" Traubel, *With Walt Whitman in Camdem*, I,223.

13 Whitman, himself, saw it as "The Great construction of the New Bible" *Daybooks and Notebooks*, (New York: New York University Press, 1978), 1:353, quoted in Gregory Eiselein, "An Introduction to the 1860 Edition," *The Walt Whitman Archive*, Ed. Ed Folsom and Kenneth M. Price, July 2004, <http://www.whitmanarchive.org>.

14 *Leaves of Grass* (1860), 23.

15 *Leaves of Grass* (1860), 291.

16 *Leaves of Grass* (1860), 122.

17 Lawson, "Spending on Vast Returns: Sex, Class and Commerce in *Leaves of Grass*," 336-337.

18 Eiselein, *The Walt Whitman Archieve*, http://www.whitmanarchive.org.

19 This common nickname for Whitman was coined by William Douglas O'Connor in the book *The Good Grey Poet: A Vindication* (New York: Bunce and Huntington, 1866).

20 Traubel, *With Walt Whitman in Camden*, VII, 386, quoted in Reynolds, *Walt Whitman's America*, 569.

21 For convenient comparison between the first and last editions, see Justin Kaplan, ed., *Walt Whitman: The Complete Poetry and Collected Prose*, (New York: Library of America, 1982). All nine editions can be found online at the Walt Whitman Archive, http://www.whitman archive.org/.

Bibliography

Allen, Gay Wilson. *A Reader's Guide to Walt Whitman*. Syracuse: Syracuse University Press, 1970.

———. "History of My Whitman Studies," *Walt Whitman Quarterly Review*. 9:2 (Fall 1992) 91-100.

———. *The Solitary Singer: A Critical Biography of Walt Whitman*. New York City: New York University Press, 1967.

Arvin, Newton. *Whitman*. New York: The Macmillan Company, 1938.

Asselineau, Roger, "My Discovery and Exploration of the Whitman Continent," *Walt Whitman Quarterly Review*. 9:1 (Spring 1991): 15-23.

Baker, Paula, "The Domestication of Politics: Women and American Political Society, 1780-1920," *The American Historical Review*, 89:3 (June 1984), 620-647.

Baldasty, Gerald J., "The Press and Politics in the Age of Jackson," *Journalism Monographs*, 89, August 1984.

Barth, Gunther. *City People: The Rise of Modern City Culture in Nineteenth-Century America*. Oxford: Oxford University Press, 1980.

Beach, Christopher. *The Politics of Distinction: Whitman and the Discourses of Nineteenth-Century America*. Athens, Georgia: The University of Georgia Press, 1996.

Belgrad, Daniel. *The Culture of Spontaneity: Improvisation and the Arts in Postwar America*. Chicago: The University of Chicago Press, 1998.

Benson, Lee. *The Concept of Jacksonian Democracy: New York as a Test Case*. New York: Atheneum,1967.

Bernbrock, John E., SJ. "Walt Whitman and Anglo-Saxonism." Ph.D. diss., North Carolina, 1961.

Blewett, Mary H. *Men, Women, and Work : Class, Gender, and Protest in the New England Shoe Industry, 1780-1910*. Urbana: University of Illinois Press, 1988.

Bohan, Ruth L. *Looking into Walt Whitman: American Art, 1850-1920*. University Park, PA: The Pennsylvania State University Press, 2006.

Brasher, Thomas L. *Whitman as Editor of the Brooklyn Daily Eagle*. Detroit: Wayne State University Press, 1970.

Bridges, Amy. *A City in the Republic: Antebellum New York and the Origins of Machine Politics.* Cambridge: Cambridge University Press, 1984.

Bucke, R.M. *Walt Whitman.* New York: Dutton, 1883.

Burroughs, John. *Whitman: A Study.* Boston: Houghton, Mifflin, 1896.

Burrows, Edwin and Mike Wallace. *Gotham: A History of New York City.* Oxford: Oxford University Press, 1999.

Buinicki, Martin T. "'Boz's Opinions of Us': Whitman, Dickens, and the Forged Letter," *Walt Whitman Quarterly Review* (Summer, 2003) 21:1.

Bushman, Richard Lyman. *The Refinement of America: Persons, Houses, Cities.* New York: Alfred A. Knopf, 1992.

Chase, Richard. *Walt Whitman Reconsidered.* New York: William Sloane Associates Inc., 1955.

Cliff, Nigel. *The Shakespeare Riots: Revenge, Drama, and Death in Nineteenth-Century America.* New York: Random House, 2007.

Cohen, Patricia Cline, Timothy J. Gilfoyle, and Helen Lefkowitz Horowitz. *The Flash Press: Sporting Male Weeklies in 1840s New York.* Chicago: University of Chicago Press, 2008.

Crawley, Thomas Edward. *The Structure of Leaves of Grass.* Austin: University of Texas, 1971.

Cremin, Lawrence A. *American Education: The National Experience, 1783-1876.* New York: Alfred A. Knopf, 1980.

―――――. *The American Common School: An Historic Conception.* New York: Teachers College Press, 1951.

Cummings, Glenn N. "Placing the Impalpable: Walt Whitman and Elias Hicks," *Modern Language Studies*, 28:2. (Spring, 1998), pp. 69-86.

Dawley, Alan. *Class and Community: The Industrial Revolution in Lynn.* Cambridge, Massachusetts: Harvard University Press, 1976.

Dewey, John. *Democracy and Education.* New York: Free Press, 1916.

Dougherty, James. *Walt Whitman and the Citizen's Eye.* Baton Rogue, LA: Louisiana State University Press, 1993.

Degler, Carl. "The Locofocos: Urban 'Agrarians'" *Journal of Economic History* 16 (1956): 322–33.

Dimock, Wai Chee. "Whitman, Syntax, and Political Theory," *Breaking Bounds: Whitman and American Cultural Studies.* Betsy Erkkila, Jay Grossman, eds., Oxford: Oxford University Press, 1996.

Earle, Jonathan H. *Jacksonian Antislavery and the Politics of Free Soil, 1824-1854.* Chapel Hill and London: University of North Carolina Press, 2004.

Emerson, Ralph Waldo. *The Essential Writings of Ralph Waldo Emerson.* Brooks Atkinson, ed., New York: The Modern Library, 2000.

Erkkila, Betsy. *Whitman: The Political Poet.* New York: Oxford University Press, 1989.

Faner, Robert D. *Walt Whitman & Opera*. Carbondale, IL: Southern Illinois University Press, 1951.

Florence, Don. *Persona and Human in Mark Twain's Early Writings*. Columbia: University of Missouri Press, 1995.

Folsom, Ed. "The Census of the 1855 *Leaves of Grass*: A Preliminary Report," *Walt Whitman Quarterly Review* 24:2-3, (Fall 2006/Winter 2007): 71-84.

———— and Kenneth M. Price., eds. *The Walt Whitman Archive*. <http://www.whitmanarchive.org>.

————, ed., *Walt Whitman: The Centennial Essays*. Iowa City: University of Iowa Press, 1994.

Foner, Eric. *Free Soil, Free Labor, Free Men: The Ideology of the Republican Party Before the Civil War*. Oxford: Oxford University Press, 1970.

Foner, Philip. *Organized Labor and the Black Worker*. New York: International Publisher, 1982.

Fishkin, Shelley. *From Fact to Fiction: Journalism and Imaginative Writing in America*. Baltimore: Johns Hopkins University Press, 1985.

Freedman, Florence B. *Walt Whitman Looks at Schools*. New York: King's Crown Press, 1950.

Freehling, William. *Prelude to Civil War: The Nullification Controversy in Southern Carolina, 1816-1836*. Oxford: Oxford University Press, 1965.

Fulghum, Walter. "Quaker Influences on Whitman's Religious Thought," Ph.D. diss., Northwestern University, 1943.

Gohdes, Clarence. *Faint Clews and Indirections: Manuscripts of Walt Whitman and His Family*. Durham, NC: Duke University Press, 1949.

Gorn, Eliot. *The Manly Art: Bare-Knuckle Prize Fighting in America*. Ithaca, New York: Cornell University Press, 1986.

Gilfoyle, Timothy. *City of Eros: New York City, Prostitution, and the Commercialization of Sex 1790-1920*. New York: W.W. Norton and Company, 1992.

Gilje, Paul, ed. *Wages of Independence: Capitalism in the Early American Republic*. Madison: Madison House, 1997.

Gravil, Richard. "'The Discharged Soldier' and 'the Runaway Slave': Wordsworth and the Definition of Walt Whitman," *Symbiosis* 1, April 1997.

Greenspan, Ezra. "An Undocumented Review of the 1860 Leaves of Grass in the Liberator," *Walt Whitman Quarterly Review*, 24:4 (Spring 2007), 201-207.

————. *Walt Whitman and the American Reader*. New York: Cambridge University Press. 1990.

Gutman, Herbert. *Work, Culture and Society in Industrializing America*. New York: Vintage, 1977.

Habermas, Jürgen. *The Structural Transformation of the Public Sphere: An Inquiry into a Category of Bourgeois Society*. Cambridge, Mass: MIT Press, 1989.

Halttunen, Karen. *Confidence Men and Painted Women: A Study of Middle-class Culture in America, 1830-1870*. New Haven: Yale University Press, 1982.

————. *Murder Most Foul: The Killer and the American Gothic Imagination*. Cambridge, Massachusetts: Harvard University Press, 1998.

Hamm, Thomas. *The Transformation of American Quakerism: Orthodox Friends 1800-1907*. Bloomington, IN: The University of Indiana Press, 1988.

Hartsock, John C. *A History of American Literary Journalism: The Emergence of a Modern Narrative Form*. Amherst, MA: University of Massachusetts Press, 2000.

Herreshoff, David Sprague. *Labor into Art: The Theme of Work in Nineteenth-Century American Literature*. Detroit: Wayne State University Press, 1991.

Higham, John. *Strangers in the Land: Patterns of American Nativism 1960-1925*. New York: Atheneum, 1955.

————. *Hanging Together: Unity and Diversity in American Culture*. New Haven: Yale University Press, 2001.

Hirsch, Susan E. *Roots of the American Working Class: The Industrialization of Crafts in Newark, 1800-1860*. Philadelphia: University of Pennsylvania Press, 1978.

Holloway, Emory, ed. *The Uncollected Poetry and Prose of Walt Whitman vols. I and II*. Gloucester, Mass: Peter Smith, 1972.

Horowitz, Helen Lefkowitz. *Rereading Sex: Battles over Sexual Knowledge and Supression in Nineteenth-Century America*. New York: Vintage Books, 2002.

Howe, Daniel Walker. *The Political Culture of the American Whigs*. Chicago: The University of Chicago Press, 1979.

————. *What Hath God Wrought The Transformation of America, 1815-1848*. Oxford: Oxford University Press, 2007.

Hudson, Frederick. *Journalism in the United States from 1690-1872*. New York: Routledge, 2000.

Ingle, H. Larry. *Quakers in Conflict: The Hicksite Reformation*. Knoxville: The University of Tennessee Press, 1986.

Jancovich, Mark. *The Cultural Politics of New Criticism*. Cambridge: Cambridge University Press, 1993.

Kaestle, Carl. *Pillars of the Republic: Common Schools and American Society. 1780-1860*. New York: Hill and Wang, 1983.

Killingsworth, M. Jimmie. *The Growth of Leaves of Grass: The Organic Tradition in Whitman Studies*. Columbia, S.C.: Camdem House, 1993.

Kim, Heidi Kathleen. "From Language to Empire: Walt Whitman in the Context of Nineteenth-Century Popular Anglo-Saxonism," *Walt Whitman Quarterly Review*, 24:1 (Summer 2003), 1-18.

Klammer, Martin. *Whitman, Slavery, and the Emergence of Leaves of Grass*. University Park: Pennsylvania State University Press, 1995.

Kohl, Lawrence Frederick. *The Politics of Individualism: Parties and the American Character in the Jacksonian Era*. New York: Oxford University Press, 1989.

Krieg, Joann P. *Whitman and the Irish*. Iowa City: University of Iowa Press, 2000.

Kuebrich, David. *Minor Prophecy: Walt Whitman's New American Religion*. Bloomington: Indiana University Press, 1989.

Larson, Kerry. *Whitman's Drama of Consensus*. Chicago: University of Chicago Press, 1988.

Lang, Amy Schrager. *The Syntax of Class: Writing Inequality in Nineteenth-Century America*. Princeton: Princeton University Press, 2003.

Laurie, Bruce. *Artisans into Workers: Labor in Nineteenth Century America*. New York: Hill and Wang, 1989.

Lawrence, D.H. *Studies in Classic American Literature*. New York: Penguin, 1977.

Lawson, Andrew. "'Spending on Vast Returns': Sex, Class, and Commerce in the First *Leaves of Grass*," *American Literature* (June 2003) 75:2, 335-365.

————. *Walt Whitman and the Class Struggle*. Iowa City: University of Iowa Press, 2006.

Levine, Lawrence. *Highbrow/Lowbrow: The Emergence of Cultural Hierarchy in America*. Cambridge: Harvard University Press, 1988.

Levinson, Marjorie. *Rethinking Historicism: Critical Readings in Romantic History*. Oxford: Basil Blackwell Ltd, 1989.

Loving, Jerome. *Emerson, Whitman, and the American Muse*. Chapel Hill: University of North Carolina, 1982.

————. *Walt Whitman: Song of Himself*. Berkeley: University of California Press, 1999.

McCormick, Richard Patrick. *The Second American Party System; Party Formation in the Jacksonian Era*. Chapel Hill, University of North Carolina Press, 1966.

Margadant, Jo Burr, ed. *The New Biography: Performing Femininity in Nineteenth-Century France*. Berkeley and Los Angeles: University of California Press, 2000.

Matthiessen, F.O. *American Renaissance*. London: Oxford University Press, 1941.

Miller, James. *A Critical Guide to Walt Whitman*, Chicago: University of Chicago Press, 1957.

————. "Whitman Then and Now: A Reminiscence," *Walt Whitman Quarterly Review*. 8:2, (Summer 1990) 92-101.

Miller, Matt. "The Cover of the First Edition of Leaves of Grass," *Walt Whitman Quarterly Review*, 24:2-3 (Fall 2006/Winter 2007): 85-97.

Mindich, David T.Z., "Edwin M. Stanton, the Inverted Pyramid, and Information Control," *Journalism Monographs*, no. 140, August 1993.

————. *Just the Facts: How Objectivity Came to Define American Journalism*. New York: New York University Press, 1998.

O'Connor, William Douglas. *The Good Grey Poet: A Vindication*. New York: Bunce and Huntington, 1866.

Pannapacker, William. *Revised Lives: Walt Whitman and Nineteenth-Century Authorship*. New York: Routledge, 2004.

Perlman, Helen Harris. *Persona: Social Role and Personality*. Chicago: The University of Chicago Press, 1968.

Pessen, Edward. *Most Uncommon Jacksonians: The Radical Leaders of the Early Labor Movement*. Albany: State University of New York, 1967.

―――. *The Many-Faceted Jacksonian Era: New Interpretations*. Westport, Conn: Greenwood Press, 1977.

Pound, Louise, "Peter Funk: The Pedigree of a Westernism," *American Speech*, Vol. 4, No. 3. (Feb., 1929), pp. 183-186.

Reynolds, David S. *Beneath the American Renaissance: The Subversive Imagination in the Age of Emerson and Melville*. Boston: Harvard University Press, 1988.

―――, ed. *George Lippard: The Profit of Protest*, New York: Peter Lang, 1986.

―――. ed. *A Historical Guide to Walt Whitman*. Oxford: Oxford University Press, 2000.

―――. *Walt Whitman's America: A Cultural Biography*. New York: Alfred A. Knopf, 1995.

―――. "Walt Whitman and the new York Stage." *Thesis: The Graduate School Magazine*, 9:1 (1995), 5-11.

Roediger, David R. *The Wages of Whiteness: Race and the Making of the American Working Class*. New York: Verso, 1991.

Rorabaugh, W. J. *The Craft Apprentice: From Franklin to the Machine Age in America*. New York : Oxford University Press,1986.

Rubin, Joseph Jay, Charles H. Brown, eds. *Walt Whitman of the New York Aurora*. State College, PA: Bald Eagle Press, 1950.

Ryan, Mary. *Civic Wars: Democracy and Public Life in the American City During the Nineteenth Century*. Berkeley: University of California Press, 1997.

Safranski, Rüdiger. *Nietzsche: A Philosophical Biography*. Translated by Shelley Frisch. New York: W.W. Norton and Coompany, 2002.

Saxton, Alexander *The Rise and Fall of the White Republic: Race, Politics, and Mass Culture in Nineteenth Century America*. New York: Verso, 2003.

Schyberg, Frederick. *Walt Whitman*. New York: Columbia University Press, 1933.

Shamir, Milette. *Inexpressible Privacy: The Interior Life of Antebellum American Literature*. Philadelphia: University of Pennsylvania Press, 2006.

Sellers, Charles. *The Market Revolution: Jacksonian America*. Oxford: Oxford University Press, 1991.

Shephard, Esther. *Walt Whitman's Pose*. New York: Harcourt, Brace and Company, 1938.

―――. "Walt Whitman's Whereabouts in the Winter of 1842-1843," *American Literature* (November 1957) 29:3.

Smarr, Janet. *Historical Criticism and the Challenge of Theory*. Urbana: The University of Illinois Press, 1993

Smith, Adam. *An Inquiry into the Nature and Causes of the Wealth of Nations*. New York: The Modern Library, 1937.

Spann, Edward. *Ideas and Politics: New York Intellectuals and Liberal Democracy 1820-1880*. Albany: State University of New YorkPress, 1972.

———. *The New Metropolis: New York City 1840-1857*. New York: Columbia University Press, 1981.

Stansell, Christine. *City of Women: Sex and Class in New York, 1789-1860*. New York: Knopf, 1986.

Stott, Richard. *Workers in the Metropolis: Class, Ethnicity and Youth in Antebellum New York City*. Ithaca: Cornell University Press, 1990.

Stovall, Floyd. *The Foreground of Leaves of Grass*. Charlottesville: University of Virginia, 1974.

Templin, Lawrence, "The Quaker Influence on Walt Whitman." *American Literature*, 42:2 (May 1970), pp. 165-180

Thomas, M. Wynn. *The Lunar Light of Whitman's Poetry*. Cambridge: Harvard University Press, 1987.

Todd, John Emerson. *Emily Dickenson's Use of the Persona*. The Hague: Mouton, 1973.

Tolles, Frederick B. "A Quaker Reaction to Leaves of Grass." *American Literature* 19, May 1947.

Traubel, Horace. *Walt Whitman in Camden, vols. 1-3*. New York: Rowman and Littlefield, 1961.

———. *With Walt Whitman in Camden, vol. 4*. Sculley Bradley, ed., Philadelphia: University of Pennsylvania Press, 1953.

———. *With Walt Whitman in Camden, vol. 5*. Gertrude Traubel, ed., Carbondale: Southern Illinois University Press, 1964.

Traubel, Horace, *With Walt Whitman in Camden, vol. 6*. Gertrude Traubel, William White, ed., Carbondale: Southern Illinois University Press, 1982.

———. *With Walt Whitman in Camden, vol. 7*. Jeanne Chapman and Robert MacIsaac., eds., Carbondale: Southern Illinois University Press, 1992.

———. *With Walt Whitman in Camden, vol. 8*. Jeanne Chapman and Robert MacIsaac., eds., Oregon House, CA: W. L. Bentley, 1996.

———. *With Walt Whitman in Camden, vol. 9*. Jeanne Chapman and Robert MacIsaac eds.; Foreword by Ed Folsom. Oregon House, CA: W.L. Bentley, 1996

Tyrrell, Ian R. *Sobering Up : From Temperance to Prohibition in Antebellum America, 1800-1860*. Westport, Conn: Greenwood Press, 1979.

Warner, Sam Bass. *The Private City: Philadelphia in Three Periods of its Growth*. Philadelphia: University of Philadelphia Press, 1987.

Waskow, Harold. *Whitman: Explorations in Form*. Chicago: University of Chicago. (1966).

Weber, Robert J. *The Created Self: Reinventing Body, Persona, and Spirit*. New York: W.W. Norton and Company, 2000.

Welter, Barbara. "The Cult of True Womanhood 1820-1860." *American Quarterly 18*, 1966, 151-174.

Whitman, Walt. *Leaves of Grass: The First Edition*. New York: Penguin, 2005.

————. *Notes and Fragments*. Richard Maurice, ed., New York: Burke Publishing, 1899.

————. *Daybooks and Notebooks*. William White, ed., New York: New York University Press. 1978.

————. *The Complete Prose Works of Walt Whitman*. New York: Putnam, 1902.

————. *The Collected Whitman: Prose and Poetry*. New York: The Library of America, 1999.

————. *The Collected Writings of Walt Whitman: The Journalism, vol. I, 1834-1846*. Bergman, Herbert, et al, eds. New York: Peter Lang, 1998.

————. *The Collected Writings of Walt Whitman: The Journalism, vol. II, 1846-1848*. New York: Peter Lang, 2003.

————. *The Uncollected Poetry and Prose of Walt Whitman*. Emory Halloway, ed., Gloucester, Mass: Peter Smith, 1972.

Widmer, Edward. *Young America: The Flowering of Democracy in New York City*. Oxford: Oxford University Press, 1999.

Wilentz, Sean. *Chants Democratic : New York City & the Rise of the American Working Class, 1788-1850*. New York : Oxford University Press, 1984.

————. *The Rise of American Democracy: Jefferson to Lincoln*. New York: W.W. Norton and Company, 2005.

Zweig, Paul. *Walt Whitman: The Making of a Poet*. New York: Basic Books, 1984.

Index